Model Letters for Personal Injury Lawyers

Second Edition

Model Letters for Personal Injury Lawyers

Second Edition

John McQuater
Solicitor

Published by
Jordan Publishing Limited
21 St Thomas Street
Bristol BS1 6JS

British Library Cataloguing-in-Publication Data

A catalogue record for this book is available from the British Library.

ISBN 978 184661 052 3

Typeset by Letterpart Ltd, Reigate, Surrey

Printed in Great Britain by Antony Rowe Limited, Chippenham, Wiltshire

PREFACE

The APIL Guides are intended to assist lawyers dealing with personal injury claims by giving practical advice on law and procedure.

Whilst this book takes the format of letters these, when read together, should help to provide a work-flow path, from initial enquiry by the client to resolution of the claim, reflecting law and practice in this area of work.

Guidance on using the letters is provided by the general convention, adopted throughout the book, of indicating optional or alternative paragraphs by the use of square brackets.

Although many personal injury claims will follow a broadly similar path, the letters in this book can be no more than a guide to the matters which may need to be considered at each stage of any particular case. The lawyer with day-to-day conduct of the claim must always decide what is appropriate for the individual case. Letters, especially the longer letters, should be edited to focus on relevant issues. Conversely, it may often be necessary to include further matters to ensure all issues in the case are dealt with.

When dealing with clients some firms may prefer to write with advice on complex issues while others may prefer face-to-face meetings or discussions on the telephone. The approach to adopt in any particular case may depend upon the requirements of the individual client.

Just as every case, and every client, is different so every opponent will have a particular way of working. Whilst keeping in mind the need to always act in the best interests of the client it is often helpful to allow flexibility to accommodate the reasonable requirements of the opponent given that, ultimately, the parties should be working together towards achieving a fair resolution of the claim at the earliest stage.

There are key stages in any case which demand the use of fairly complex letters. That will inevitably involve spending more time on the case at that stage but should result in an overall saving of time by ensuring all relevant matters are dealt with and that the claim continues to progress logically by anticipating, and moving towards, the following stages.

I am grateful for the help I have had from many people in the preparation of the book. Particular thanks go to Nigel Tomkins, Martin Bare and Roger Bolt, for their ideas, and to members of the team at Atherton Godfrey. I could not have completed the book without the encouragement, and patience, of Tony Hawitt at Jordans and the invaluable help of my secretaries Gill Drohan and Diane Wood.

I have tried to reflect, in these letters, the law, as I understand it, up to 1 January 2008.

I hope this further edition of the book will be useful to you in the important job of recovering compensation for injured people.

John McQuater

Doncaster
March 2008

ASSOCIATION OF PERSONAL INJURY LAWYERS (APIL)

APIL is the UK's leading association of claimant personal injury lawyers, dedicated to protecting the rights of injured people.

Formed in 1990, APIL now represents over 5,000 solicitors, barristers, academics and students in the UK, Republic of Ireland and overseas.

APIL's objectives are:

- to promote full and just compensation for all types of personal injury;
- to promote and develop expertise in the practice of personal injury law;
- to promote wider redress for personal injury in the legal system;
- to campaign for improvements in personal injury law;
- to promote safety and alert the public to hazards;
- to provide a communication network for members.

APIL is a growing and influential forum pushing for law reform, and improvements, which will benefit victims of personal injury.

APIL has been running CPD training events, accredited by the Solicitors Regulation Authority and Bar Standards Board, for well over fifteen years and has a wealth of experience in developing the most practical up-to-date courses, delivered by eminent leading speakers, either publicly or in-house.

APIL training now runs almost 200 personal injury training events nationally each year, plus up to a further 100 meetings of our regional and special interest groups. Topics cover a wide range of subjects and are geared towards giving personal injury lawyers a thorough grounding in the core areas of personal injury law, whilst keeping lawyers thoroughly up-to-date in all subjects.

APIL is also an authoritative information source for personal injury lawyers, providing up-to-the-minute PI bulletins, regular newsletters and publications, information databases and online services.

For further information contact:

APIL
11 Castle Quay
Nottingham
NG7 1FW
DX 716208 Nottingham 42
Tel 0115 9580585
Email mail@apil.org.uk
Website www.apil.org.uk

CONTENTS

SECTION 1

CLIENT CARE AND INSTRUCTIONS

CONTENTS

INITIAL LETTERS

1.1   Letter to Client – Confirming Initial Appointment

Thank you for your enquiry about pursuing a claim for compensation.

I look forward to [meeting] [talking on the telephone to] you on [*day and date*] at [*time*]. I confirm that you are welcome to this [free] initial interview which will allow me to obtain further details and, I hope, agree with you how best to proceed with any claim.

To help me advise you as fully as possible on the options for funding a claim it would be helpful if you could [bring with you] [have available when we speak] details of any legal expenses insurance you may have. This might be a specific policy to cover legal expenses or cover as an 'add-on' to a home contents, car insurance or other policy which you or your spouse/partner may have. [Please could you also, if possible, try to have available a copy of the motor insurance policy of the driver of the vehicle.] I will be happy to make further enquiries about availability of legal expenses cover so you do not need to contact any insurers meanwhile.

If you have already been contacted by other solicitors purporting to act for you or if you have previously instructed other solicitors on this claim please let me know.

I look forward to [meeting] [speaking to] you.

Yours sincerely

1.2   Letter to Client's Legal Expenses Insurers – Seeking Clarification of Cover

Our Client: [*name of client*]

[**Policy Number:** [*number of relevant insurance policy*]]

We have been consulted by [*name of client*] in connection with a claim for personal injuries arising out of [a motor accident][an accident at work] [an accident that occurred when [*details*]] on [*date*].

We are establishing what, if any, cover our client may have for legal expenses, so that all available funding options can be considered. We consider our client may have cover for legal expenses [under the above] [associated with an insurance] policy.

Accordingly, we write to request certain information so that we can advise our client on the options available. Please deal with the following points when replying so that we are able to advise our client as fully as possible.

(1) Please confirm whether our client is covered for legal expenses under any policy with you to pursue claims arising out of [the accident on [*date*]] [industrial disease].

(2) If so will our client be indemnified for legal costs incurred by us under the policy? If not, why not?

(3) Do you require us to seek authority before instructing experts, instructing Counsel or incurring any other disbursements?

(4) Are we free to select experts and Counsel or limited to specified experts/Counsel or panels of experts/Counsel?

(5) Will disbursements be funded by you as the case progresses or do you expect us or our client to fund these?

(6) Is there any requirement as to the status or qualification of the fee earner dealing with the case on a day-to-day basis? If so, please specify.

(7) Are we able to issue proceedings on our client's behalf if necessary and, if so, is this subject to any specific reporting/review of the case?

(8) Will you provide a full indemnity in respect of any liability our client may have for the costs of the opponent in the event of the claim not succeeding? If not, what is the limit on the indemnity?

(9) In the event of the opponent making a Part 36 offer or payment which, on our advice, our client rejects but subsequently fails to beat, would you indemnify our client in respect of any costs of the opponent incurred as a result of that advice?

(10) Are there any further conditions relating to the policy, limiting what we can do for our client, of which we should be aware? If so, please advise.

We look forward to hearing from you in reply to these points and, if appropriate, with any further relevant terms.

So that the matter can proceed, as promptly as possible, we shall be grateful for your response to these points by [*date*] to help our make an informed decision as to the most appropriate funding option.

Yours faithfully

CLIENT CARE LETTERS

1.3 Letter to Client – Client Care (Offering Conditional Fee Agreement)

Thank you for consulting me.

I outlined, when we talked, the legal work I consider appropriate to deal with this matter for you. I hope this letter will usefully confirm the matters we discussed, though to provide as much information as I can for you at this stage that does mean writing at some length.

[You have already indicated you would like to proceed under a conditional fee, or 'no win–no fee', agreement. However, I hope you do not mind me setting this out in more detail, and also confirming how this contrasts with other methods of funding the case, so that I can be sure you are making a considered and informed decision about how to proceed.]

To confirm the legal work that seems appropriate, and the basis on which the firm will carry out that work, I need to deal with a number of important matters in turn.

1.   Advice and action

I confirm that, given the background I consider compensation for injuries, expenses and losses should be sought from [*name of opponent*] (who I shall described as 'the Opponent'). Accordingly, you are quite right to seek advice on the matter.

I should also confirm, at the outset, that any court action seeking compensation should normally be commenced before the [third anniversary of the date the injuries were suffered] [twenty-first birthday of [*name of child*]] (although in a claim arising out of injuries suffered the court may, in certain circumstances, extend this time limit).

That is a brief summary of the advice given and the legal work that appears appropriate. I will write explaining exactly how the matter will proceed once the best way to fund the case has been confirmed.

2.   People responsible for your work

It is important to let you have details about the people in the firm responsible for your work [, arrangements for referral of that work to the firm] and how people outside the firm may be involved as the matter progresses.

(1)   I have principal responsibility for dealing with this matter for you, on a day-to-day basis. I am a [*eg partner, solicitor, legal executive,*

litigation assistant]. If anyone needs to know who is dealing with the matter on your behalf you can tell them that it is [*name*].

[(2)   I will be assisted by [*name*].]

(3)   The partner with responsibility for overall supervision is [*name*].

(4)   Once the matter is under way I will keep in touch with you, usually by letter, as it progresses.

(5)   The address for any letters you wish to send me is [*address*] and the reference is [*reference*]. It is helpful if you can quote this reference when writing or calling.

(6)   The telephone number is [*telephone number*]. To help deal with any telephone enquiries as promptly as possible calls [will usually be dealt with by [*name of assistant*]]/[may be answered by a colleague].

(7)   My e-mail address is [*insert e-mail address*]. Please note any e-mails that are sent will not be encrypted.

(8)   At various stages I will suggest we review the case. If, at other times, you would like to arrange an appointment please contact [*name of assistant*] [me].

(9)   The firm tries to avoid changing the people you are dealing with but if it should seem appropriate at any stage for the matter to be referred to another member of the team I will let you know.

(10) During the case it may be helpful to get some assistance from others, outside the firm. For example, it is sometimes helpful to involve experts, who can advise on and help deal with certain aspects of the case, and it may become appropriate to instruct counsel (a barrister) to advise or to represent you. I will let you know if it seems appropriate to seek such further assistance and give you details of who will be involved in providing this.

I hope this is all the information you need to ensure we are able to keep in touch with each other. If you should change your name, address or telephone number please let me know as soon as you can.

[The firm has an arrangement with [*name*] for referral of enquiries. For your referral a payment, of £[*figure*], will be made to [*name*]. You will not have to contribute in any way to this payment.]

3. *Identity and disclosure requirements*

Government regulations require the firm to obtain confirmation of your identity. It would be helpful, therefore, if you could let me have sight of documentation confirming your name, such as a passport or driving licence, and also address, for example a copy of a recent utility bill.

You need to be aware the firm has responsibilities under money laundering legislation to make reports in certain circumstances and that where this is required the firm cannot be held responsible for any loss, damage or delay resulting from compliance with such requirements.

4. *Charges, expenses and funding*

I need to provide you, at the outset, with important information about costs and funding. This includes information about how costs are incurred, how those costs may be funded, any liability that might arise to pay the costs of the Opponent and measures that might be taken to obtain protection against any liability for the costs of the Opponent.

That information will, I hope, allow us to agree the best way, for you, of funding the case and to help ensure the cost of carrying out the legal work is justified by the likely benefits of that work.

I discussed with you whether you had any legal expenses insurance, membership of a Union or other organisation which might provide legal assistance and any other cover or support for the cost of legal work [as Public Funding, formerly Legal Aid, is not available for the claim].

I understand you [do not] [are not aware that you] [may] have such cover.

To confirm I shall be grateful, unless these documents have already been provided, if you could let me have a look at all documentation relating to any insurance you, your spouse/partner or anyone else in your household may have. This is because such cover might be provided not only by a specific policy to cover legal expenses but as an 'add on' to a home contents, car insurance or other policy or even as part of a credit card agreement. [Please could you also, if possible, try to obtain and let me have a copy of the motor insurance policy of the driver.]

[I am, therefore, checking to see whether you do have any cover and, if so, what cover is provided so that you can assess that in the context of the options set out in this letter. I have asked for a prompt response to these enquiries which I hope will allow quick progress to be made with the necessary arrangements for funding.

If you should hear direct from any legal expenses insurers, or solicitors instructed through the insurers, suggesting your choice of solicitor is restricted please let me know straightaway as, whatever may be said, you might well have the right to choose which representation you prefer.

I will go on to set out, in this letter, the funding options available but you need to bear in mind that, if you do have cover, this may offer some protection against liability for your own costs, and any potential liability for the costs of the opponent, if proceeding on a private basis.]

I will deal in turn with the options for funding the legal work.

(1)   On a private basis

I enclose details of the terms that will apply if you wish to proceed on a private basis.

[If you have insurance or other cover for the cost of legal work that should, wholly or partly, meet the obligation you would have for those costs and the costs of the opponent. However, it is important to appreciate that these costs would remain your obligation whether or not any indemnity is provided.]

(2)   On a conditional fee (or 'no win–no fee') agreement

If you were to decide to enter a conditional fee, or 'no win–no fee', agreement there are a number of important points to note.

(i)   You only pay the firm a fee if you win the claim (the meaning of 'win' is explained in the enclosed information about entering a conditional fee agreement).

(ii)   You would not, provided you kept to the terms of the agreement, pay a fee unless you did win the claim. However, if the claim did not succeed you would still potentially be responsible for:
   (a)   the cost of reports or other outlays incurred by my firm on your behalf (whether or not court proceedings were issued against the Opponent); and
   (b)   (if court proceedings had to be issued) the costs of the Opponent.
   Accordingly, I would arrange for an insurance policy to be taken out which will cover any liability you may have for outlays and also the costs of the opponent if the claim is unsuccessful.
   I believe, on the information available, that a policy with [*insurer*] would be appropriate for these potential liabilities. There is a premium for the policy [but I will not need you to pay this now as, if you win, that premium will be sought from the Opponent or, if you do not win, payment of the premium will be waived] [the cost of which I will let you know as soon as I can] [the cost of which is [*figure*]].

Please note that the firm does [not] have an interest in recommending this policy [as [*details of interest*] [and your agreement, in writing, to the firm retaining any commission is sought, by returning a signed copy of this letter. If commission is payable it will be the sum of £[*figure*]].

Please also note that this recommendation is made without the firm having conducted a fair analysis of the insurance market.

I enclose demands and needs statement relating to the policy.

(iii) If you win, costs become payable by you, calculated in the same way as on a private basis but with a success fee payable in addition. The success fee reflects the risk of the firm not being paid if the claim is not successful. The opponent will, however, have to pay most, although probably not all, of these costs, including the success fee (but not any part of the success fee that reflects the delay in payment of costs until the end of the case). [To provide as much certainty as possible, but subject to you following all advice given and complying with all terms of the agreement, I confirm that you will not get less than [*figure*]% of the compensation received from the Opponent.]

Either

[(iv) Outlays to others necessary to pursue the case, such as to experts or to the court, are, strictly, payable by you as and when incurred as the case progresses. Outlays of several hundred pounds can easily be incurred in a case of this kind, although these outlays will be recouped at the conclusion of the case either from the Opponent, if the case is successful, or under the insurance policy, if the case is not successful As I do not want you to be financing these outlays as the claim progresses, even though they will recovered one way or another at the conclusion of the case, I confirm they will be met by the firm, on your behalf, until such time as the claim is concluded (subject to using any interim payment to help meet those outlays).

Or

[(iv) Outlays to others necessary to pursue the case, such as to experts or the court, will be payable by you when incurred as the case progresses. I estimate, in your case, that those outlays will be in the region of £[*figure*] to £[*figure*]. Accordingly, I would ask for a payment of say, £[*figure*] on account of these outlays, although I would hope to refund that to you at the conclusion of the case.]

[Whatever method of funding is appropriate the firm may make use of arrangements with agencies who specialise in obtaining expert medical reports. If the firm uses such an agency payment of the fee for the report is usually deferred for a fixed period or until the end of the case.

Sometimes a commission is payable and if so it will be in the sum of £[*figure*]. Signing a copy of this letter will be your agreement to the firm retaining any such commission.]

I enclose, for your information, important information about entering a conditional fee agreement entitled 'Conditional Fee Agreements: What you need to know about a CFA' which is intended to accompany any agreement entered into.

You do need to bear in mind that under a conditional fee agreement the firm is effectively sharing the risks of the case with you which gives a say in how the case should be run to the extent that the case will be reviewed at appropriate stages and if it is considered you are not likely to win the firm may decide to end the agreement. On a private basis, where you alone are running the risk, such decisions would be largely yours alone. If you consider it is important to retain full control of the case, rather than sharing this and the risks with the firm, then you do need to take that into account when assessing the best funding option.

It is important to keep in mind, whatever method of funding is appropriate, that the likely benefits of the proposed legal work should justify the likely cost of carrying out that work.

5.   *Documents*

It is important that you keep all documents which relate in any way to this matter.

For present purposes, the term 'documents' includes anything recorded, whether in permanent, semi-permanent or electronic form, such as letters, contracts, receipts, diaries, computer records, photographs, videos, and anything else of that kind.

Whilst I do not need to see all of those documents at this stage, such documents may have to be produced in court proceedings, and a duty is owed to the court to ensure the documents are preserved in case they should be required. Similarly, any documents you subsequently obtain which relate to the matter should also be kept. Also, if you have any other property connected with the matter in any way, you should preserve that property until the case is concluded.

[I acknowledge safe receipt of the documents handed over at our meeting, which I have placed in my file for safekeeping, comprising [*details*].]

[I am grateful for sight of the documents you handed over at our meeting and I now return the original documents, having retained copies for my file.]

After completing the work, the firm is entitled to keep all papers and documents while there is money owing for charges and expenses. The firm keeps papers (except for any papers you ask to be returned to you) for no more than 6 years and keeps the file on the understanding that the firm has authority to destroy it after 6 years from the date of the final bill, although documents you ask to deposit in safe custody will not, of course, be destroyed.

If it becomes necessary to retrieve papers or documents from storage in relation to continuing or new instructions to act on your behalf the firm would not normally charge for such retrieval. However, the firm will make a charge, based on time spent producing stored papers or documents to you or to another person at your request, in other circumstances. The firm may also charge for reading correspondence or other work necessary to comply with instructions given by you or on your behalf in this connection.

6. *Termination*

Termination will depend upon arrangements made for funding.

(1) Under a conditional fee agreement

You will see that the conditions applicable to a conditional fee agreement provide for termination and its consequences.

The firm can end the agreement if it is no longer thought likely you will win the case or if you do not keep to your responsibilities under the agreement.

You can end the agreement at any time.

It is particularly important to note that if you end the agreement, or the firm ends the agreement because you have not kept to your responsibilities, you would then be responsible to pay costs, under that agreement, whether or not the matter had then reached a successful conclusion.

(2) Otherwise

You may terminate your instructions in writing at any time but the firm will be entitled to keep all your papers and documents while there is money owing for charges and expenses.

In some circumstances I may consider I ought to stop acting for you, for example if you cannot give clear or proper instructions on how to proceed or if it is clear you have lost confidence in how the work has been carried out.

I may only decide to step acting for you with good reason, for example if I do not receive instructions from you or otherwise do not have the assistance I need to progress the claim properly or if costs are not paid. I will, however, always give reasonable notice before ceasing to act so that, if possible, any problems can be dealt with and I can continue to act on your behalf.

If the costs are covered by any insurance the insurer may well have the right to withdraw funding if there are no longer reasonable prospects of success.

Under the Consumer Protection (Distance Selling) Regulations 2000 you may have the right to withdraw, without charge, within 7 working days of the date on which you asked the firm to act for you **but** if I start work with your consent, within that period, you lose that right to withdraw. Your acceptance of the firm's terms of business, set out in this letter, will amount to such consent.

7.   *Communication and suggestions*

We are confident of providing a high quality service.

We do, of course, welcome any suggestions you might wish to make which you think could help to improve our service.

If, at any time, you are not happy with the service you are receiving from the firm, please let us know. You are valued client of the firm and I should like the opportunity to put matters right if any problems do arise. In the first instance, please contact me and I will do what I can to resolve the problem promptly. If, however, I am not able to resolve matters to your satisfaction you should then contact [*name*], who is responsible for the firm's complaints procedure.

This firm is not authorised by the Financial Services Authority. However, we are included on the Register maintained by the Financial Services Authority so that we can carry on insurance mediation activity, which is broadly the advising on, selling and administration of insurance contracts. This part of our business, including arrangements for complaints or redress if something goes wrong, is regulated by The Law Society. The Register can be accessed via the Financial Services Authority website at ww.fsa.gov.uk/register.

Sometimes personal injury work involves investments. If, during this transaction, you need advice on investments we may have to refer you to someone who is authorised by the Financial Services Authority, as we are not. However, as we are regulated by the Law Society, we may be able to provide certain limited investment services where these are closely linked to the legal work we are doing for you. If you have any problem with the service we provide for you then please let us know. We will try to deal with any problem quickly and operate an internal complaints handling system to help us resolve matters between ourselves. The Law Society also provides a complaints and redress scheme.

8. *Video surveillance*

Although this occurs in only a few cases you should be aware that anyone pursuing a personal injury claim may be subject to covert surveillance by enquiry agents acting on behalf of the opponent.

If, at any stage, you believe you are the subject of video surveillance please advise.

9. *Internet information*

You should also be aware that the opponent may, as the claim progresses, look for any available information about you on the internet, particularly those sites where people are invited to share personal information.

10. *What happens next?*

I look forward to hearing from you with confirmation of how you would like to proceed with the claim.

If you do need any further information before reaching a decision please feel free to telephone [*name*].

If you are now able to reach a decision please could you return the copy of this letter, with the appropriate box ticked, as confirmation and I will then be able to proceed with the claim.

This letter sets out the firm's terms of business with you, and so your continuing instructions in this matter will amount to acceptance by you of the terms. Even so, I shall be grateful if you would sign and date, in the space provided, the enclosed copy letter as I can then be sure you understand, and are happy with, the basis on which the firm will act for you. I enclose a pre-paid envelope for your use.

As this letter is an important document, please keep it in a safe place for future reference.

I hope this letter usefully confirms the advice given and action agreed upon, as well as dealing with any immediate queries about the day-to-day handling of the matter and the firm's terms of business.

I look forward to hearing from you.

Yours sincerely

A copy of this letter should be enclosed with the following attached.

Receipt of this letter is acknowledged.

☐   I agree to the terms of, and wish to proceed on, a conditional fee basis [whether or not there is suitable insurance or other cover available for legal costs]

☐   I agree to the terms of, and wish to proceed on, a private basis [whether or not there is suitable insurance or other cover available for legal costs]

☐   I agree to the terms of, and wish to proceed on, a private basis provided I have suitable insurance or other cover available for legal costs

☐   I do not wish to proceed with the claim on the terms offered.

Please tick appropriate box to confirm your wishes.

Signed:

1.4   Details of Charges and Expenses on a Private Basis

Charges and Expenses

These are the arrangements for costs that will apply on a private basis.

[If you would rather enter a conditional fee agreement you should still refer to the details of how charges are calculated, as these apply equally to work done under a conditional fee agreement but subject to the terms of such an agreement.]

1.   *Charging rates*

I need to explain the basis, and calculation, of charges for which, if you instruct my firm to proceed you would become responsible irrespective of whether or not those costs can be recovered from the Opponent.

The firm's charges are based on the time spent dealing with the case and certain other factors.

That charge will be £[*figure*] per hour for all time, calculated in units of 1/10 of an hour that we are engaged on the case. The hourly rate will be reviewed on [*date*]. You will be advised, in writing, of any increased rate from the review date.

When calculating charges the firm may, in addition to the time spent, take into account a number of factors including the complexity of the issues, the speed at which action must be taken, the expertise or specialist knowledge that the case requires and, if appropriate, the value of the property or subject matter involved. On the basis of the information currently available it is expected that these factors will be adequately covered by the hourly rate already referred to. However, the rate may be higher if the matter becomes more complex than expected or if your instructions mean we have to work outside normal office hours. You will be notified if this should happen. If you were then to have any query about the level of any revised rates I would ask you to contact me immediately.

VAT will be added to the charge at the rate that applies when the work is done. At present VAT is 17.5%.

[Details of other expenses which you are likely to have to pay, when they are likely to become due and an estimate of their costs are as follows:

Expense	*When payment is likely to be needed*	*Costs*
[*details*]	[*details*]	£[ ]

VAT is payable on certain expenses.]

The amount of costs which you will have to pay may well be greater than the amount you can recover from the Opponent (for reasons set out later in this letter).

The time spent, for which a charge will be made, includes:

(i)   time spent seeing you or others involved in the case (including travelling if necessary);

(ii)   time spent writing letters to you and others (with routine letters being charged at 1/10 of an hour, and other letters on a time basis);

(iii)   time spent making or receiving telephone calls (with routine calls being charged at 1/10 of an hour, and other calls on a time basis);

(iv)   time spent drafting statements and other documents;

(v)   time spent considering and reviewing documents and/or the matter generally; and

(vi)   time spent travelling to and being at court.

The firm will also be entitled to claim for the cost of payments made to other people involved in the case, such as experts and Counsel, as well as any court fees paid.

We aim to give the best possible value for money, although we will always spend the time necessary to deal properly with your case. Your co-operation in helping, wherever possible, to save time spent on the matter and so keep costs to a minimum will always be appreciated. In particular, if you can let us have any information requested as soon as possible, that will help both to speed up the case and save costs.

I will have discussed with you whether the firm's charges and expenses may be covered by insurance.

2.   *Estimate*

Because I do not know, in advance, what response your opponent will make to the claim I cannot be specific about the costs that would actually need to be incurred to reach a satisfactory conclusion. So, on a private basis, I would need to adopt a stage-by-stage approach and estimate accordingly.

Initially, it will be necessary to obtain detailed instructions, make a number of preliminary enquiries and begin correspondence with the Opponent.

[Additionally, it will also be necessary to take [steps in the] court action whilst further enquiries are being carried out.]

It is estimated, based on the time likely to be spent dealing with the first stage of work in this matter, that charges and expenses would be [about £[*figure*]]/[between £[*figure*] and £[*figure*]]. (This estimate is not intended to be fixed.)

Further estimates of likely charges and expenses would be given as the matter progresses at least every 6 months. You would be informed if it appeared the estimate would be exceeded.

You would be informed if any unforeseen additional work became necessary (for example, due to unexpected difficulties or if your requirements or the circumstances were to change significantly during the course of the matter). If that should happen you would be informed in writing of the estimated costs of that additional work before any extra charges and expenses were incurred.

If, for any reason, the matter did not proceed to completion, you would be charged for the work done and expenses incurred.

Either

[You may set a limit on the charges and expenses to be incurred.]

Or

[We have agreed to set a limit of £[*figure*] on charges and expenses to be incurred. This means that you must pay those charges incurred up to the agreed limit without our needing to refer back to you. We will inform you as soon as it appears that the limit may be exceeded and will not exceed the limit without first obtaining your consent.]

Once the first stage of the work has been dealt with, you will be advised further so that you can decide, given the likely costs but taking account of the potential benefit, whether to proceed.

When proceeding on a private basis it is normal practice to ask clients to pay sums of money from time to time on account of the charges and expenses which are expected in the following weeks or months. This helps to avoid delay in the progress of the case. Given the work which is likely to be required in dealing with the first stage of the case I would need to ask for £[*figure*] on account of charges, and to enable payment of expenses, before starting work on the case. It may be necessary to request further payments on account for charges and expenses to be incurred as the matter progresses. When these payments are put towards bills you will be sent a receipted bill. Such payments will be offset against the final bill, but it is important that you understand that the total charges and expenses may be greater than any advance payments.

3. *Billing arrangements*

To help you budget you would be sent an interim bill for charges and expenses at regular intervals while the work is in progress. You would be sent a final bill after completion of the work.

Payment is due within one month of the final bill. You would be charged interest on the bill at 4% above the base rate prevailing at the time on a daily basis, from the date on which payment of the bill is due if the bill is not paid by the due date.

If you have any query about a bill please always contact me immediately.

4. *Recovery of costs from the opponent*

If you are successful I will try to recover costs from the Opponent as part of any court judgment or settlement.

However:

(1) recovery of costs cannot be guaranteed (for example, the Opponent may be unable to pay costs or may be granted legal aid which would make recovery of costs very difficult);

(2) the court expects the costs incurred to be proportionate to the claim, and will not make the Opponent pay any of the costs that are disproportionate meaning. that the work undertaken must reflect, and be justified by, the nature of the case and the extent of the dispute, as well as the value of the claim which may effectively limit some potential enquiries or courses of action, on the basis either that the court will not allow such action, or that any costs incurred would certainly not be recovered from the Opponent;

(3) costs that may be recovered from the Opponent are unlikely to cover all costs incurred.

Accordingly, it is important you understand that, if you proceed on a private basis, you will be responsible for paying the firm's bills whether or not any part of the costs can be recovered from the Opponent.

You will also be responsible for paying the charges and expenses of seeking to recover any costs that the court orders the Opponent to pay. Interest can be claimed on any costs the Opponent is ordered to pay by the court, from the date of the court order. To the extent that you have paid charges or expenses on account you will have the benefit of such interest, but the firm is entitled to the rest of that interest.

5. *Responsibility for payment of the Opponent's costs*

The comments made so far in this letter concern only the costs of pursuing the claim, not the costs of the Opponent.

Either

[Until proceedings are issued it is unlikely the Opponent could recover any costs against you, even if the claim is not successful. If proceedings are issued, and they are not successful, the court can order you to pay the costs, or part of the costs, of your Opponent.]

Or

[If you are not successful the court can order you to pay the costs, or part of the costs, of your Opponent.]

I will have discussed with you whether any liability for the Opponent's costs may be covered by insurance and, if not, whether it would be advisable to have insurance to meet the Opponent's costs.

6. *Making payment*

Any payment you need to make to the firm can be accepted in cash (up to £[*figure*]) or by cheque [or by Switch/Visa/Mastercard].

7. *Summary*

So, to summarise the position if you were to instruct my firm to proceed on a private basis:

(1) you would be responsible for the costs of pursuing the claim, initially on the basis of the estimate already given, but that might have to be reviewed and, as already indicated, the total costs could end up being quite substantial;

(2) if [court proceedings have to be issued and] the claim fails, you would potentially be liable for the costs of the Opponent;

(3) if your claim succeeds I would expect to get most, though probably not all, of your costs paid by the Opponent.

1.5 Letter to Client – Client Care (Not Offering Conditional Fee Agreement)

Thank you for consulting me about this matter.

I should like to confirm the matters discussed and provide as much information as I can for you at this stage.

This letter explains the basis on which all necessary work will be carried out. Whilst that does mean writing at some length, I hope the information will be useful.

I will deal with a number of important matters in turn:

1.   *Advice and action*

When we met I advised you upon and summarised the legal action I believe is appropriate concerning this matter.

I confirm that, if a claim is to be pursued, compensation should be sought from [*name of opponent*] (who I shall describe as 'the Opponent').

I should also confirm, at the outset, that any court action seeking compensation should normally be commenced before the [third anniversary of the date the injuries were suffered] [twenty-first birthday of [*name of child*]] (although in a claim arising out of injuries suffered the court may, in certain circumstances, extend this time limit).

That is a brief summary of the advice and the action that appears appropriate. I will write at more length, explaining exactly how the matter could proceed, once we have arranged the best way of funding the case for you (which I will deal with later in this letter).

2.   *People responsible for your work*

It is important to let you have details about the people in the firm responsible for your work[, arrangements for referral of that work to the firm] and how people outside the firm may be involved as the matter progresses.

(1)   I have principal responsibility for dealing with this matter for you, on a day-to-day basis. I am a [*eg partner, solicitor, legal executive, litigation assistant*]. If anyone needs to know who is dealing with the matter on your behalf you can tell them that it is [*name*].

[(2)   I will be assisted by [*name*].]

(3)   The partner with responsibility for overall supervision is [*name*].

(4)   Once the matter is under way I will keep in touch with you, usually by letter, as it progresses.

(5)   The address for any letters you wish to send me is [*address*] and the reference is [*reference*]. It is helpful if you can quote this reference when writing or calling.

(6) The telephone number is [*telephone number*]. To help deal with any telephone enquiries as promptly as possible calls [will usually be dealt with by [*name of assistant*]]/[may be answered by a colleague].

(7) My e-mail address is [*insert e-mail address*]. Please note any e-mails that are sent will not be encrypted.

(8) At various stages I will suggest we review the case. If, at other times, you would like to arrange an appointment please contact [*name of assistant*] [me].

(9) The firm tries to avoid changing the people you are dealing with but if it should seem appropriate at any stage for the matter to be referred to another member of the team I will let you know.

(10) During the case it may be helpful to get some assistance from others, outside the firm. For example, it is sometimes helpful to involve experts, who can advise on and help deal with certain aspects of the case, and it may become appropriate to instruct counsel (a barrister) to advise or to represent you. I will let you know if it seems appropriate to seek such further assistance and give you details of who will be involved in providing this.

I hope this is all the information you need to ensure we are able to keep in touch with each other. If you should change your name, address or telephone number please let me know as soon as you can.

[The firm has an arrangement with [*name*] for referral of enquiries. For your referral a payment, of £[*figure*], will be made to [*name*]. You will not have to contribute in any way to this payment.]

3. *Identity and disclosure requirements*

Government regulations require the firm to obtain confirmation of your identity. It would be helpful, therefore, if you could let me have sight of documentation confirming your name, such as a passport or driving licence, and also address, for example a copy of a recent utility bill.

You need to be aware the firm has responsibilities under money laundering legislation to make reports in certain circumstances and that where this is required the firm cannot be held responsible for any loss, damage or delay resulting from compliance with such requirements.

4. *Charges, expenses and funding*

It is important to let you have details, at the outset, of how costs are incurred, how those costs may be funded, and any liability that might arise to pay the costs of the Opponent.

I hope this will allow us to agree the best way of funding the case.

I discussed with you whether you had any legal expenses insurance, membership of a Union or other organisation which might provide legal assistance and any other cover or support for the cost of legal work [as Public Funding, formerly Legal Aid, is not available for the claim].

I understand you [do not] [are not aware that you] [may] have such cover.

[To confirm, I shall be grateful if you could let me have any documentation relating to any insurance that you or your spouse/partner may have, as this cover might be provided, as well as a specific policy to cover legal expenses, as an 'add on' to a home contents, car insurance or other policy.] [Please could you also, if possible, try to obtain and let me have a copy of the motor insurance policy of the driver.]

[I am, therefore, checking to see whether you do have any cover and, if so, what cover is provided so that you can assess that in the context of the options set out in this letter. Meanwhile, I will set out in this letter the funding options on the basis that there is no further cover available, but will, of course, let you know if and when I do hear anything further and hope this letter will allow you to confirm your wishes on the basis of the available options.]

I have put forward details of your case to my firm's risk assessment panel, to see if we could offer you a conditional fee (or 'no win–no fee') agreement. Unfortunately, looking at all the factors involved in the case, this is not a matter in which the panel are prepared to authorise entry of a conditional fee agreement to pursue the claim (although there may be solicitors who would be willing to proceed on this basis).

[The reason the risk assessment panel cannot authorise entry of a conditional fee agreement at this stage is that a proper assessment of the risks of the claim cannot be made on the information presently available. However, I would be happy to refer the matter back to the risk assessment panel, as and when further information is available, if you are prepared to meet the cost of obtaining that information which, as you will see from the enclosed details, I estimate would commit you to costs in the region of £[*figure*].]

That means the only method of funding the case (with this firm)[, at least initially,] is on a private basis.

If you have insurance or other cover for the cost of legal work that should, wholly or partly, meet the obligation you would have for those costs and the costs of the opponent. However, it is important to appreciate that these costs would remain your obligation whether or not any indemnity is provided.

I enclose, for you to refer to if necessary, a summary of the terms that would apply if you wished to proceed on private basis[, at least initially].

[Whatever method of funding is appropriate the firm may make use of arrangements with agencies who specialise in obtaining expert medical reports. If the firm uses such an agency payment of the fee for the report is usually deferred for a fixed period or until the end of the case. Sometimes a commission is payable and if so it will be in the sum of £[*figure*]. Signing a copy of this letter will be your agreement to the firm retaining any such commission.]

It is important to keep in mind, whatever method of funding is appropriate, that the likely benefits of the proposed legal work should justify the likely cost of carrying out that work.

5. Documents

It is important that you keep all documents which relate in any way to this matter.

For present purposes, the term 'documents' includes anything recorded, whether in permanent, semi-permanent or electronic form, such as letters, contracts, receipts, diaries, computer records, photographs, videos, and anything else of that kind.

Whilst I do not need to see all of those documents at this stage, such documents may have to be produced in court proceedings and a duty is owed to the court to ensure the documents are preserved in case they should be required. Similarly, any documents you subsequently obtain which relate to the matter, should also be kept. Also, if you have any other property connected with the matter in any way, you should preserve that property until the case is concluded.

[I acknowledge safe receipt of the documents handed over at our meeting, which I have placed in my file for safekeeping, comprising [*details*].]

[I am grateful for sight of the documents you handed over at our meeting and I now return the original documents, having retained copies for my file.]

After completing the work, the firm is entitled to keep all papers and documents while there is money owing for charges and expenses. The firm keeps papers (except for any papers you ask to be returned to you) for no more than 6 years and keeps the file on the understanding that the firm has authority to destroy it after 6 years from the date of the final bill, although documents you ask to deposit in safe custody will not, of course, be destroyed.

If it becomes necessary to retrieve papers or documents from storage in relation to continuing or new instructions to act on your behalf, the firm would not normally charge for such retrieval. However, the firm will make a charge, based on time spent producing stored papers or documents to you or to another person at your request, in other circumstances. The firm may also charge for reading correspondence or other work necessary to comply with instructions given by you or on your behalf in this connection.

6.   Termination

If you decide to proceed you may subsequently terminate your instructions in writing at any time, but the firm will be entitled to keep all your papers and documents while there is money owing for charges and expenses.

In some circumstances you may consider that I ought to stop acting for you, for example if you cannot give clear or proper instructions on how to proceed, or if it is clear that you have lost confidence in how the work has been carried out.

I may only decide to stop acting for you with good reason, for example if I do not receive instructions from you or otherwise do not have the assistance I need to progress the claim properly or if costs are not paid. I will, however, always give reasonable notice before ceasing to act so that, if possible, any problems can be dealt with and I can continue to act on your behalf.

Under the Consumer Protection (Distance Selling) Regulations 2000 you may have the right to withdraw, without charge, within 7 working days of the date on which you asked the firm to act for you. But if I start work with your consent, within that period, you lose that right to withdraw. Your acceptance of the firm's terms of business, set out in this letter, will amount to such consent.

7.   Communication and suggestions

We are confident of providing a high quality service.

We do, of course, welcome any suggestions you might wish to make which you think could help to improve our service.

If, at any time, you are not happy with the service you are receiving from the firm, please let us know. You are valued client of the firm and I should like the opportunity to put matters right if any problems do arise. In the first instance, please contact me and I will do what I can to resolve the problem promptly. If, however, I am not able to resolve matters to your satisfaction you should then contact [*name*], who is responsible for the firm's complaints procedure.

This firm is not authorised by the Financial Services Authority. However, we are included on the Register maintained by the Financial Services Authority so that we can carry on insurance mediation activity, which is broadly the advising on, selling and administration of insurance contracts. This part of our business, including arrangements for complaints or redress if something goes wrong, is regulated by The Law Society. The Register can be accessed via the Financial Services Authority website at ww.fsa.gov.uk/register.

Sometimes personal injury work involves investments. If, during this transaction, you need advice on investments we may have to refer you to someone who is authorised by the Financial Services Authority, as we are not. However, as we are regulated by the Law Society, we may be able to provide certain limited investment services where these are closely linked to the legal work we are doing for you. If you have any problem with the service we provide for you then please let us know. We will try to deal with any problem quickly and operate an internal complaints handling system to help us resolve matters between ourselves. The Law Society also provides a complaints and redress scheme.

8. *Video surveillance*

Although this occurs in only a few cases you should be aware that anyone pursuing a personal injury claim may be subject to covert surveillance by enquiry agents acting on behalf of the opponent.

If, at any stage, you believe you are the subject of video surveillance please advise.

9. *Internet information*

You should also be aware that the opponent may, as the claim progresses, look for any available information about you on the internet, particularly those sites where people are invited to share personal information.

10. *What happens next?*

Subject to hearing from you with confirmation of your instructions to proceed on the basis of this letter, as requested below, I will write to confirm how the matter will proceed.

[If you wish to proceed, I should be grateful if you could let me have the sum of £[*figure*] on account of costs.]

[I assume you would like to proceed on the basis of any cover you may have for legal expenses, although, as I have already indicated, I do need to have confirmation of this cover. If cover is not available I will seek your further instructions, and authority to incur costs on a private basis, before those costs are incurred.]

This letter sets out the firm's terms of business with you, and so your continuing instructions in this matter will amount to acceptance by you of the terms. Even so, I shall be grateful if you would sign and date, in the space provided, the enclosed copy letter I can then be sure you understand, and are happy with, the basis on which the firm will act for you. I enclose a pre-paid envelope for your use.

As this letter is an important document, please keep it in a safe place for future reference.

I hope this letter usefully confirms the advice given and action agreed upon, as well as dealing with any immediate queries about the day-to-day handling of the matter and the firm's terms of business.

I look forward to hearing from you.

Yours sincerely

A copy of this letter should be enclosed with the following attached.

Receipt of this letter is acknowledged.

☐ I agree to the terms of this letter and wish to proceed on a private basis whether or not there is suitable insurance or other cover available for legal costs

☐ I agree to the terms of this letter and wish to proceed on a private basis provided I have suitable insurance or other cover available for legal costs

☐ I do not wish to proceed with the claim on the terms offered.

[Please tick appropriate box to confirm your wishes.]

Signed:

1.6 Letter to Client – Following Arrangement for Funding

Either

[Thank you for confirming that you would like to proceed with this matter under a conditional fee agreement with my firm.

I explained the nature and effect of a conditional fee agreement in earlier correspondence and sent, with that correspondence, a copy of the conditions which will apply to the agreement.

I have now prepared an agreement, for your claim, incorporating the conditions already notified to you. I should like to speak to you again at this stage so that the agreement, assuming it is approved by you, can be signed.]

Or

[Thank you for confirming that you would like to proceed with this matter on a private basis.

[I am pleased to report that I have confirmation from your legal expenses insurers that my firm can proceed with this matter on your behalf under the cover you have with them. I should mention, however, that even though you have the benefit of legal expenses insurance you retain the responsibility for the payment of my firm's costs and if, for any reason, the insurers refuse to make a payment for costs the firm would have to look to you for payment. The limit of the indemnity for costs is [presently] £[*figure*] and it is important to note that this indemnity level does not restrict your responsibility for costs.]

So that I can obtain your further instructions, and outline how the matter will then proceed, I should be grateful if you would contact [me]/[*name*].

I look forward to hearing from you.

Yours sincerely

AUTHORITIES AND CONFIRMATION OF INSTRUCTIONS

1.7   Authority to Confirm Instructions on Advice Given

[client's address]

I acknowledge receipt of your letter dated *[date of letter]* with which this authority was enclosed.

Please tick the appropriate box.

☐   I accept the advice given.

☐   I do not accept the advice given (if you would like to state what you would prefer, please do so in the space below).

[client's title, initials and surname]

Dated:

1.8   Authority to Confirm Instructions on Report

[client's address]

I acknowledge receipt of your letter dated *[date of letter]* enclosing the report of *[name of expert]*.

Please tick the appropriate box.

☐   I approve the report and wish to rely on it.

☐   I do not approve the report (if you would like to state why, please set out details in the space below) [and wish to obtain a further opinion].

[client's initials and surname in capitals]

Dated:

1.9   Authority Confirming Information

[client's address]

I acknowledge receipt of your letter dated *[date of letter]* and the enclosed information.

Please tick the appropriate box.

☐   I confirm that the information is correct.

☐   I confirm that the information is not correct as (please set out details in the space below).

[client's initials and surname in capitals]

Dated:

1.10   Authority for Release of Information

[address]

To: *[name]*
         [address]

Dear Sir

Name: *[client's full name]*

Address: *[client's address]*

Date of Birth: *[client's date of birth]*

I hereby authorise and request you to release to my solicitors, *[name and address]*, such information as they may require relating to me and copies of any documents held by you relating to me.

Yours faithfully

SECTION 2

INITIAL INVESTIGATIONS

CONTENTS

Advising the Client

CLIENT STATEMENT

2.1   Letter to Client – Sending Statement

I have now had the opportunity of completing a full and up-to-date statement which I hope accurately reflects all you are able to tell me.

I enclose the statement for your approval and shall be grateful if you could read it carefully to check the content.

It is very important that facts in the statement are accurate as I shall base my advice, and the action taken to pursue the matter, on your instructions as set out in the statement. Furthermore, to comply with court rules to which the statement may later be subject, your signature is confirmation that the facts stated are true. If, at a later stage, the court took the view that facts were stated without an honest belief in the truth of those facts, proceedings for contempt of court could be taken against you. I am sorry to give a warning at this early stage in such terms, but I am sure you will appreciate that it is my duty to do so.

Once you have read the statement, please make any amendments on the statement itself, or by a covering letter, that may be required to correct any errors or to cover points that may have been omitted.

After amendment please return the statement, if necessary with any covering letter, to me so that I can arrange for a further version, incorporating the amendments, to be sent out to you.

If the amendments are such that it would be easier to discuss the matter please telephone [*name*] [me].

If the statement is correct in its present form I shall be grateful if you would just sign and date it, in the space provided at the end, prior to returning it to me.

For the moment, the statement is intended for use only in the further investigation of the claim. At a later stage it may be necessary to disclose your statement to [*name of opponent*] ('the Defendant'). Usually, a further, up-to-date, statement will be prepared in a format for disclosure. However, as the statement enclosed with this letter might have to be disclosed, and any further statement will largely follow the same format, it is important that this statement is as full and accurate as possible.

[You will see that the statement refers to a sketch. I think it will be useful if you can prepare a rough sketch plan illustrating how the accident occurred. Please draw the sketch on the last page of the statement, which has been left blank for that purpose. I confirm that all I require at this stage is a very rough sketch.]

I enclose a pre-paid envelope and look forward to receiving the statement back, either signed and approved or with appropriate amendments, as soon as possible.

Either

[Once the statement is in approved form I shall write to you at more length detailing how the matter will proceed.]

Or

[Additionally, I find there are some further points which I would like to include in the statement and upon which I require your instructions. Perhaps it would be convenient to telephone me so that we may discuss these points. It may be sensible to return the statement to me only after we have spoken. Should the statement otherwise be approved you can no doubt confirm as much when we speak. I look forward to hearing from you.]

Yours sincerely

2.2   Letter to Client – Sending Amended Statement

Thank you for returning your draft statement with details of the amendments which are required.

I have prepared a further statement, incorporating those amendments, which I enclose for your approval.

Again, I shall be grateful if you would read the amended statement carefully to check that the content is complete and accurate. May I remind you of the importance of this given the statement of truth in the statement.

If further amendments are required, please correct the statement again and return it to me. If the statement is now in fully approved form, would you please sign and date it at the end, in the space provided, prior to return to me.

Either

[I have retained the exhibit referred to in the statement and will, of course, put this with the statement once that has been returned by you in approved form.]

Or

[You do, of course, still have the exhibit to the statement and I shall be grateful if this could be returned along with the statement, once that is approved.]

I enclose a pre-paid envelope for your use in returning the statement.

Yours sincerely

WITNESSES

2.3   Letter to Witness

Our Client: [*name of client*]

We are instructed by [*name of client*].

We understand that you may be able to confirm some matters relating to the injuries suffered by our client [in the accident on [*date*]].

Either

[In particular, it would assist us to know:

(1)   [*details*]

(2)   [*details*]

We enclose a pre-paid envelope for your use should you like to write with these details. Alternatively, please telephone [*name*] to confirm the details or to let us know if dealing with this request presents any difficulty.

We look forward to hearing from you.]

Or

[Accordingly, we enclose a questionnaire and shall be grateful if you could answer applicable questions either in the space provided on the questionnaire itself or on a separate sheet of paper if necessary.

Once complete, would you please sign and date the questionnaire and then return this to us in the pre-paid envelope also enclosed.

If you would prefer, we shall be happy to take these details from you and prepare a statement for your approval. If you would like to deal with the matter in this way, please telephone [*name*].

Please contact [*name*] if dealing with this request presents any difficulty.

We look forward to hearing from you.]

Yours faithfully

2.4   Letter to Witness – Sending Statement for Approval

Our Client: [*name of client*]

Thank you for letting me have details of the circumstances in which my client suffered injury.

I should like to record what you are able to say in a formal written statement. Accordingly, I have prepared a draft statement which I hope accurately sets out the information you are able to provide. I enclose that draft statement for approval.

I shall be grateful if you would read the statement carefully to check the content. It is likely that I will disclose the statement, once fully approved by you, as your evidence. It is essential, therefore, that the statement is full and accurate. In particular:

(1)   I hope this statement sets out, in your words, the information you are able to give.

(2)   The statement should not only be accurate in the actual content, but should also include all matters to reflect fairly everything that you think may be relevant.

(3)   To comply with court rules, to which this statement may later be subject, your signature will be confirmation that the facts stated are true. If, at a later stage, the court took the view that facts were stated without an honest belief in the truth of those facts proceedings for contempt of court could be taken against you. I am sorry to give a warning in such terms, but I am sure you will appreciate that it is my duty to do so.

Once you have read the statement, please make any amendments on the statement itself, or by a covering letter, that may be required to correct any errors or to cover points that may have been omitted.

After amendment please return the statement, if necessary with any covering letter, to me so that I can arrange for a further version, incorporating the amendments, to be sent out to you.

If the amendments are such that it would be easier to discuss the matter please telephone [*name*] [me].

If the statement is correct in its present form I shall be grateful if you would just sign and date it, in the space provided at the end, prior to returning it to me.

I hope that by disclosing the statement, once fully approved, I will be able to rely on your evidence in that written form and, if possible, not trouble you further. There is, of course, always a possibility (and it is no more than a possibility at this stage) that I would need you to give evidence at court. Very few cases reach a final court hearing, and even if that did occur, I would still hope that it would not be necessary for you to attend. If, at any stage, it seems likely that I will need you to attend a hearing, I will let you know.

Yours sincerely

POLICE

2.5   Letter to Police – Requesting Police Accident Report

Road Traffic Accident: [*place of accident*]

On: [*date of accident*]

We are instructed by [*name*], one of the parties involved in the above accident.

We understand that the police have investigated the circumstances of the accident and shall be grateful if you would let us know whether a copy of the police report is yet available.

[If the report is not yet available, we shall be grateful if you could confirm the name, address and insurance details of any other parties involved.]

[We would expect images relating to the accident to have been recorded on CCTV. Please confirm relevant images will be preserved and, meanwhile, all such material will be preserved. If images from the CCTV are stored by anyone else please identify who that is, by name and address, and notify any such person the material should be retained for the purpose of disclosure in court proceedings.]

We look forward to hearing from you.

Yours faithfully

2.6   Letter to Client – Sending Copy of Police Report

I have now received from the police a copy of the report relating to the accident.

The police report contains most of the background information, and much of the evidence, necessary to pursue a claim arising out of a road traffic accident.

It may be useful if I summarise the content.

(1)   The report confirms that the accident occurred at [*location of accident*] on [*date of accident*].

(2)   The report confirms that the vehicle, driven by the party you hold responsible for the accident, was a [*type of vehicle*], registration [*registration number*] driven by [*name of opponent*].

(3)   The report notes that the weather conditions were [*give details*].

(4)   The driver told the police, after caution, that [*give details*].

Either

[(5)   No criminal proceedings were taken against any party.]

Or

[(5)   Following the police investigation, criminal proceedings were taken against [*name*] who was convicted of [*insert details of conviction*] by [*name of Court*] Magistrates' Court on [*date convicted*]. That conviction is evidence of negligence unless, and this is unlikely, the conviction can be shown to be either erroneous or irrelevant.]

The police report may well be relied upon as evidence and, accordingly, I enclose a copy for you to check the content. Please let me know if you think there are any significant factual errors.

Either

[Generally, the report confirms the details you have given me concerning the accident and, I believe, supports the claim against the insurers of [*name of opponent*]. Accordingly, I consider that the police report is useful evidence.]

Or

[The report is helpful in confirming the general circumstances of the accident, but it is of limited assistance in showing the accident was the fault of [*name of opponent*]. Even so, it is useful to have this information on what happened.]

Yours sincerely

HEALTH AND SAFETY EXECUTIVE

2.7 Letter to Health and Safety Executive – Checking for Report of Accident

Accident to: [*name of client*]

Employed by: [*name of opponent*]

On: [*date of accident*]

Location: [*location of accident*]

We are instructed by [*name*] in connection with a claim for personal injuries arising out of the above accident.

We write to enquire whether the incident has been reported to you. If so, we shall be grateful for details of any investigation of the circumstances of the accident or inspection that may have been carried out, together with copies of factual statements and photographs.

If any investigation or inspection was not conducted by you, we shall be grateful if this letter could be referred to the appropriate department or office for a reply in due course.

We look forward to hearing in response to this enquiry.

Yours faithfully

2.8 Letter to Client – When the Health and Safety Executive Has No Information

I have made enquiries of the Health and Safety Executive to establish whether the accident was reported to and investigated by the Executive.

Either

[I am told that the accident was not reported and, accordingly, no information is available from this source.]

Or

[I am told that, although reported, no investigation was carried out and, accordingly, no information is available from this source.]

Whilst it has been right to make this enquiry I anticipate that we will be able to obtain, from other sources, confirmation of the circumstances of the accident. Accordingly, I hope the absence of information from the Health and Safety Executive will not present any particular difficulty.

Yours sincerely

2.9   Letter to Client – On Receipt of Health and Safety Executive Information

The accident was, as you know, reported to and investigated by the Health and Safety Executive.

Accordingly, I requested the Executive to disclose documents relating to that investigation for my use in pursuing the claim against [*name of opponent*] ('the Defendant').

I am pleased to report that I have now heard further from the Health and Safety Executive. I enclose copies of the documents received for your information.

I shall be grateful if you would check the content of the documentation produced and let me know if you disagree with any of the factual information this contains.

I should like you to check the documentation as this information is likely to be taken into account as the claim progresses.

I should like you to check the documents as I intend, in turn, to disclose copies to the Defendant in support of the claim as I consider these contain useful information.

Please would you complete and return the enclosed authority, to confirm whether or not you consider the information provided by the Health and Safety Executive is correct.

Yours sincerely

PHOTOGRAPHS

2.10   Letter to Photographer – to Illustrate Injuries

Our Client: [*name of client*]

Address: [*client's address*]

Telephone No: [*client's telephone number*]

We are instructed by [*name*] in a claim for personal injuries.

The injuries have left our client with [*details of injuries to be photographed*] and we think it would be useful to have photographs to assist the court at a later stage and for the purpose of negotiations meanwhile.

Accordingly, we shall be grateful if you would act on our behalf in taking a selection of photographs illustrating the present effect of the injuries.

Would you please let us have colour prints which should, of course, be printed unaltered from the images taken.

It will be helpful if, either on the prints themselves or by covering letter, you could state when, where and by whom the photographs were taken.

We invite you to contact our client direct at the above address to arrange a mutually convenient appointment for the photographs to be taken.

We confirm that we shall, of course, be responsible for your reasonable fee in acting on our behalf.

We look forward to receipt of photographs taken, together with a note of your fee in due course.

Would you please keep all negatives or other original images in case further prints are required for any court hearing.

Yours faithfully

2.11   Letter to Photographer – To Illustrate Scene of Accident

Our Client: [*name of client*]

Address: [*client's address*]

Telephone No: [*client's telephone number*]

We are instructed by [*name*] in a claim for personal injuries.

The circumstances of the accident are set out in our client's statement which we enclose for your information.

We think it will be useful to have photographs[, and a sketch plan,] illustrating the scene of the accident.

Accordingly, we shall be grateful if you would act on our behalf in taking a selection of photographs of the scene of the accident, putting that accident in context[, and in preparing a suitable sketch plan].

If you need further information from our client, or would like our client to be present when the photographs are taken, we would invite you to write direct to the above address.

[Facilities for inspection have been granted and, to confirm a mutually convenient time, we shall be grateful if you would contact [*contact name, address, telephone number and reference*].]

Would you please let us have a selection of colour prints which should, of course, be printed unaltered from the images taken.

It will be helpful if, either on the prints themselves or by covering letter, you could state when, where and by whom the photographs were taken.

We confirm that we shall, of course, be responsible for your reasonable fee in acting on our behalf.

Would you please keep all negatives or other original images in case further prints are required for any court hearing.

Yours faithfully

2.12   Letter to Client – Confirming Instructions to Photographer

Either

[I think it will be helpful to have photographs illustrating the cosmetic effect that, unfortunately, remains as a result of the injuries.]

Or

[I think it would be helpful to have photographs illustrating the place where the injuries were suffered as this will help to explain to the Defendant how those injuries occurred.]

I have, therefore, commissioned [*name*] to take a selection of suitable photographs and I anticipate that the photographer will be in touch with you, in due course, to make the appropriate arrangements.

I hope this letter explains why I have asked a photographer to help with the claim.

Yours sincerely

2.13   Letter to Client – On Receipt of Photographs

I am pleased to report that I now have available the photographs which I recently arranged for.

I enclose copies of the photographs for your information.

I shall assume, unless I hear to the contrary, that you accept that these photographs accurately show [the remaining effect of the injuries] [the scene of the accident] [the [*details*] involved in the accident].

I intend to disclose further copies of the photographs to the insurers of [*name of opponent*] ('the Defendant') by way of illustration.

Yours sincerely

OTHER ENQUIRIES

2.14   Letter to Non-defendant – Locus/Documents

We are instructed by [*name of client*] in connection with a claim for compensation for personal injuries suffered in an accident on [*date of accident*].

[At the time of the accident, our client was, during the course of employment with [*name of opponent*], working on your premises at [*location of accident*].]

Our instructions are to pursue a claim for personal injury compensation against [*name of opponent*]. On the information presently available we do not envisage a claim against you but, until our enquiries are complete, we must reserve our position in this respect.

The circumstances of our client's accident may have been investigated and relevant documents brought into being.

Accordingly, we write to request disclosure of any documents in the following categories.

(1)   The entry in your accident book.

(2)   Any entries there may be in the book concerning similar accidents over, say, the preceding year.

(3)   Any copies of enquiries into the circumstances of the accident.

(4)   Any relevant photographs.

(5)   Any relevant CCTV or other video images.

(6)   Any relevant instructions issued to those on your premises either before or since the date of the accident.

(7)   Any relevant correspondence or other documentation passing between you and [*name of opponent*].

If there are any relevant CCTV or other video images please can you ensure these are preserved pending disclosure.

We shall take production of the documents to mean that we have your consent for such documents to be produced to our client, all legal advisers, all experts instructed and [*name of opponent*].

[We also request facilities, should the need arise, for our client, ourselves and any expert instructed on our client's behalf, to enter onto the premises at [*location of accident*] for the purpose of inspecting the scene of the accident and taking photographs, and for any expert to obtain such information as may be necessary to prepare a report.]

We confirm that we shall, of course, be responsible for your reasonable copying charges.

We look forward to hearing from you in due course.

Yours faithfully

2.15   Letter to Non-defendant – Property/Documents

We are instructed by [*name of client*] in connection with a claim for compensation for personal injuries suffered in an accident on [*date of accident*].

At the time of the accident, our client was, during the course of employment with [*name of opponent*], using [*describe equipment, vehicle, or other property, as appropriate*].

Our instructions are to pursue a claim for personal injury compensation against [*name of opponent*]. On the information presently available we do not envisage a claim against you but, until our enquiries are complete, we must reserve our position in this respect.

To investigate the circumstances of the claim we should like facilities to have [*details of property*] inspected by experts instructed on our client's behalf.

[We have been advised that the [*details of property*] is no longer in the possession of [*name of opponent*] and that it is now in your possession.]

Accordingly, we write to request facilities for our client, ourselves, and experts instructed on our client's behalf to inspect the [*details of property*] at a place and time convenient to you and, so far as may be necessary, permission to enter your premises to carry out such an inspection.

We confirm that the purpose of the inspection is so that a report may be prepared by experts for use in our client's claim against [*name of opponent*].

Additionally, if you have any documentation relating to the [*details of property*] it would be most helpful if this could be made available at the time of inspection and, if possible, copied and sent to us meanwhile. We confirm that we shall, of course, be responsible for your reasonable copying charges.

If there are any relevant CCTV or other video images please can you ensure these are preserved pending disclosure.

We shall take production of any documents to mean that we have your consent for such documents to be produced to our client, all legal advisers, all experts instructed and [*name of opponent*].

If you require any further information at this stage, please let us know.

We look forward to hearing from you.

Yours faithfully

2.16   Letter to School – For School Report

Our Client: [*name*]

We are instructed by [*name of parent*] (on behalf of [*name of child*]) in a claim following the injuries suffered in an accident on [*date of accident*].

We understand that [*name of child*] attends your school and, accordingly, write to request a report dealing with any consequences of the accident on education and other school activities.

We shall be grateful if this letter can be referred to a teacher with personal knowledge of [*name of child*] and if any report can deal with the following matters.

(1)   A summary of pre-accident academic abilities and performance.

(2)   The academic consequences of the absence from school following the accident.

(3)   Whether the absence is likely to have any permanent effect on academic performance and, if so, what that might be.

(4)   The effect of the absence on any exam results stating, if appropriate, anticipated results against actual results.

(5)   The effect of the absence on other activities at school.

We look forward to hearing from an appropriate member of staff in due course.

Yours faithfully

2.17   Letter to HM Coroner

Our Client: [*name of client*]

Inquest into the death of: [*name of deceased*]

On: [*date of inquest*]

We are instructed by [*name of client*] on behalf of the Estate of [*name of deceased*] (Deceased).

The deceased died on [*date*] [as a result of injuries suffered in an accident on [*date*]]. We understand that you subsequently held an inquest on the above date.

So that we may fully advise our client, we shall be grateful if you would let us have the following information.

(1)   Notes of evidence given at the inquest.

(2)   Details of the verdict.

(3)   A copy of the pathologist's report.

[We understand that similar circumstances led to the death of [*name of other deceased*] and that an inquest into that death was held on [*date of that inquest*]. Accordingly, we would invite you to rule that our client is a person properly interested in the death of [*name of other deceased*] and, if so, to provide us with notes of evidence given at that inquest and details of the verdict.]

We assume we may have your permission for any expert instructed on our client's behalf to refer to the pathologist's report in preparing his or her own report.

We confirm that we shall, of course, be responsible for your reasonable fee in providing these details.

We look forward to hearing from you in due course.

Yours faithfully

ADVISING THE CLIENT

2.18   Letter to Client – Summary of Initial Steps

Thank you for returning the signed and approved statement. I enclose a copy of that statement for your future reference.

Now that I have your full and approved instructions, I should like to outline the further action I am taking on your behalf to pursue the claim against [*name of opponent*] (whom I shall describe as 'the Defendant').

Either

[I think there is a good case against the Defendant, but it is important that I obtain information to support the case and review the matter once all that information is available.]

Or

[On the information presently available I think the claim against the Defendant ought to be fully investigated, but I cannot advise you on the strength of the case until further information is available.]

Accordingly, I am making a number of enquiries which should help advance the claim and, in due course, allow me to advise further on the strength of the case and the appropriate level of compensation.

These enquiries will concentrate on the two most important elements of the case: first, that the Defendant is, as a matter of law, responsible for what has happened – this is termed 'liability'; secondly, the implications of what has happened, which will determine the amount payable by way of compensation (assuming liability is established) – this is termed 'quantum'.

There is a protocol, designed to help resolve claims of this kind as quickly and fairly as possible, which, in the event of proceedings being issued, the Court will have expected each party to have complied with.

Under the protocol appropriate details of the claim should be given to the Defendant so that a decision on the claim can be made. The Defendant is then expected to investigate the claim properly and make a timely decision how to deal with it. The enquiries now being made, as well as investigating the case, will help to comply with the protocol which, in turn, should assist in resolving the matter, or at least narrowing the issues, before any court proceedings are commenced.

I will now explain the enquiries I am making on liability and quantum, and how the protocol will apply to these, in turn.

1. *Liability*

The first objective is to establish the Defendant's liability for the injuries.

The enquiries on liability will concentrate mainly on the factual background and will involve the following steps.

(1) I have, as required by the protocol, sent a formal letter of claim to the Defendant which:
  (a) gives a summary of the factual background and the reasons why the Defendant is blamed for what happened;
  (b) summarises the injuries, losses and expenses;
  (c) confirms that compensation is sought;
  (d) asks that the claim be referred to the Defendant's insurers; and
  (e) reminds the Defendant of the timescale for dealing with the claim under the protocol.
  The protocol requires the Defendant, or the Defendant's insurers, to acknowledge the letter of claim within 21 days.

(2) If the claim is not acknowledged I will advise further on the action that will then be appropriate. However, I hope the Defendant will comply with this aspect of the protocol.

(3) Assuming that the Defendant does comply with the protocol by acknowledging the claim, I will pursue further correspondence with the Defendant's insurers with a view to resolving, or at least narrowing, the issue of liability. Under the protocol, the Defendant's insurers are expected, within 3 months from the 21day time limit for acknowledging the claim, to make a decision on liability so that either:
  (a) liability is admitted (which will allow us to enter negotiations towards outright settlement of the claim); or
  (b) reasons are given why liability is denied and relevant documents disclosed.

Either

[(4) Meanwhile, in case liability is not admitted, I have written to witnesses asking for a short statement about what happened.]

Or

[(4) Meanwhile, in case liability is not admitted, I should like to write to witnesses and would appreciate confirmation of the relevant details as discussed at our meeting.]

Or

[(4) I note that there are no witnesses[, or at least no witnesses who would be available to assist,] concerning [the direct circumstances of the accident]/[the events leading to the death of [*name of deceased*]].]

Or

[(4) I note that there may be witness evidence to confirm the circumstances in which the injuries occurred, but think that we should await a decision on liability before deciding whether or not this evidence will be required.]

[(5) I have asked the police for a copy of the accident report which, in a case of this kind, will provide most of the background information I need, including details of witnesses.]

[(6) I am establishing if any evidence to confirm the background can be obtained from [*relevant source, eg Health and Safety Executive*].]

(7) If liability is not admitted, it may be necessary to obtain a report from a suitable expert to help explain exactly how the injuries occurred as that, in turn, may help to support the case. I will write to you in more detail if and when an expert is instructed.

If no decision on liability is made by the Defendant I will advise further on the action that will then be appropriate. However, again, I hope the Defendant will comply with the protocol.

If you feel that there are any other lines of enquiry I should be pursuing at this stage, please let me know.

I shall, if possible, try to establish that the Defendant is entirely responsible for what happened. It may be, however, that these enquiries will suggest that the Defendant is only partly responsible for the injuries suffered. In this event, the compensation payable would be only a proportion of the compensation that would be received if the Defendant was fully responsible: that proportion being equal to the degree of responsibility. I will advise you further, in due course, if we shall need to consider making any such concession but it is, perhaps, right to explain at the outset that there is this degree of flexibility if necessary.

Either (accident)

2. Quantum

Secondly, it is necessary to prove the extent of the injuries, losses and expenses suffered as a result of the accident. This raises a number of points.

(1) Compensation (termed 'Damages') in cases of this kind, falls under
     two broad heads, which are:
     (a) *General damages*:
          These are claims that cannot readily be quantified in monetary
          terms and cover such matters as pain and suffering,
          inconvenience and the general effects of the injuries on various
          aspects of life. This part of the claim will usually be established
          by medical evidence.
          I will advise further on this aspect when I make arrangements
          to obtain medical evidence.
          The medical evidence will usually be provided by a suitable
          medical expert. The protocol also encourages parties, with a
          view to saving duplication of evidence, to agree selection of
          experts in any particular field and, accordingly, I will suggest
          some names to the Defendant, who must object if any are not
          agreed as suitable for joint selection.
     (b) *Special damages*:
          These are claims that can be quantified precisely, being
          financial losses. I have already obtained details of these
          expenses from you and they are summarised in the approved
          statement. The calculation may need to be revised at a later
          stage and, if necessary, I shall prepare a more detailed
          calculation of all losses and expenses. It may be necessary,
          again at a later stage, to obtain further evidence in support of
          the calculations. For the time being, the information contained
          in the statement will be sufficient, although you should retain
          any receipts or other documents relating to the claim for special
          damages.

(2) I have summarised the injuries, losses and expenses to the Defendant
     at this stage so that the Defendant can assess what investigation is
     necessary, given the nature of the claim. Once further enquiries on
     quantum have been completed, I will disclose to the Defendant any
     medical evidence to be relied on, so that the Defendant can form a
     view on the appropriate level of general damages. I will also supply a
     'Schedule of Special Damages', so that the Defendant can assess
     what claims are made for losses and expenses.

(3) Once this information is available, I will also be able to advise you in
     broad terms as to the likely level of compensation so that, if offers of
     settlement are made, you will be in a position to judge these.

(4) If liability has been accepted, even if this is for the purpose of
     negotiation only, I hope that will allow negotiations towards outright
     settlement to proceed. If liability is not accepted, it will be sensible to
     let the Defendant have this information in any event, as it will need
     to be disclosed if and when any court proceedings are commenced.

(5) An important matter, concerning the level of compensation, is that the Defendant, who will have to repay to the Government any State benefits received as a result of the injuries, may be entitled to reduce certain parts of the claim if corresponding State benefits have been paid. This is because the court, when assessing compensation, should try to put the injured person in the position that they would have been in had the injuries never occurred. Since, if the injuries had been avoided, benefits would not have been paid as a result of those injuries, it is appropriate for this allowance to be made.

To clarify the position, I am asking the Compensation Recovery Unit to let me have details of any benefits paid as a result of the injuries or confirmation that no such benefits have been paid. Once I hear further from the Unit I will send to you the information they have supplied with further advice on the possible effect of the scheme for recovery of State benefits. It will not, of course, be possible to confirm the position finally until such time as compensation is paid and so, from time to time, I will continue to check the position with the Compensation Recovery Unit as the claim proceeds. You will appreciate that, in some cases, the recovery of State benefits can have a significant effect on the compensation which is ultimately paid.

Or (fatality)

2. Quantum

Secondly, it is necessary to assess fully the implications of what has happened.

(1) I recognise that it is both impossible and inappropriate to put a value on the life of [*name of deceased*] but, nevertheless, the only remedy the courts can provide is by the payment of compensation and, so, I do have to consider how the court would make up any award of compensation, and direct my enquiries accordingly. In cases of this kind, there are a number of heads under which the court can award compensation although not all are applicable in any particular case. To summarise:
   (a) you are entitled to be reimbursed for the financial losses and expenses of [*name of deceased*] details of which I already have from you;
   (b) you are entitled to be reimbursed in respect of the funeral expenses;
   [(c) compensation for your bereavement is fixed by Parliament at a figure of £[*figure*];]
   [(d) to the extent that anyone was dependent upon [*name of deceased*], the court can award compensation to reflect that dependency;]

[(e) to the extent that [*name of deceased*] suffered any pain and discomfort before the untimely death, the court can award compensation. To assess this aspect of the matter further I have asked [*name of expert*] to let me have a written medical report. I anticipate that our medical expert will want to review the GP notes and records relating to the deceased. Accordingly, I enclose a suitable authority and should be grateful if you would kindly sign this and return it to me with the name of the GP and address of the surgery endorsed.]

(2) I have, for the moment, summarised the implications of what has happened to the Defendant, so that the Defendant can assess what investigation is necessary. As and when further relevant information becomes available, I will disclose this to the Defendant so that the Defendant can form a view on the appropriate level of damages.

(3) If liability has been accepted, even if this is for the purpose of negotiation only, I hope that this will allow negotiations towards outright settlement to proceed. If liability is not accepted, it will be sensible to let the Defendant have this information in any event, as it will need to be disclosed if and when any court proceedings are commenced.

(4) An important matter, concerning the level of compensation, is that the Defendant, who will have to repay to the Government any benefits received by [*name of deceased*] as a result of what happened, may be entitled to reduce certain parts of the claim if [*name of deceased*] received corresponding State benefits. To clarify the position, I am asking the Compensation Recovery Unit to let me have details of any benefits paid to [*name of deceased*] as a result of what happened, or confirmation that no such benefits have been paid. Once I hear further from the Unit, I will advise further.

I hope this letter usefully summarises the action being taken on your behalf to pursue the claim and also the likely timescale within which these further events will take place.

Once we have made progress under the protocol, I will, if the Defendant is prepared to accept liability, try to negotiate a settlement of the claim. If liability is not accepted, or the Defendant is not prepared to make realistic proposals to pay compensation, I will advise whether it is appropriate to issue court proceedings to pursue the claim.

Meanwhile, as information becomes available, I shall keep you advised of developments.

Yours sincerely

SECTION 3

MEDICAL EVIDENCE

CONTENTS

ADVISING THE CLIENT AND GETTING MEDICAL RECORDS

3.1   Letter to Client – Advising on Instructions to Medical Expert

To confirm the injuries suffered, the effect of those injuries and the prognosis, it will be helpful to have medical evidence. That medical evidence will be in the form of a written report prepared by an appropriate expert, usually after seeing [*you*] [*name of child*] and reviewing relevant medical records.

Given the injuries suffered, I recommend that a report be obtained from a [*specialism*]. I would suggest, as a suitable expert in that field, [*name of expert*] [or] [*name of further expert*] [or] [*name of further expert*]. [I will be able to confirm which expert will be asked to report once I have established, for reasons set out later in this letter, whether any is objected to].

[To ensure evidence on all aspects of the injuries is available, I recommend we also obtain a report from a [*specialism*]. I would suggest [*name of expert*] as a suitable expert in this field [or] [*name of further expert*] [or] [*name of further expert*]. [I will, once again, be able to confirm which expert has been asked to report once I have established whether any is objected to.] [I am sorry to trouble you with a number of appointments, but I am sure you will appreciate just how important it is to establish the full extent and effect of the injuries. In the rest of this letter, the comments I make about 'the doctor' will apply to each doctor I have asked to report.]

The doctor will send out an appointment in due course and I would ask you to liaise with the doctor's secretary if that appointment presents any difficulty for you.

I have sent, with my instructions, a copy of your statement to confirm the general background to the matter. However, you should feel free to discuss any further matters with the doctor when you meet.

I anticipate that the doctor will need to review both hospital and GP's records to prepare a report so I think it sensible to obtain copies of those notes at this stage.

[Accordingly, unless you have any objection, I would ask you to deal with the enclosed authorities for release of records in the following way.]

(1)   The application for records addressed to [*name of hospital*] just needs your signature (on the last page in the space provided between the marked crosses).

(2)   The authority to obtain GP records just needs your signature (again, in the space provided between the marked crosses).

If treatment has been given elsewhere please would you let me have details of the place concerned so that I can obtain any records from that source also.]

If you have any objection to records, or any part of the records, being produced, please let me know why. I appreciate that these records are confidential, and that there may be matters quite unrelated to the injuries with which the claim is concerned. However, it is usually best for any report to be prepared on the basis of all records having been reviewed by the doctor, although it will often only be necessary for relevant records to be referred to in the report.

The opinion of an expert, given in a formal written report, should help to explain the nature and extent of the injuries suffered which, in turn, will help in an assessment of the amount of compensation a court would award. Furthermore, if the court later gives permission, the report can be used as evidence at any hearing.

When the medical report is available I will send a copy to you for your information and approval. It may then be appropriate to disclose a copy to the insurers of [*name of opponent*] ('the Defendant'), to confirm the injuries suffered and the effect of those injuries.

Once medical evidence is disclosed to the Defendant I will invite the Defendant to agree that disclosed evidence. It will help to narrow the issues if the evidence is agreed, although, if it is not, the Defendant should explain which points are not agreed and the reasons why.

Meanwhile, it is appropriate to advise the Defendant that we intend to obtain expert opinion of this kind. That is because the court would expect the parties to have been in touch with each other, when an expert is to be instructed, so that the Defendant has the opportunity of objecting to any proposed expert. By giving the Defendant the opportunity of objecting now, it is hoped that this will avoid the need to duplicate the evidence from another expert in the same field.

Either

[I am pleased to confirm that there has been no objection to the doctor by the Defendant. It will now be more difficult, although not necessarily impossible, for the Defendant to argue successfully, at a later stage, that facilities should be given to obtain a report from a corresponding expert instructed by the Defendant.]

Or

[Unfortunately, the Defendant has objected to the doctor, together with other experts suggested in the same field. In these circumstances, I think we should obtain a report from the doctor, but the Defendant may have grounds, at a later stage, for requesting facilities to obtain a report from a corresponding expert instructed by the Defendant. I am sorry that it has not proved possible to agree on arrangements for joint selection of an expert but, of course, there can be cases when it is important that each party is able to obtain the evidence they think necessary.]

Or

[I will let you know if there is an objection by the Defendant.]

If, for whatever reason, it does become appropriate for the Defendant to request facilities to obtain a report from a corresponding expert I will advise further, at that stage, on whether I think it appropriate for the Defendant to take such a step. Should the Defendant wish to make arrangements to obtain such evidence, I expect that the Defendant will ask for copies of all medical records to be produced to the expert instructed and, possibly, the insurers concerned. I recognise that all such records are confidential but stress that, like any other documents disclosed by one party to the other during the progress of your claim, whoever receives those records is under a duty to keep the content confidential (unless and until any details are referred to at a court hearing).

Occasionally, it may be appropriate for an expert to act as a joint expert. If that should happen the expert will send the written report at the same time to me and to the Defendant. I will let you know if this should happen but, otherwise, the expert will report to me and I will, as already outlined, disclose the evidence to the Defendant with a request that the evidence be agreed or specific points of disagreement identified.

The doctor, like any expert involved in the case, will charge a fee for the preparation of the report.

[Should the claim not succeed, the insurance policy, which you took out when the conditional fee agreement was entered into, will meet the expert's fee so that you remain fully protected on costs.]

The doctor, like any expert involved in the case, has a duty to help the court on matters within his expertise and this duty overrides any obligation to the person who instructs the expert. Accordingly, the written report will be addressed to the court and will need to contain a statement that the expert understands, and has complied with, this duty to the court.

Unless I hear from you to the contrary, I shall assume you are content for me to send out instructions for expert involvement on the terms of this letter.

[I enclose a pre-paid envelope for your use in returning the enclosed authorities.]

[Finally, I should explain that the doctor will be instructed through an agency, [*name of agency*], so you may hear direct from the doctor or through that agency. [The agency will also arrange to obtain the medical records for the doctor.]]

Yours sincerely

3.2   Authority for Production of GP Records

[*address of client*]

[*date authority typed up*]

[*name of GP and address of surgery if known – otherwise leave blank*]

Dear [*Sir or Madam*]

Our Client: [client's full name]

Address: [client's address]

Date of Birth: [client's date of birth]

I hereby authorise and request you to release all notes, records and other documents held by you relating to [me] [*name of child*], or copies, to my solicitors, [*name*] of [*address*].

I confirm that production of the notes is not sought in connection with any claim against you or any of your employees.

Yours faithfully

3.3   Letter to Hospital – Requesting Records

Our Client: [*client's full name*]

Address: [*client's address*]

Date of Birth: [*client's date of birth*]

Access to Health Records – Data Protection Act 1998

We are instructed by our client in connection with a personal injury claim.

We understand our client has received hospital treatment and we expect, therefore, that you will be holding relevant records.

Accordingly, our client requests access, by copies, of [all] medical records [relating to treatment resulting from the injuries suffered on [*date of accident*]].

We enclose formal application, in the agreed Law Society and Department of Health format, duly signed by our client.

Either

[We confirm that, in addition to paper records, our client also seeks copies of all X-rays, CT scans, MRI scans and similar records.]

Or

[When replying please would you let us have details of any X-rays, CT scans, MRI scans and the like, so that we can assess whether copies of these are required.]

This request is made under the Data Protection Act 1998. We confirm that we will be responsible for the appropriate fee (if any) under the Act.

We look forward to hearing from you with the records.

Yours faithfully

3.4   Letter to GP – Requesting Records

Our Client: [*client's full name*]

Address: [*client's address*]

Date of Birth: [*client's date of birth*]

Access to Health Records – Data Protection Act 1998

We are instructed by our client in connection with a personal injury claim.

We understand that you hold records relating to our client.

Either

[Accordingly, we enclose authority signed by our client and shall be grateful for either:

(1)   copies of all records; or

(2)   the original records which we will copy ourselves prior to returning the originals to you forthwith.]

Or

[Accordingly, we enclose authority signed by our client and shall be grateful for copies of relevant records. We anticipate that the only relevant records will be those that relate to treatment for the injuries suffered on [*date of accident*], unless there is any history of particular relevance. We shall be grateful for:

(1)   copies of relevant records (if these can be easily identified); or

(2)   copies of all records over the relevant period (if that would be easier for you to provide); or

(3)   copies of all notes or the original notes and records for us to copy and return to you if it is not viable, for any reason, to identify and produce only relevant records.]

We confirm that the notes are not to be used in connection with any claim against you or your practice.

This request is made under the Data Protection Act 1998. We confirm that we will be responsible for the appropriate fee (if any) under the Act.

We look forward to hearing from you with the records.

Yours faithfully

INSTRUCTIONS TO MEDICAL EXPERT

3.5   Letter to Expert – Instructions to Provide Medical Report

Our Client: [*name*] [whose parent and contact is [*name*]]

Address: [*details*]

Date of Birth: [*date*]

Telephone No: [*number*]

We are instructed by our client in connection with a personal injury claim.

We shall be grateful if you would act as an expert in this case.

[It is intended that you act as a single joint expert. Accordingly, these instructions are also sent on behalf of the representatives of [*name of opponent*] who are [*name of firm*] of [*address*] under reference [*reference*] and we shall be grateful if you could copy to them any correspondence sent to us and, of course, the report.]

At this stage we ask you to prepare a written report, although it may, of course, become necessary for you to give evidence at any future court hearing.

[We anticipate that you will wish to focus on matters within your specialist field. We are content to rely on your judgment as to whether you deal with all aspects of the injuries or matters within your particular field. We would ask you to read the instructions later in this letter subject to that.]

We recognise that you will be familiar with the approach of the court to expert evidence under both the Civil Procedure Rules and the Protocol for the Instruction of Experts to Give Evidence in Civil Claims. However, we hope you do not object if we remind you of the duties of an expert witness, and some points relating to the format of an expert's report, before going on to outline some specific matters we would ask you to deal with and concluding with some more general points.

1.   *Overriding duty to the court*

(1)   It is, of course, the duty of an expert to help the court on all matters within the expertise of the expert. This duty is paramount and overrides any obligation to the person from whom instructions have been received.

(2)   Expert evidence should, of course, be the independent product of the expert uninfluenced by the pressures of litigation to assist the

court in providing objective, unbiased opinion on matters within the expertise of the expert and without assuming the role of an advocate.

(3) An expert should consider all material facts, including those which might detract from the opinion, and should make it clear:
(a) when a question or issue falls outside the expert's expertise; and
(b) when the expert is not able to reach a definitive opinion, for example because of insufficient information.

(4) If, after producing a report, an expert has a change of view on any material matter, that change of view should be communicated without delay.

(5) The report should be addressed to the court.

(6) The court should be made aware of any possible conflict of interest by production of a current CV giving details of any employment or activity raising a possible conflict (and if you think there may be such a conflict we would appreciate details at the outset).

(7) Failure to comply with these duties may result in costs penalties and the court debarring our client from relying on the evidence.

2. *Form and content of experts' reports*

(1) Details of qualifications should be given.

(2) Details of any literature or other material relied on in making the report should be given.

(3) There should be a statement setting out the substance of all material instructions, whether written or oral, and that statement should summarise the facts and instructions given to the expert which are material to the opinions expressed in the report or upon which those opinions are based. Please note that these instructions, though not privileged, do not have to be disclosed, unless the court so orders. Accordingly, these instructions can be referred to in the report but should not be attached or exhibited to it.

(4) The report should make clear which of the facts stated are within the expert's own knowledge.

(5) Anyone who carried out a test or experiment used for the report should be identified and the report should confirm whether or not the test or experiment was carried out under the expert's supervision.

(6)   The qualifications of the person who carried out any such test or experiment should be given.

(7)   Where there is a range of opinion on the matters dealt with in the report, the expert should:
      (a)   summarise the range of opinion; and
      (b)   give reasons for the expert's own opinion.

(8)   There should be a summary of the conclusions reached.

(9)   There should be a statement that the expert understands the duty to the court, has complied with that duty and will continue to comply with that duty.

(10) The report must be verified by a statement of truth, as well as containing the statements referred to in the preceding sub-paragraphs. The form of the statement of truth is:

> 'I confirm that insofar as the facts stated in my report are within my own knowledge I have made clear which they are and I believe to them to be true, and that the opinions I have expressed represent my true and complete professional opinion.'

3.   Documentation

Either

[We enclose a copy of our client's statement. We are taking steps to obtain relevant medical records and, once available, we will forward these for review when preparing your report.]

Or

[We enclose copies of the following.

(1)   Our client's statement which details the background, our client's account of the injuries sustained and present complaints.

[(2) Statement of [*name of witness*].]

[(3) Report prepared by [*name of expert*] (on our instructions).]

(4)   Hospital records.

(5)   GP records.

(6)   X-rays (which we shall be grateful if you could return to us after review as these are the only ones in our possession).]

We think it is appropriate for you to have sight of all available medical records as we consider you are best able to assess which records, or entries, are relevant and should therefore be relied upon and referred to when reporting. We do, of course, wish to balance the need for disclosure of relevant information against the confidential nature of medical records and the need to keep our client's privacy in relation to matters not relevant to your report. In these circumstances, it would be helpful if your report can either specifically identify relevant entries/records or, if possible, be accompanied by a core bundle containing only relevant entries/records. This should help to ensure that disclosure of records is kept relevant and proportionate.

4.   The background

Either

[The background is set out in the enclosed factual evidence.]

Or

[Our client's instructions on relevant matters are as follows: [*details*].]

5.   Your opinion

It would be helpful if you could, in your report, let us have your opinion on the following matters.

Either

[(1) The nature and extent of the initial injuries with details of immediate treatment given for each.

(2)   Subsequent progress with details of further treatment.]

Or

[(1) The link between our client's working environment and [his]/[her] present condition. Essentially we need to know if it is more likely than not that the environment has caused or materially contributed to that condition or materially increased the risk of our client developing that condition.

(2)   Your diagnosis of that condition.

(3)   The nature of any further treatment envisaged and prospects this may offer by way of improvement.

(4) The period over which the injuries have affected our client [particularly justifying any absence from work].]

Either

[(5) Confirmation our client has now made a full recovery.]

Or

[(5) Present complaints.]

(6) The extent which our client's ability to enjoy social, recreational and domestic activities [is]/[has been] impaired as a result of the injuries.

(7) The extent to which, as a result of the injuries, our client's working capacity [is]/[has been] restricted and/or our client is at any disadvantage on the labour market.

(8) Whether our client is disabled as a result of the injuries suffered, meaning that:
  (1) Our client has a progressive illness or an illness which has lasted or is expected to last for over a year; and
  (2) Our client satisfies the Disability Discrimination Act definition that the impact of the disability substantially limits the ability to carry out normal day-to-day activities; and
  (3) The condition affects either the kind or amount of paid work our client can do.

(9) Confirmation, if this is justified on medical grounds, our client [requires]/[has required] day-to-day care and attendance with personal needs and tasks as a result of the injuries.

(10) The risk of any deterioration in health and risk, or increased risk, of the onset of some connected or resulting condition. If there is such a risk, please can you, if possible, assess the risk in percentage terms and let us know if that risk is likely to increase or decrease materially in the future.

(11) Exclusion of any relevant previous history or relevant details and the contributory effect, if any, on our client's present condition.

(12) Your prognosis.

[(13) Whether our client's life expectancy has been reduced as a result of the injuries and, if so, to what extent.]

(14) If a further report would be appropriate at a subsequent stage. If so, an estimate of when that might be.

(15) If a report from another specialist, on any aspect of the injuries or subsequent management and treatment, would be useful.

6. *Further matters*

(1) We anticipate that you will wish to carry out an examination (though we are happy to leave this to your discretion) and, accordingly, invite you to write direct to our client ['s parent] with a view to making a mutually convenient appointment.

(2) If there is specific information, not presently available to us but to which another party has access, we may ask the court to direct that party to provide details. Accordingly, please let us know if any information of this kind is required.

(3) We would remind you that, if necessary, an expert always has the right to seek directions from the court to assist in carrying out the function of an expert. Whilst we are not entitled to notice of any such request, it would be helpful to know if this should be necessary.

(4) May we also remind you that, as and when any report is disclosed, written questions may be put to you about the report for the purpose of clarification. Should such a request be made by any other party, we expect that this will be through us, but if you should receive any request directly from another party, we would appreciate a copy of the request when made and any subsequent reply.

7. *Timescale*

Either

[At this stage we are not faced with any particular time limits and, accordingly, are content to await receipt of the report as soon as you are able to produce it.]

Or

[We are faced with a time limit which requires us to have your report, if possible, by [*date*]. If this presents any particular difficulty, can you please let us know as soon as possible.]

8. *Funding*

[We confirm that we shall be responsible for your reasonable fee in acting on our behalf.]

[This is on the basis that we are jointly and severally responsible for the fee, although we will make arrangements to share this with the representatives of [*name of opponent*].]

[These instructions are submitted through [*name of agency*] who will deal with arrangements for the fee.]

We hope that you are able to proceed with these instructions though please let us know if they present any difficulty.

Yours faithfully

APPOINTMENT WITH MEDICAL EXPERT

3.6   Letter to Client – Confirming Appointment with Expert

I understand you have an appointment to see [*name of expert*], a medical expert I have instructed on your behalf, on [*date*] at [*time*].

You should receive details of the appointment and the venue direct from the expert.

If the appointment is not convenient, or becomes inconvenient, please contact either the expert's secretary or, if this is not possible for any reason, [*name*] to arrange another appointment.

[I stress the importance of keeping the appointment, or making alternative arrangements meanwhile, as the expert will otherwise charge a cancellation fee. It is unlikely that the cost of any cancellation fee would be recovered as part of the costs of the claim and could result in that cost being deducted from any compensation recovered.]

I would expect to receive the medical report within a few weeks of your meeting with the expert and will advise further once that report is available.

Yours sincerely

RECEIPT OF MEDICAL REPORT

3.7 Letter to Expert – Acknowledging Receipt of Report

Thank you for your report relating to our client.

Payment of your fee will follow, under separate cover, in due course.

[Having carefully reviewed your report, and the matter generally, it would assist us if you could answer the following points:

(1) [*details*]

(2) [*details*]

We look forward to hearing from you in reply and confirm that we shall, of course, be responsible for your reasonable fee in dealing with this request.]

[Having considered the report on the basis of the factual instructions given by our client we would invite you to amend the report by [*details*].

Please let us know if this request presents you with any difficulty. Whilst we do wish to correct any errors we certainly have no wish to rewrite your report or to ask that this be amended so it no longer properly reflects your opinion or the information given to you.]

Yours faithfully

3.8 Letter to Client – Sending Medical Report

I am pleased to confirm that, following your meeting with [*name of medical expert*], I have now received the written medical report. I enclose a copy of the report for your information and consideration.

I shall be grateful if you would check the content of the report carefully to make sure that all factual points, upon which the report is based, are correct. Please let me know if there are any inaccuracies.

You will note the opinion of the expert. I hope that you feel this is a fair assessment of the situation, but if you do have any particular observations please let me know.

[Having carefully considered the report, there are some points I should like [*name of expert*] to clarify, so that we are aware of the expert's opinion on relevant matters. These are [*details*].]

Either

[As the doctor has been acting on instructions from me, the report has not yet been sent to the Insurers of [*name of opponent*] ('the Defendant'). However, I anticipate disclosing a copy of the report to the Defendant as confirmation of the injuries suffered and the effect of those injuries. Accordingly, I should like you to have this opportunity of carefully reviewing the report. When the report is disclosed I shall invite the Defendant to agree the content or identify any points of disagreement with reasons.]

Or

[As the Doctor has acted as a joint expert, a copy of the report has also been supplied to [*name of opponent*] ('the Defendant') confirming the injuries suffered and the effect of those injuries.]

The Defendant may ask for facilities to obtain a report from an expert in a similar field to [*name of medical expert*]. I shall advise further should such facilities be sought.

As I mentioned at an earlier stage, I hope the report will be useful in the negotiation of a settlement of the claim. The report may also be used, if the court later gives permission, as evidence and become part of the formal written case before the court.

[As it is not yet possible to give a final opinion on the long-term effect of the injuries, I will need the expert to report again in due course. At that stage I hope it will be possible for a final report to be prepared. I will advise further as and when instructions to prepare a supplemental report are sent out to the expert.]

[Given the content of the report, I think it is appropriate to make some further enquiries to assess properly all effects of the injuries. Accordingly, I am now instructing [*details*].]

Either

[I now propose, on the basis of the report, to make some assessment of the appropriate level of compensation for pain and suffering. I will let you have my advice on this aspect of the matter in due course.]

Or

[Although this report is helpful in confirming the injuries, I do not consider that sufficient information is yet available to make any realistic assessment of the appropriate level of compensation for pain and suffering, although I will, of course, let you know once that assessment can be made.]

[I am making this report available to [*name or names of experts who have not yet reported*] as the content may be useful in preparing further reports.]

I shall be grateful if, after reviewing the report, you could let me have your instructions. If the report is approved or you can confirm any specific reasons why the report should not be approved, I would ask you to complete the enclosed confirmation accordingly and then, after signature in the space provided, return this to me by the pre-paid envelope also enclosed.

If it is not possible to let me have your instructions by returning the confirmation form please telephone [*name*] [me] to discuss matters further.

I look forward to hearing from you.

Yours sincerely

3.9   Letter to Client – Sending Supplemental/Further Report

I am pleased to confirm that, following your further meeting with [*name of medical expert*], I have now received the written report supplementing the earlier medical report. I enclose a copy of the report for your information and consideration.

As with the earlier report, I shall be grateful if you would check the content carefully to make sure that all factual points upon which the report is based are correct. Please let me know if there are any inaccuracies.

You will note the current opinion and conclusions of the expert. I hope that you feel this is a fair assessment of the current situation, but if you do have any particular observations please let me know.

Either

[As the evidence of [*name of expert*] has already been disclosed, and so relied upon, it is necessary to disclose this further report to the representatives of [*name of opponent*] ('the Defendant') in order to confirm the current opinion of the expert (if this report were not disclosed, the court would expect us not to rely on the opinion of [*name of expert*] at all). Accordingly, I shall disclose a copy of the report to the Defendant, but I should like you to be aware of the expert's current expert opinion as well.]

Or

[As the doctor has acted as a joint expert, a copy of the report has also been supplied to [*name of opponent*] ('the Defendant') to confirm the current opinion of the expert.]

I will invite the Defendant to agree the report or, if that is not possible, to identify any particular points of disagreement and the reasons for these.

[I shall, now that we have a more definite prognosis, review the appropriate level of compensation for pain and suffering and write with my advice in due course.]

I shall be grateful if, after reviewing the report, you could let me have your instructions. If the report is approved or you can confirm any specific reasons why the report should not be approved, I would ask you to complete the enclosed confirmation accordingly and then, after signing in the space provided, to return this to me by the pre-paid envelope also enclosed.

If it is not possible to let me have your instructions by returning the confirmation form, please telephone [*name*] [me] to discuss matters further.

I look forward to hearing from you.

Yours sincerely

SECTION 4

EXPENSES AND LOSSES

CONTENTS

EARNINGS DETAILS

4.1   Letter to Non-defendant Employer – For Earnings Details

Our Client: [*name of client*]

We are instructed by [*name of client*] in connection with a personal injury claim.

Our instructions are to pursue a claim against [*name of opponent*] ('the Defendant').

We understand that our client [has been] [is [now]] employed by you as a [*job description*]. Accordingly, we write to request certain information so that a claim for loss of earnings can be properly calculated.

We shall be grateful if you would let us have the following information.

[(1)   The exact period of our client's absence from work [following the accident on [*date of accident*]].

(2)   Our client's gross and net earnings for the 13 weeks preceding the absence.

(3)   Any other financial losses arising from the absence. For example:
  –   bonus payments (whether seasonal or otherwise);
  –   commission;
  –   car and/or fuel benefit;
  –   free/reduced-price food at work;
  –   concessionary fares;
  –   accommodation;
  –   cheap loans;
  –   clothing/uniform allowance;
  –   telephone expenses;
  –   insurance benefits;
  –   pension provision;
  –   profit shares.
Please provide details of any of the above together with any financial benefits of any other kind.]

[(4)   The date our client's employment with you commenced.

(5)   Full details of gross and net earnings to date.]

[(6)   If our client has lost the chance of promotion as a result of the injuries:
  –   how great was the chance – in percentage terms if possible;
  –   when would promotion have been likely;

> – is there still any chance of promotion and, if so, what prospect (again in percentage terms if possible), when and to what position;
> – what is the annual difference in remuneration between our client's present position and that if promoted.]

[(7) Is there, at present, any risk to our client's future employment, whether as a result of the injuries sustained or other unrelated factors? If so, as much information as possible would be appreciated.

(8) Details of the current selection criteria used for redundancies.]

[(9) Any general pay award since the date of the accident.

(10) Comparative earnings – that is, current average net earnings for a selection of employees engaged in the same position as our client. We appreciate that you may wish to give figures anonymously, although if you can identify the employees concerned that would be helpful.]

[(11) Any payments made to our client during absence from work including sick pay, statutory sick pay and tax refunds.

(12) If any payments of sick pay have been made, please advise whether these are due under a contributory or non-contributory scheme. Please also advise if there is any relevant contractual provision requiring repayment in the event of damages being recovered and, if so, producing a copy of that provision.]

We shall, of course, wish to produce copies of the information provided to our client, experts involved in the case and the Defendant.

We confirm that our client's claim is not directed against you.

We look forward to hearing from you in due course.

Yours faithfully

4.2 Letter to Client – To Check Earnings Details

I have now received earnings details from [*name of source*]. I anticipate using this information to help confirm the calculation of the claim for lost earnings and, accordingly, enclose copy details for you to check.

If the details are correct, would you please confirm by completion and return of the enclosed authority. If, however, the information is inaccurate or, perhaps, requires some explanation to ensure I have a fair picture of lost earnings resulting from the injuries, please complete the form accordingly. Should you need to discuss any matters before returning the authority, please telephone [*name*] [*me*].

I also enclose a pre-paid envelope for your use in returning the authority.

Either

[When seeking this information I specifically enquired whether there is any contractual entitlement to recover, out of any compensation, monies paid during the absence from work.

I understand there is such an entitlement. Accordingly, whilst I shall aim to recover, as part of the claim, lost earnings as though no payments were made during your absence from work, you need to remember that, out of any compensation received, a sum representing earnings received during absence from work will have to be paid over to [*name of relevant employer*].

I mention this now as I will subsequently ignore, for the purposes of assessing the value of the claim and any offers, sums for which you will have to account to [*name of relevant employer*] out of any compensation received at the conclusion of the claim.

I understand that the amount to be recouped is £[*figure*].

I look forward to hearing from you.]

Or

[When seeking this information I specifically enquired whether there is any contractual entitlement to recover, out of any compensation, monies paid during the absence from work.

I understand that there is no such provision, but please let me know if you think otherwise.

I look forward to hearing from you.]

Or

[I look forward to hearing from you.]

Yours sincerely

TAX AND NI RECORDS

4.3   Letter to Client – Sending Authorities for HM Revenue & Customs and Department for Work and Pensions Information

To help establish the earnings achieved before the injuries, I think it would be helpful to obtain confirmation of those earnings from government departments holding appropriate records.

HM Revenue & Customs and the Department for Work and Pensions are likely to have records, relating to Income Tax and National Insurance Contributions respectively, that should help confirm your employment history and, accordingly, help substantiate the claim for lost earnings.

Government departments will not release information without your written approval and, accordingly, I enclose forms of authority which I would ask you to sign and return to me in the pre-paid envelope also enclosed.

It will be helpful, if you know it, to complete the relevant authority with the name and address of the Tax Office which currently, or last, dealt with your income tax.

It may well be appropriate to disclose to [*name of opponent*] any information obtained, although please let me know if you have any objection to this.

I look forward to receiving back from you, duly signed, the enclosed forms of authority.

Yours sincerely

4.4   Letter to HM Revenue & Customs – Requesting Schedule

Our Client: [*client's name*]

Address: [*client's address*]

Tax Reference: [*client's tax reference*]

National Insurance No: [*client's National Insurance number*]

We are instructed by our client in connection with a personal injury claim.

To quantify our client's claim for loss of earnings properly, we would appreciate a schedule of earnings over the last, say, 5 tax years. Would you please include details of the following:

(1)   the names and addresses of employers throughout this time;

(2)   the dates between which our client was employed by each employer;

(3)   gross and net earnings with each employer, or for individual tax years if this is more convenient;

(4)   our client's code number throughout this time.

Our client is [presently employed by]/[was last employed by] [*name of employer*]. We hope our client's National Insurance number is sufficient for you to trace the whereabouts of relevant records, and if necessary to forward this letter to the appropriate office for reply, if those records are not with you.

We enclose our client's signed authority for release of information contained in your records.

Yours faithfully

4.5   Letter to HM Revenue & Customs (NI Contributions Office) – Requesting National Insurance Records

HM Revenue & Customs
NI Contributions Office
Special Section A
Room 145B
Long Benton
Newcastle-upon-Tyne
NE98 1ZZ

Dear Sirs

Our Client: [*client's name*]

Address: [*client's address*]

Tax Reference: [*client's tax reference*]

National Insurance No: [*client's National Insurance number*]

We are instructed by our client in connection with a personal injury claim.

To quantify our client's claim for loss of earnings properly, we shall be grateful if you could provide the following details from your records:

(1) all periods of employment (other than self-employment) and details of which employer paid National Insurance contributions during these periods;

(2) periods of self-employment;

(3) periods of unemployment;

(4) a breakdown, on an annual basis, of the type and amount of National Insurance contributions.

We enclose our client's signed authority for release of information contained in your records.

Yours faithfully

4.6   Letter to Client – With Tax/National Insurance Information

I am pleased to report that I have now heard from HM Revenue & Customs in response to my enquiry for details of past earnings.

I enclose a copy of the information provided for you to check.

If the details are correct, would you please confirm by completion and return of the enclosed authority. If, however, the information is inaccurate or, perhaps, requires some explanation please complete the form accordingly. Should you need to discuss any matters before returning the authority, please telephone [*name*] [me].

I also enclose a pre-paid envelope for your use in returning the authority.

Yours sincerely

THE SCHEDULE

4.7   Letter to Client – Sending Schedule of Expenses and Losses for Approval

When I prepared your statement I included a summary of the financial losses and expenses incurred as a result of the injuries and mentioned that, once further information was available, I might want to prepare a more detailed and up-to-date calculation of those losses and expenses.

On the basis of the information which is now available, I have been able to make a further calculation of the financial losses and expenses resulting from the injuries. Accordingly, I am pleased to enclose a copy of that calculation.

In addition to the expenses and losses set out in the calculation, I would remind you that there will be an award of compensation to reflect the pain, suffering and loss of amenity caused by the injuries [and I have already advised on what I believe to be the appropriate level of compensation for that]/[and I will advise on what I believe to be the appropriate level of compensation for this as soon as I can].

May I ask you to bear in mind that the calculation of expenses and losses I have prepared puts forward your case on the most reasonably optimistic basis possible. Whilst it is right to put the case at its best to the insurers of [*name of opponent*] ('the Defendant'), it is likely that the Defendant will argue that lower figures are appropriate on certain aspects of the claim and, accordingly, you do need to keep an open mind on the level at which a settlement might be achieved should sensible proposals be put forward by the Defendant. I will advise further on this as and when the Defendant responds to the calculation.

[Meanwhile, my view is that, allowing for arguments the Defendant is likely to advance, it is likely that the court might not award more than £[*figure*] for expenses and losses. Accordingly, you do need to read the calculation with this in mind.]

Furthermore, the calculation does not make any allowance for State benefits paid as a result of the injuries.

Either

[I mention this just for the sake of completeness, although it seems, from information supplied by the Compensation Recovery Unit, that no recoverable benefits, which the Defendant might deduct against appropriate heads of claim, have been paid; therefore, unless the position should change, the rules relating to recovery of benefit should not have an impact on the claim.]

Or

[As you know, the Defendant must repay all recoverable benefits when a settlement is reached or an award of compensation made by the court and, insofar as benefits that correspond to relevant heads of the claim for special damages have been paid, the Defendant may reduce payments under the relevant head by the amount of corresponding benefit paid.]

[This calculation of your expenses and losses may need further amendment in due course as additional information becomes available. I will, of course, let you have a copy of any future calculations, but hope it is useful for you to have sight of this calculation meanwhile.

I shall be grateful if you could check the calculation, and in particular let me know if there have been any further items of expenditure or loss incurred but not yet included.

If there are any further items to be included, or the calculation needs correcting in any other respect, please could you amend the calculation accordingly. Alternatively, if it would be easier to explain or discuss any amendments please contact [*name*] [me].

Should the calculation be approved, as presently drafted, please would you sign the statement, to this effect, in the space provided between the marked crosses and then return the calculation to me.

The calculation is required to contain a statement of truth. Your signature amounts to confirmation that the facts in the calculation are true and I must remind you that if the court took the view any facts were stated without an honest belief in them proceedings for contempt of court could be taken against you.

I enclose a pre-paid envelope for you to return the calculation, either signed and approved or with details of amendments, and look forward to hearing from you accordingly.

Yours sincerely

COMPENSATION RECOVERY

4.8   Letter to Compensation Recovery Unit – Notifying Claim

The Manager
Compensation Recovery Unit
DX 68560 WASHINGTON 4

Dear Sir

Our Client: [*client's name*]

Address: [client's address]

Date of Birth: [client's date of birth]

National Insurance No: [client's National Insurance no]

We are instructed by our client in connection with a personal injury claim.

We shall be grateful if you would note our interest and also forward details of all benefits paid as a result of the injuries.

We enclose Form CRU1 accordingly.

Yours faithfully

4.9   Letter to Client – On Receipt of Compensation Recovery Unit Information

I enclose a copy of a statement issued by the Compensation Recovery Unit detailing any State benefits which the Unit understand have been paid since the date the claim arose and as a result of the injuries.

[The certificate indicates that no recoverable benefits have been paid as a result of the injuries. Accordingly, if that remains the position, recovery of benefits is not likely to have any impact on the claim. However, I would prefer to set out, in some detail, the operation of the Compensation Recovery Scheme just in case the position should change and any future certificate indicate that recoverable benefits have been paid.]

It is the responsibility of the insurers of [*name of opponent*] ('the Defendant') to refund to the Department for Work and Pensions, at such time as any compensation is paid, any recoverable benefits.

The repayment of recoverable benefits, therefore, is made by the Defendant, in addition to any compensation paid. However, the Defendant may be entitled to reduce any compensation which is ultimately paid insofar as, meanwhile, corresponding benefits have been paid. This is because the objective, in providing compensation, is to put the injured person in the financial position that he or she would have been in had the injuries never occurred (and, of course, had the injuries not occurred, State benefits, received as a result of those injuries, would not have been paid).

In these circumstances, it is important to be aware of, and to keep under review, the payment of State benefits, and I therefore requested the Compensation Recovery Unit to provide details of any benefits already paid. It is the response to this enquiry which I enclose.

Having set out the general background to the scheme for recovery of benefits, I should now like to deal with the detail of the scheme, as this is important for you to understand the possible impact of any entitlement by the Defendant to reduce compensation paid in due course.

(1)   When compensation is paid by the Defendant, either as an interim payment or as part of a final award, the Defendant must repay to the Compensation Recovery Unit the total amount of recoverable benefits paid up to that time.

(2)   The Defendant is entitled to reduce the compensation paid insofar as corresponding benefits have been paid as a result of the injuries (and in effect have already provided some compensation). The requirement that only 'corresponding' benefits are relevant for these purposes means that any State benefits paid can only reduce those parts of the claim to which they relate and cannot be used to reduce other parts of the claim. Those parts of the claim from which relevant recoverable benefits can be deducted are as follows.
      Compensation for lost earnings can be reduced by any of the following benefits paid as a result of the injuries:
      (a)   disability working allowance;
      (b)   disability pension;
      (c)   incapacity benefit;
      (d)   income support;
      (e)   invalidity pension;
      (f)   invalidity allowance;
      (g)   jobseeker's allowance;
      (h)   reduced earnings allowance;
      (i)   severe disablement allowance;
      (j)   sickness benefit;
      (k)   unemployment supplement;
      (l)   unemployment benefit;

(m) statutory sick pay (but only that paid up to 5 April 1994 – and only a proportion of payments made between April 1991 and April 1994).

Compensation for care and attendance can be reduced by any of the following benefits paid as a result of the injuries:

(a) attendance allowance;

(b) care component of disability living allowance;

(c) constant attendance allowance;

(d) exceptionally severe disablement allowance.

Compensation for loss of mobility can be reduced by any of the following benefits paid as a result of the injuries:

(a) mobility allowance;

(b) mobility component of disability living allowance.

So, in assessing offers of settlement, we will need to bear in mind any allowance the Defendant can make, when formulating that offer, in respect of relevant recoverable benefits. It is too early to assess the exact impact of any such entitlement, but I think it right to make you aware of the position at this stage.

(3) The Defendant is only liable to repay benefits, and to use any benefits paid to reduce the compensation payable, insofar as those benefits have been paid as a result of the injuries and to the extent of those benefits received up to the time compensation is paid or for 5 years after the injuries were suffered, whichever is the soonest.

(4) To confirm the possible impact of recoupment, the Compensation Recovery Unit will continue to issue, from time to time, certificates of recoverable benefits. As and when certificates are issued, I will send copies to you so that:

(a) you can check that any benefits shown in the certificate are accurate – in terms of the benefit paid, the amount and the period over which payment has been made;

(b) you can check that those benefits have been paid as a result of the injuries which are the subject of the claim and not for any other reason;

(c) you can keep up to date, so far as the benefits listed above are concerned, on the potential impact of these benefits being used to reduce the compensation that may be received from the Defendant in respect of relevant parts of the claim.

Unless I hear from you to the contrary, at the time, I shall assume that the details of certificates are correct. If not, please let me know, as an application can be made to the Unit seeking a review of the certificate if it contains an error in relation to any benefit paid or the amount or period over which payment has been made.

If, when compensation is paid, there is a dispute as to whether the Defendant is entitled to make a deduction to allow for relevant benefits paid, you may appeal that deduction. This is a matter I will advise on, if necessary, at that stage.

I think it right to advise you on details of the rules relating to recovery of benefits, even though it may not be appropriate for the Defendant to make any deduction in your case as, of course, in some cases, the entitlement to make a deduction can have a significant effect on the compensation receivable.

If you disagree with the information in the certificate, please contact [*name*] [me] to advise.

Yours sincerely

4.10   Letter to Client – Sending up-to-date Compensation Recovery Unit Statement

At an earlier stage I explained how, as and when you receive payment of any compensation, [*name of opponent*] ('the Defendant') would have to repay any recoverable benefits to the Compensation Recovery Unit of the Department for Work and Pensions and might be entitled, insofar as you have received corresponding benefits, to reduce certain parts of your claim by the amount of those benefits paid.

I mentioned that, from time to time, the Department would issue up-to-date statements of any benefit paid, either to me or to the Defendant.

I have recently received a further statement giving details of benefits paid to date and, to keep you in the picture, I enclose a copy of that statement herewith. Once again, I shall be grateful if you would check its accuracy.

Either

[Unless I hear from you to the contrary, I shall assume that the statement correctly gives details of the type of benefit, rate of benefit and period over which that benefit has been paid as a result of the injuries. If, however, you do not agree with any of this information, please contact [*name*] [me] to give details of any errors.]

Or

[I note that the certificate indicates there are still no recoverable benefits paid as a result of the injuries and, if this remains the position, the recovery of benefits is still unlikely to have any impact on the claim. If, however, you consider the information is wrong, please contact [*name*] [me] to give details of any errors.]

Yours sincerely

SECTION 5

THE PROTOCOL AND LIABILITY

CONTENTS

Preliminaries: Disease and Illness

5.1   Letter to Opponent – Enquiries under the Pre-action Protocol for Disease and Illness claims

5.2   Disease Questionnaire

Letter of Claim

5.3   Letter to Opponent – Generic Letter of Claim

5.4   Paragraphs for the Letter of Claim – Documents

5.5   Paragraphs for the Letter of Claim – Earnings

5.6   Paragraphs for the Letter of Claim – Identity

5.7   Paragraphs for the Letter of Claim – Insurance

Acknowledgment and decision on liability

5.8   Letter to Opponent – Following Acknowledgment of Letter of Claim

5.9   Letter to Client – Following Acknowledgment of Letter of Claim

5.10   Letter to Opponent – Following Decision on Liability

5.11   Letter to Client – Following Decision on Liability by Admission

5.12   Letter to Client – Following Decision on Liability by Denial

Documents

5.13   Letter to Opponent – Dealing with Documents

5.14   Letter to Client – Enclosing Documents Disclosed by Defendant Under the Protocol

Failure to comply with the protocol

5.15   Letter to Opponent – Non-Compliance with Protocol

PRELIMINARIES: DISEASE AND ILLNESS

5.1   Letter to Opponent – Enquiries under the Pre-action Protocol for Disease and Illness claims

We are instructed by [*name*].

Our client complains has developed [disease] and we are investigating whether this may have been caused [during the course of employment with [you] [*name*]]/[whilst at your premises at [*address*]]/[as a result of your product [*name*]].

We write this letter in accordance with the Pre-action Protocol for Disease and Illness Claims to seek [personnel records] [and] [occupational health records] [and] [*details*].

Please note your insurers may require you to advise them of this request.

We enclose a request form for the records sought.

Please would you confirm, within the next 21 days, the records requested will be produced within the next 40 days.

If you are not able to comply with this request, or not able to do so within the time stipulated, please advise us of the reason within the next 21 days.

Yours faithfully

5.2   Disease Questionnaire

Application on behalf of a potential claimant for use where a disease claim is being investigated

This should be completed as fully as possible

Company:

Name:

Address:

1.(a)	Full name of Claimant (including previous surnames)	
(b)	Address now	
(c)	Address at date of termination of employment, if different	
(d)	Date of birth (and death, if applicable)	
(e)	National Insurance number (if known)	
2.	Department(s) where Claimant worked	
3.	This application is made because the Claimant is considering:	
(a)	A claim against you as detailed in para 4	YES/NO
(b)	Pursuing an action against someone else	YES/NO
4.	If the answer to Q3 (a) is 'Yes' details of:	
(a)	The likely nature of the claim, eg dermatitis	
(b)	Grounds for the claim, eg exposure to chemical	
(c)	Approximate dates of the events involved	
5.	If the answer to Q3 (b) is 'Yes' insert:	
(a)	The names of the proposed Defendants	

(b)	Have legal proceedings been started?	YES/NO
(c)	If appropriate, details of the claim and action number	
6.	Any other relevant information of documents requested	
	Signature of Solicitor	
	Name	
	Address	
	Ref:	
	Telephone number	
	Fax number	

I authorise you to disclose all of your records relating to me/the Claimant to my Solicitor and to your legal and insurance representatives.
Signature of Claimant..

Signature of personal representative where Claimant has died

LETTER OF CLAIM

5.3   Letter to Opponent – Generic Letter of Claim

Either

[We are instructed [by] [on behalf of] [*name of client*] in connection with a claim for personal injuries suffered in an accident on [*date*].]

Or

[We are instructed by [*name of client*] in connection with a claim for personal injuries arising from the [illness]/[disease] of [*details.*]/[we write further to earlier correspondence, requesting employment records, as we are now able to confirm our client's instructions following a review of the information made available.]

Our client considers that the injuries occurred through your negligence [or the negligence of those for whom you have responsibility] and claims damages accordingly.

We enclose a copy of this letter for you to send to your insurers. Please refer the copy letter to the relevant insurers as soon as possible as if you do not this may affect insurance cover and/or the conduct of any subsequent legal proceedings.

This is a letter of claim sent in accordance with the Pre-action Protocol for [Personal Injury] [Disease and Illness] Claims. We will, therefore, deal with the matters which arise under that protocol at this stage. We trust your insurers will reciprocate, by meeting their obligations, as we consider compliance with the terms of the protocol will be the best way of resolving this matter, or at least narrowing the issues, in a timely and proportionate way.

We should, in particular, like to deal with liability as quickly as possible. We hope that will then allow us to enter negotiations on quantum and explore the possibility of outright settlement at the earliest opportunity.

We will deal with the matters arising at this stage, under the terms of the protocol and more generally, in turn.

1.   Liability

Please confirm your position on liability as soon as possible. If liability is not accepted and/or you blame anyone for our client's injuries please give full details so that we may consider what you have to say.

2. Summary of the Claim

This letter gives a summary of the factual background and the reasons why it is considered you are liable for our client's injuries.

However, this summary should not be taken to be comprehensive and we reserve the right to plead such particulars as may be appropriate when we have a response, in accordance with the protocol, to this letter and when any further investigations that may then be required have been concluded.

We are instructed that [*factual background*].

Our client contends injuries, losses and expenses were caused by the matters already outlined and that, for the following reasons, you are liable for these.

(1) [*allegation*].

(2) [*allegation*].

(3) [*allegation*].

[Furthermore, our client considers that the accident is of a kind which should not occur, in the ordinary course of events. Accordingly, it is alleged the very fact of the accident is evidence of your negligence. If you contend otherwise please explain why.]

[Our client also relies on the conviction by [*name*] Court on [*date*] of [*details of conviction*] which is considered relevant. If you contend otherwise please give full reasons when replying.]

[Our client also considers that you are responsible as the employers of [*name*] for the injuries. Please confirm that vicarious liability for [*name*] is not an issue. If you are unable to give that confirmation, please explain why, identify [*name*] by full name and address, and tell us now if it is contended that [*name*] was, at the time, working for anyone else.]

We consider this summary is sufficient for the claim to be investigated, and a decision on liability given, so that the timescale provided for under the protocol has started to run. We would remind you that if you contend otherwise we should be advised accordingly within 21 days of this letter.

[3. Police Report

We [are establishing the availability of a Police Report and, if one is available,]/[have obtained a copy of the Police Report and] will be happy to supply a copy provided we receive half the cost, which [we anticipate] will be £[*figure*].]

[4. Investigations

Please confirm that we may, with our client and an expert instructed on our client's behalf, have access to your premises for the purposes of inspecting [*describe locus and/or relevant property*], taking photographs and preparing any necessary plans.

We consider that evidence of this kind will be appropriate, unless liability is admitted in full, and that the evidence is best obtained by someone with suitable expertise so that any photographs and plans are as meaningful as possible.

We would suggest, as suitable experts to instruct, [*name of expert*] [and [*name of further expert*]]. Please let us know if you have any objection.

We ask you not to carry out a unilateral investigation but to liaise with us over the selection of a suitable expert who can assist in and save duplication of investigation, in accordance with the spirit of the pre-action protocol.

Please confirm that the [*describe locus and/or relevant property*] involved in the accident will be preserved in its present condition until seen and photographed on our client's behalf and that, thereafter, the property will be retained by you until such time as our client's claims have been resolved.]

5. *Documents*

Unless liability is fully admitted we will expect disclosure of documents, in accordance with the protocol, to be given. Compliance with this aspect of the protocol will also ensure that all relevant documents are preserved.

Given the background to the matter, as already set out in this letter, we consider documents within the following categories are relevant and that, accordingly, copies should be supplied to us which, in accordance with the protocol, should be provided without making a charge.

[*List documents required – examples are given in* **5.2**.]

If there are documents, within these categories, you contend are privileged please state the grounds of the claim for privilege and identify the documents with sufficient detail for us to assess the validity of the claim for privilege.

Should you fail to give disclosure, insofar as that is required by the protocol, we reserve the right to make appropriate application to the court, whether pre-action or in the main action. We will also, if necessary, draw the content of this letter to the court's attention at a later stage should any document not be preserved on the basis that, having specifically requested the same at this stage, any disposal of documents would be a deliberate non-compliance with the obligations to the court both under the protocol and the Civil Procedure Rules.

6. *Injuries and loss*

We should like to get liability dealt with as quickly as possible, hence the request for information already made in this letter, so that we may move on, we hope, to negotiations on quantum.

Presently, we can only summarise, under broad heads, the nature of our client's claim.

(1) *General damages*
Our client has suffered [*details of injury*]. This is, however, just a summary and should not be regarded as a comprehensive description of the injuries pending receipt of expert medical opinion. We wish to obtain medical evidence and would suggest, as suitable experts to instruct, [*name*], Consultant [*speciality*], [*name*], Consultant [*speciality*], and [*name*], Consultant [*speciality*].
[We propose to submit instructions through [*agency*] as we anticipate that will assist in making the necessary arrangements for obtaining medical evidence.]
Please let us know if you have any objections.

(2) *Expenses and losses*
We expect the claim for expenses and losses will include the following heads.
(i) [*details*]
(ii) [*details*]

We will provide further details in due course and meanwhile it may be helpful if we indicate our preliminary view is that this claim will be suitable for the [multi-track]/[fast track].

[7. *Earnings*

[*If the Defendant is the employer insert paragraphs from* **5.3**]

8. *CRU*

We confirm that we will provide your insurers with appropriate details for the claim to be reported to the CRU.

9.   Identity

[*Insert appropriate paragraph from 5.4.*]

10.   Insurance

[*Insert appropriate paragraph from 5.5.*]

11.   Alternative Dispute Resolution (ADR)

We should like to see if it is possible to resolve, or at least narrow, any issues by ADR. We consider the appropriate means of ADR to be negotiation, though please let us know if you contend any other method to be suitable. Accordingly we hope you will comply with your obligations under the pre-action protocol and act on our invitation to negotiate within its framework. Should you decline to do so we do reserve the right to refer to this, and further relevant, correspondence when seeking any orders that may be necessary from the court, on case management, and also in connection with the costs of any specific application and, indeed, the matter generally.

[12.   Other parties

We have also sent a letter of claim to [*name*] and enclose a copy for your information.]

13.   Funding

The claim is funded by a conditional fee agreement dated [*date*], which provides for a success fee, supported by an insurance policy issued on [*date*] by [*insurer*] (policy number [*number*]).

We enclose Notice of Funding, in Form N251, to confirm.

14.   Timetable

We consider that this letter commences the timetable applicable under the pre-action protocol and, accordingly, would ask for an acknowledgment of this letter, from you or the relevant insurers, by [*date which is 21/42 days after the date of this letter*] and a decision on liability by [*date which is 3/6 calendar months after the last date for acknowledgement*] at the latest.

We look forward to receiving a response to this letter of claim in accordance with the pre-action protocol.

Yours faithfully

5.4 Paragraphs for the Letter of Claim – Documents

Road Traffic

(1) Documents identifying nature, extent and location of damage to defendant's vehicle where there is any dispute about point of impact.

(2) MOT certificate.
If vehicle defect is alleged or it is alleged by defendant that there was an unforeseen defect which caused or contributed to the accident

(3) Maintenance records.
If an accident involving a commercial vehicle as defendant

(4) Tachograph charts or entry from individual control book.

(5) Maintenance and repair records required for operators' licence.

Workplace

(1) Accident book entry.

(2) First aider report.

(3) Surgery record.

(4) Foreman/supervisor accident report.

(5) Safety representative's accident report.

(6) RIDDOR (Reporting of Injuries, Diseases and Dangerous Occurrences Regulations) report to HSE.

(7) Other communications between defendants and HSE.

(8) Minutes of Health and Safety Committee meeting(s) where accident/matter considered.

(9) Report to DSS.

(10) Documents listed above relative to any previous accident.

(11) Photographs and/or videos relating to the accident.

(12) Documents produced to comply with requirements of the Management of Health and Safety at Work Regulations 1999 including:
  (i)   Pre-accident Risk Assessment required by Regulation 3(1).
  (ii)   Post-accident Re-Assessment required by Regulation 3(2).
  (iii) Accident Investigation Report prepared in implementing the requirements of Regulations 4 and 5.
  (iv)   Health Surveillance Records in appropriate cases required by Regulation 6.
  (v)   Information provided to employees under Regulation 10.
  (vi)   Documents relating to the employees health and safety training required by Regulation 8.
  (vii) Documents relating to the appointment of competent persons to assist required by Regulation 7.
  (viii) Documents relating to necessary contacts with external services required by Regulation 9.

If applicable

(13) Documents produced to comply with requirements of the Workplace (Health, Safety and Welfare) Regulations 1992 including:
  (i)   Repair and maintenance records required by Regulation 5.
  (ii)   Housekeeping records to comply with the requirements of Regulation 9.
  (iii) Hazard warning signs or notices to comply with Regulation 17 (Traffic Routes).

If applicable

(14) Documents produced to comply with requirements of the Provision and Use of Work Equipment Regulations 1998 including:
  (i)   Manufacturers' specifications and instructions in respect of relevant work equipment establishing its suitability to comply with Regulation 5.
  (ii)   Maintenance log/maintenance records required to comply with Regulation 6.
  (iii) Documents providing information and instructions to employees to comply with Regulation 8.
  (iv)   Documents provided to the employee in respect of training for use to comply with Regulation 9.
  (v)   Any notice, sign or document relied upon as a defence to alleged breaches of Regulations 14 to 18 dealing with controls and control systems.
  (vi)   Instruction/training documents issued to comply with the requirements of Regulation 22 insofar as it deals with maintenance operations where the machinery is not shut down.

(vii) Copies of markings required to comply with Regulation 23.

(viii) Copies of warnings required to comply with Regulation 24.

If applicable

(15) Documents produced to comply with requirements of the Personal Protective Equipment at Work Regulations 1992 including:

    (i)   Documents relating to the assessment of the Personal Protective Equipment to comply with Regulation 6.

    (ii)   Documents relating to the maintenance and replacement of Personal Protective Equipment to comply with Regulation 7.

    (iii) Record of maintenance procedures for Personal Protective Equipment to comply with Regulation 7.

    (iv) Records of tests and examinations of Personal Protective Equipment to comply with Regulation 7.

    (v)   Documents providing information, instruction and training in relation to the Personal Protective Equipment to comply with Regulation 9.

    (vi) Instructions for use of Personal Protective Equipment to include the manufacturers' instructions to comply with Regulation 10.

If applicable

(16) Documents produced to comply with requirements of the Manual Handling Operations Regulations 1992 including:

    (i)   Manual Handling Risk Assessment carried out to comply with the requirements of Regulation 4(1)(b)(i).

    (ii)   Re-assessment carried out post-accident to comply with requirements of Regulation 4(1)(b)(i).

    (iii) Documents showing the information provided to the employee to give general indications related to the load and precise indications on the weight of the load and the heaviest side of the load if the centre of gravity was not positioned centrally to comply with Regulation 4(1)(b)(iii).

    (iv) Documents relating to training in respect of manual handling operations and training records.

If applicable

(17) Documents produced to comply with requirements of the Health and Safety (Display Screen Equipment) Regulations 1992 including:

    (i)   Analysis of work stations to assess and reduce risks carried out to comply with the requirements of Regulation 2.

    (ii)   Re-assessment of analysis of work stations to assess and reduce risks following development of symptoms by the claimant.

(iii) Documents detailing the provision of training including training records to comply with the requirements of Regulation 6.

(iv) Documents providing information to employees to comply with the requirements of Regulation 7.

If applicable

(18) Documents produced to comply with requirements of the Control of Substances Hazardous to Health Regulations 1992 including:

(i)   Risk assessment carried out to comply with the requirements of Regulation 6.

(ii)   Reviewed risk assessment carried out to comply with the requirements of Regulation 6.

(iii) Copy labels from containers used for storage handling and disposal of carcinogenics to comply with the requirements of Regulation 7(2A)(h).

(iv)   Warning signs identifying designation of areas and installations which may be contaminated by carcinogenics to comply with the requirements of Regulation 7(2A)(h).

(v)   Documents relating to the assessment of the Personal Protective Equipment to comply with Regulation 7(3A).

(vi)   Documents relating to the maintenance and replacement of Personal Protective Equipment to comply with Regulation 7(3A).

(vii) Record of maintenance procedures for Personal Protective Equipment to comply with Regulation 7(3A).

(viii) Records of tests and examinations of Personal Protective Equipment to comply with Regulation 7(3A).

(ix)   Documents providing information, instruction and training in relation to the Personal Protective Equipment to comply with Regulation 7(3A).

(x)   Instructions for use of Personal Protective Equipment to include the manufacturers' instructions to comply with Regulation 7(3A).

(xi)   Air monitoring records for substances assigned a maximum exposure limit or occupational exposure standard to comply with the requirements of Regulation 7.

(xii) Maintenance examination and test of control measures records to comply with Regulation 9.

(xiii) Monitoring records to comply with the requirements of Regulation 10.

(xiv) Health surveillance records to comply with the requirements of Regulation 11.

(xv)   Documents detailing information, instruction and training including training records for employees to comply with the requirements of Regulation 12.

(xvi) Labels and Health and Safety data sheets supplied to the employers to comply with the CHIP Regulations.

If applicable

(19) Documents produced to comply with requirements of the Construction (Design and Management) Regulations 2007 including:
   (i)   Notification of a project form (HSE F10).
   (ii)   Health and Safety Plan.
   (iii) Health and Safety file.
   (iv)   Information and training records provided.
   (v)   Records of advice from and views of persons at work.

If applicable

(20) Documents produced to comply with requirements of the Pressure Systems and Transportable Gas Containers Regulations 1989 including:
   (i)   Information and specimen markings provided to comply with the requirements of Regulation 5.
   (ii)   Written statements specifying the safe operating limits of a system to comply with the requirements of Regulation 7.
   (iii) Copy of the written scheme of examination required to comply with the requirements of Regulation 8.
   (iv)   Examination records required to comply with the requirements of Regulation 9.
   (v)   Instructions provided for the use of operator to comply with Regulation 11.
   (vi)   Records kept to comply with the requirements of Regulation 13.
   (vii) Records kept to comply with the requirements of Regulation 22.

If applicable

(21) Documents produced to comply with requirements of the Lifting Operations and Lifting Equipment Regulations 1998 including the record kept to comply with the requirements of Regulation 6.

If applicable

(22) Documents produced to comply with requirements of the Noise at Work Regulations 1989 including:
   (i)   Any risk assessment records required to comply with the requirements of Regulations 4 and 5.

(ii)   Manufacturers' literature in respect of all ear protection made available to claimant to comply with the requirements of Regulation 8.
(iii) All documents provided to the employee for the provision of information to comply with Regulation 11.

If applicable

(23) Documents produced to comply with requirements of the Construction (Head Protection) Regulations 1989 including:
   (i)   Pre-accident assessment of head protection required to comply with Regulation 3(4).
   (ii) Post-accident re-assessment required to comply with Regulation 3(5).

If applicable

(24) Documents produced to comply with requirements of the Construction (General Provisions) Regulations 1961 including report prepared following inspections and examinations of excavations etc to comply with the requirements of Regulation 9.

If applicable

(25) Documents produced to comply with requirements of the Gas Containers Regulations 1989 including:
   (i)   Information and specimen markings provided to comply with the requirements of Regulation 5.
   (ii)   Written statements specifying the safe operating limits of a system to comply with the requirements of Regulation 7.
   (iii) Copy of the written scheme of examination required to comply with the requirements of Regulation 8.
   (iv)   Examination records required to comply with the requirements of Regulation 9.
   (v)   Instructions provided for the use of operator to comply with Regulation 11.

If applicable

(26) Documents produced to comply with requirements of the Work at Height Regulations 2005 including:
   (i)   Documents relating to planning, supervision and safety carried out for Regulation 4.
   (ii)   Documents relating to training for the purposes of Regulation 5.
   (iii) Documents relating to the risk assessment carried out for Regulation 6.

(iv) Documents relating to any inspection carried out for Regulation 12.

(v) Documents relating to any inspection carried out for Regulation 13.

Occupiers

(1) The accident book for the premises where the accident occurred covering the date of the accident.

(2) Entries in other accident books relating to accidents on the premises.

(3) All documents relating to any safety checks carried out.

(4) All documents submitted to, or received from, the Health and Safety Executive or other authority with the appropriate investigative function concerning the accident.

(5) All statements relating to the accident.

(6) All invoices, receipts and other documents relating to the purchase of relevant safety equipment to prevent a repetition of the accident.

(7) All correspondence, memoranda or other documentation received, or created, concerning the condition or repair of the premises where the accident occurred.

(8) All correspondence, instructions, estimates, invoices and other documentation submitted or received concerning repairs, remedial works or other works to the scene of the accident, since the date it occurred.

(9) Work sheets and all other documents recording work done completed by those responsible for maintaining the premises.

(10) All reports, conclusions or recommendations following any enquiry or investigation into the accident.

(11) Any photographs or videos illustrating the accident or scene.

(12) All documents brought into being or correspondence sent, or received, relating to the accident.

Highway

For a period of 12 months prior to the accident:

(1) Records of inspection for the relevant stretch of highway.

(2)   Maintenance records including records of independent contractors working in relevant area.

(3)   Records of the minutes of Highway Authority meetings where maintenance or repair policy has been discussed or decided.

(4)   Records of complaints about the state of highways.

(5)   Records of other accidents which have occurred on the relevant stretch of highway.

If highway design defect is alleged

(6)   Documents produced to comply with Section 39 of the Road Traffic Act 1988 in respect of the duty designed to promote road safety to include studies into road accidents in the relevant area and documents relating to measures recommended to prevent accidents in the relevant area.

5.5   Paragraphs for the Letter of Claim – Earnings

We should like to accurately quantify our client's claim for expenses and losses. Accordingly, would you please provide the following information and, where appropriate, relevant documentation.

(1)   The exact period of our client's absence from work.

(2)   Our client's gross and net earnings for the 13 weeks preceding the absence.

(3)   Any other financial losses arising from the injuries. For example:
(i)   Bonus payments (whether seasonal or otherwise);
(ii)   Commission;
(iii) Car and/or fuel benefit;
(iv)   Free/reduced price food at work;
(v)   Concessionary fares;
(vi)   Accommodation;
(vii) Cheap loans;
(viii) Clothing/uniform allowance;
(ix)   Telephone expenses;
(x)   Insurance benefits;
(xi)   Pension provision;
(xii) Profit shares;

(xiii) Financial benefits of any other kind whatsoever.

(4)   Whether our client has lost the chance of promotion as a result of the injuries and, if so:
   (i)   How great was the chance (in percentage terms if possible);
   (ii)   When would promotion have been likely;
   (iii)   Is there still any chance of promotion and, if so, what prospect (again in percentage terms if possible) at what time and to what position;
   (iv)   What is the annual difference in remuneration between our client's present position and if promoted.

(5)   If there is any risk to our client's future employment, whether as a result of the injuries sustained, other unrelated factors or whatever.

(6)   Any payments made to our client during the absence from work including sick pay, statutory sick pay and tax refunds.

(7)   If any payments of sick pay have been made, please advise whether these are due under a contributory or non-contributory scheme.

5.6   Paragraphs for the Letter of Claim – Identity

Road Traffic

Please confirm the identity of the driver of the vehicle at the time of our client's accident and, if the proper Defendant in any litigation should be the employer or principal of such driver, describe that party with the accuracy required for litigation. In either event please confirm the address for service of any proceedings.

Please note that, insofar as the potential Defendant in any litigation is a limited company, our client would wish to be notified, pending resolution of the claim, of any application for such company to be struck off the Companies Register and, for such purposes, we confirm that we will accept service of any appropriate notice on our client's behalf.

Workplace/Occupiers

Please confirm the identity of the party in control of the premises where the accident occurred, at the material time, whether this be the way in which such party is described for insurance purposes or otherwise.

Please fully describe such party, with the accuracy required for litigation, and confirm the address for service of any proceedings.

Please note that, insofar as the potential Defendant in any litigation is a limited company, our client would wish to be notified, pending resolution of the claim, of any application for such company to be struck off the Companies Register and, for such purposes, we confirm that we will accept service of any appropriate notice on our client's behalf.

Highway

Please confirm the identity of the Highway Authority responsible for the location where the accident occurred, at the material time, whether this be the way in which it is described for insurance purposes or otherwise.

Please fully describe such party, with the accuracy required for litigation, and confirm the address for service of any proceedings.

5.7   Paragraphs for the Letter of Claim – Insurance

Road Traffic

Please confirm details of your relevant insurers, supplying the name of the company, address and policy number. Please would you also supply us with a copy of the relevant policy of insurance so that we can ensure appropriate notice is given to those insurers, in the event of proceedings being commenced, in case our client should wish to rely upon the provisions of the Third Parties (Rights Against Insurers) Act 1930.

Alternatively, please let us have a letter from your insurers confirming that you have complied with the terms of the policy concerning this claim, and that they are happy for us to correspond directly with you, without the necessity of corresponding further with them, and that they will indemnify you in respect of our client's claim.

For the avoidance of doubt, we demand that, under the terms of s 154 of the Road Traffic Act 1988, you state:

(1)   whether you were, at the time of the accident, insured by a policy having effect for the purposes of the Road Traffic Act 1988 or had in force a security having effect for those purposes or would have been so insured, or would have had in force such a security, if the insurers or giver of the security had not avoided or cancelled the policy or security; and

(2)   (if so) particulars of the policy or security in any certificate delivered; and

(3)   (if not) the following:
       (i)   the registration mark or other identifying particulars of the vehicle concerned;
       (ii)   the number or other identifying particulars of the insurance policy issued in respect of the vehicle;
       (iii)   the name of the insurer; and
       (iv)   the period of insurance cover.

Workplace / Occupiers / Highway

Please confirm details of your relevant insurers, supplying the name of the company, address and policy number. Please would you also supply us with a copy of the relevant policy of insurance so that we can ensure appropriate notice is given to those insurers, in the event of proceedings being commenced, in case our client should wish to rely upon the provisions of the Third Parties (Rights Against Insurers) Act 1930.

Alternatively, please let us have a letter from your insurers confirming that you have complied with the terms of the policy concerning this claim, and that they are happy for us to correspond directly with you, without the necessity of corresponding further with them, and that they will indemnify you in respect of our client's claim.

ACKNOWLEDGMENT AND DECISION ON LIABILITY

5.8   Letter to Opponent – Following Acknowledgment of Letter of Claim

We thank you for your letter of [*date*] and note your interest.

We hope this will allow us to make progress in accordance with the pre-action protocol.

We will deal, in turn, with the matters which we consider arise at this stage.

1.   Liability

Please confirm your position on liability as soon as possible. If liability is not accepted and/or you blame anyone for our client's injuries, please give full reasons now so that we may consider what you have to say.

2.   Expert evidence

We are [in the absence of objections]/[having noted your objections] making arrangements to obtain expert evidence.

[We are disappointed to note your objections to all the proposed experts. We consider that, in these circumstances, you are acting unreasonably and that, in the absence of a mutually acceptable expert, it is appropriate for us to make a selection, even though this cannot be on a joint basis. You will have the opportunity to agree any expert evidence disclosed by our client, if necessary after submitting written questions, in due course and we hope that will avoid the need for you to consider obtaining any expert evidence of your own.]

[The protocol encourages joint selection, but does not provide for joint instruction, of experts. In these circumstances we do not think it appropriate to provide further information or copies of our instructions. If, however, there are any particular points you wish to be dealt with in the expert evidence please let us have details and we will pass on this information.]

[3.   Further information requested

We note that you do not deal with the points raised in paragraphs [*relevant numbers*] of our letter of [*date of letter of claim*]. Please would you now do so.]

[4. Further information provided

Thank you for the information given in response to paragraphs [*relevant numbers*] of our letter of [*date of letter of claim*].]

5. Indemnity

Either

[Thank you for confirming that you will indemnify [*name*] in respect of our client's claim.]

Or

[We assume, from the terms of your correspondence, that you will indemnify [*name of opponent*] in respect of our client's claim. If this is not correct please advise us now and explain your reasons.]

[Specifically, please confirm if you are acting on behalf of the Motor Insurers' Bureau under article 75 of the Bureau's Memorandum and Articles of Association.]

We will, of course, confirm if any court proceedings are served upon your Insured. However, if your Insured's policy has any particular provisions, relating to notification or otherwise, please let us have details, or if you prefer a copy of the policy, so that we can comply with any such provisions in the event that our client later needs to rely on the Third Parties (Rights Against Insurers) Act 1930. If that information is not given, and you later allege any failure to comply with the terms of the policy, we shall draw this correspondence to the attention of the court as confirmation that you had the opportunity to ensure any such terms were complied with by supplying appropriate details at this stage.

[6. Funding

We consider that your request for further information relating to the funding of the case is not appropriate at this stage. Such information would, in our view, be relevant only at the stage of assessment of costs.]

7. Compensation Recovery

We hope the following information assists in giving appropriate notification to the Compensation Recovery Unit.

(1) Our client's full name is [*client's full name*].

(2) Our client's address is [*client's address*].

(3)   Our client's date of birth is [*client's date of birth*].

(4)   Our client's National Insurance number is [*client's National Insurance number*].

(5)   At the material time, our client was [not employed]/[employed by you [*if the opponent is also the employer*]]/[employed by [*name of claimant's employer*]].

(6)   Our client did [not] receive hospital treatment for the injuries [at [*name of hospital*]].

No doubt you will now report the claim and confirm your interest on behalf of the compensator to the Compensation Recovery Unit.

We look forward to hearing from you again.

Yours faithfully

5.9   Letter to Client – Following Acknowledgment of Letter of Claim

I write to confirm that I have now heard from the insurers of [*name of opponent*] ('the Defendant') who will be dealing with the claim.

I am seeking confirmation that liability for the injuries will be accepted by the Defendant.

I shall let you know when I hear further with, I hope, a decision on liability.

The Defendant should make a decision on liability within 3 months of the 21 days allowed for acknowledging the formal letter of claim and I will press for a decision on liability within that timescale.

[The Defendant has now provided details relating to earnings which, as I propose to use them in helping to establish the claim for lost earnings, I enclose for you to check.

If the details are correct, would you please complete the enclosed authority accordingly. If, however, the information is inaccurate or, perhaps, requires some explanation to ensure that I have a fair picture of lost earnings resulting from the injuries, please complete the form accordingly. Should you need to discuss any matters before returning the authority, please telephone [me]/[*name*].

I also enclose a pre-paid envelope for your use in returning the authority.]

I hope this letter brings you up to date for the moment and I will advise further once I can.

Yours sincerely

5.10 Letter to Opponent – Following Decision on Liability

We thank you for your letter of [*date*].

We will deal, in turn, with the matters we consider arise at this stage.

1. Liability

Either

[We note that liability is not admitted.

[We consider you do not give adequate reasons for your stance on liability and we would ask you to do so now.]

[You have [also] failed to give disclosure of documents as sought in earlier correspondence and as you are required to do under the protocol. Please would you now do so.]

[We note that you blame [*name of third party*]. We consider that, whatever the involvement of any other party, your Insured remains responsible to our client for what happened and, accordingly, we do not consider this is an answer to our client's claim. Having said as much and, given that you consider responsibility must rest with [*name of third party*], we are obliged to make further enquiries by pursuing correspondence with [*name of third party*]. In the event that liability for the accident is found or accepted to rest with your Insured we shall seek, as part of the costs, all costs associated with directing a claim against [*name of third party*]. Accordingly, if you wish to reconsider your position please let us know as soon as possible. Meanwhile, we are submitting copy correspondence to [*name of further defendant*] with an invitation to comment on the issues arising.]]

Or

[We are pleased to note that you are prepared to admit [primary] liability in response to the letter of claim sent under the Protocol.

[However, we also note that you purport to deny causation. Unless you are contending that no injury whatsoever was caused by the breach of duty which is conceded we think it reasonable to ask for an unqualified admission of liability or, if you do not wish to give that, the reasons for your stance on causation. Unless you promptly provide such reasons we shall take, and rely upon, your stance being that you simply make, at this stage, no admission as to the extent of injuries and losses and admit causation of at least some damage as a result of the relevant breach of duty.]

[We take your letter to be an offer to admit [primary] liability which our client hereby accepts. This, therefore, amounts to a complete and unambiguous agreement on [primary] liability reached on the basis of an intention to create legal relations. Our client, in consideration, will cease, and thereby save the costs of, further enquiries on [primary] liability.

Accordingly, we consider the parties have reached a binding contract of compromise on the issue of [primary] liability namely that you will pay such damages and interest as may be agreed or assessed by the Court as a result of the injuries suffered [in the accident on [*date*]].

If you do not agree these are the terms reached please let us know straight away given that, otherwise, our client will suffer detriment as a result of reliance on the representation that you do agree with the understanding set out in this letter and we would maintain, irrespective of any other matters, that would amount to an estoppel and/or relevant change of position.]

Or

[Whilst we are grateful for the general indication of your intentions we consider that our client is entitled, under the protocol, for a clear [and open] admission of [primary] liability. We ask you to give this and, until you do so, must proceed on the basis [primary] liability remains an issue. Please advise, as soon as possible, if there is not an issue on [primary] liability.]

[2. *Allegations of Contributory Negligence*

We note the allegations of contributory negligence and the reasons given for those allegations.

We are prepared to give our client's response to these allegations, but this response should not be taken to be comprehensive and we reserve the right to plead to, and introduce such evidence as may be appropriate in relation to, your allegations when the matter has been fully investigated. Meanwhile, our client's response is as follows:

(1) [*details*].

(2) [*details*].

[You have failed to give disclosure of documents as sought in earlier correspondence and as you are required to do under the protocol unless, of course, you confirm that the allegations of contributory negligence will not be maintained. Unless you can, promptly, give that confirmation please would you give disclosure of relevant documents now.]]

[3. Witnesses

We note your request for disclosure of evidence. If witness statements are to be disclosed at this stage, please confirm that disclosure will be mutual and simultaneous so that we can consider your request further.]

4. ADR

Either

[With a view to negotiations towards settlement we have already summarised injuries, losses and expenses. Further details will follow once these are available.]

Or

[You do, of course, have information which should allow progress on quantum to be made.]

Either

[Given the way you have indicated you propose to deal with the claim we look forward to hearing from you accordingly.]

Or

[Despite your stance we invite you to enter negotiations and explore the possibility of reaching agreement, although it is a matter for you whether you wish to engage in any form of ADR in an attempt to resolve the claim without court proceedings.]

5. The Protocol

Either

[We are endeavouring to deal with this matter in accordance with the protocol which parties are encouraged to adopt, but are concerned you are not complying with your obligations.

Furthermore, you are not allowing an opportunity to resolve or narrow the matters in dispute by any form of ADR.

At this stage we need your co-operation and reserve the right, given the way we have approached the matter, to refer the court to the correspondence exchanged in connection with the costs incurred, as we cannot deal with the matter as economically and expeditiously as we would like without that co-operation.

May we please hear from you on outstanding matters as soon as possible.]

Or

[We thank you for your efforts to comply with the protocol, which we are sure will help to identify the issues and explore fully the possibility of any settlement.]

Yours faithfully

5.11   Letter to Client – Following Decision on Liability by Admission

I write to confirm that I have now heard from the insurers of [*name of opponent*] ('the Defendant') concerning liability.

Either

[I am pleased to report that the Defendant admits [primary] liability for the injuries and, accordingly, is prepared to enter negotiations towards settlement of the claim. Although it may be difficult to do so you need to be aware that the Defendant may, despite this admission, later seek to deny liability.]

Or

[I am advised that the Defendant is prepared to enter negotiations towards settlement of the claim. This is encouraging and suggests that the Defendant anticipates being liable, although I must advise you that the Defendant is still entitled to deny liability, wholly or in part, as an indication of this kind does not imply a formal admission.]

[However, the Defendant does allege contributory negligence; in other words, the Defendant considers that you were partly to blame for what happened. The reason given is that [*details of contributory negligence*].

[I am responding to these allegations on your behalf.]

[I shall be grateful for your further instructions on the allegations of contributory negligence so that I can respond to these on your behalf.]]

Either

[Once medical evidence is available that will be sent to the Defendant and will, I hope, result in some sensible proposals for settlement of the claim.]

Or

[I have already sent to the Defendant medical evidence comprising the report of [*name*] together with information on other losses and expenses resulting from the injuries. I hope that the Defendant will put forward some proposals on the basis of this evidence.]

Any initial offer may be on the low side and require further negotiations. However, provided the Defendant takes a realistic view it may be possible to achieve a settlement, although much depends upon whether the Defendant does put forward sensible proposals reasonably promptly.

Once negotiations are under way, it should be possible to assess whether the Defendant is adopting a stance such that a final settlement, after negotiation, is likely without the need to issue court proceedings or whether it is likely that court proceedings will have to be taken either to force a realistic offer of settlement from the Defendant or to have the level of compensation decided by the court. I will advise you further, at that stage, on what I consider to be the best tactic.

[Given the progress made, but as an early outright settlement of the claim seems unlikely, I think it reasonable for you to seek an interim payment from the Defendant and I have, therefore, invited the Defendant to agree this in principle and put forward some proposals. I will let you know if and when I hear further on this.]

I hope this letter brings you up to date for the moment and I will advise further once I can.

Yours sincerely

5.12   Letter to Client – Following Decision on Liability by Denial

I write to confirm that I have now heard from the insurers of [*name of opponent*] ('the Defendant') concerning liability.

I am advised that the Defendant does not accept any liability for the injuries.

Either

[The Defendant goes on to advise that the reasons for the denial of liability are [*details*].]

Or

[The Defendant does not, however, give full reasons for the denial of liability despite the requirement under the relevant protocol to do so. I am pressing for reasons to be given.]

In these circumstances you are entitled, under the protocol, to see relevant documents in the possession of the Defendant. [The Defendant has disclosed some documentation which I am reviewing and I will copy to you, with my observations, as soon as I can.]/[I am not, however, satisfied that all relevant documentation has been produced and I am asking the Defendant for some further documentation and will advise further when I hear.]/[The Defendant has, however, failed to disclose documentation and I am, therefore, reminding the Defendant that disclosure should be given and I will let you know when I hear further on this.]

I am sorry the response is not more encouraging, but at least we know what stance the Defendant takes.

Either

[Nevertheless, in the hope this may prompt the Defendant into entering negotiations, I anticipate sending medical evidence, once available, to the Defendant along with information about other losses and expenses resulting from the injuries.]

Or

[I have already sent to the Defendant medical evidence comprising the report of [*name*] together with information on other losses and expenses resulting from the injuries. It is possible that the Defendant will use this information to put forward some proposals and I will let you know if that should happen.]

If the Defendant does decide to make an offer this may be on the low side and require further negotiations.

If there are negotiations it should be possible to assess whether the Defendant is adopting a stance such that a final negotiated settlement is likely or whether it is likely that court proceedings will be required in order to force a realistic offer from the Defendant. I will advise you further, at that stage, on what I consider to be the best tactics.

In the current circumstances, unless the Defendant does enter negotiations, I will need to make a detailed review of the matter so that I can advise you on the strength of the case and whether we should commence court proceedings, initially in order to establish whether the Defendant really does intend to maintain a denial of liability and to take the first steps towards a court hearing should that prove necessary.

I hope this letter brings you up to date for the moment and I will advise further once I can.

Yours sincerely

DOCUMENTS

5.13   Letter to Opponent – Dealing with Documents

We thank you for your letter of [*date of letter received*] and are grateful for the enclosed documents.

[Unfortunately, we do not have a good quality copy of [*details of relevant document or documents*]. Please could you let us have a fully legible copy as soon as possible.]

[We are concerned that full disclosure of all relevant documents may not have taken place.

Accordingly, we shall be grateful if you would check the position and disclose any documents within the following categories.

(1)   [*details*]

(2)   [*details*]

Please let us have copies of all such documentation as soon as possible.

If possession of any such documents has not been retained please state when, and in what circumstances, the documents were parted with and also what has become of them.

We look forward to hearing from you.]

Yours faithfully

5.14   Letter to Client – Enclosing Documents Disclosed by Defendant Under the Protocol

[*Name of opponent*] ('the Defendant') has not made an admission [in full] of liability for the injuries.

In these circumstances the protocol, with which the court expects the parties to comply, requires the Defendant to disclose copies of relevant documentations.

The Defendant has, accordingly, disclosed documents and I have had the opportunity of reviewing these.

Accordingly, I now write to let you have copies of the documents disclosed along with my comments on these.

(1) The Defendant has disclosed the following documents:
    (i) [*details*]
    (ii) [*details*]
    I enclose copies for your information.

(2) My observations on these documents are:
    (i) [*comments*]
    (ii) [*comments*]
    Please let me know if you have any further observations.

[(3) It seems to me that the Defendant may have some further documentation which ought to be disclosed under the protocol comprising:
    (i) [*details*]
    (ii) [*details*]
    Given your instructions and the general background to the case, I would expect the Defendant to have, or have had, such documents. If, however, you disagree please let me know.
    I am raising this matter with the Defendant and will let you know as and when I receive a response.]

All documents sent by one party to another, during or in anticipation of litigation, are disclosed on the basis that the party receiving the document will treat the document itself, and any information contained in the document, confidentially. This will remain the position unless and until the document is referred to at a court hearing. Accordingly, you need to bear this duty of confidentiality in mind in respect of the documents now made available and any further documents that may become available as this case progresses. The Defendant is, of course, under exactly the same duty in respect of any documents disclosed by you.

I hope it is useful to have sight of these documents at this stage.

Yours sincerely

FAILURE TO COMPLY WITH THE PROTOCOL

5.15   Letter to Opponent – Non-Compliance with Protocol

We have reviewed this matter as it is now [3]/[6] months since the last date by which the letter of claim could be acknowledged within the timescale of the protocol.

We consider that you are in breach of the pre-action protocol in still [failing to make a decision on liability]/[failing to give reasons for your stance on liability] [and] [failing to give disclosure of [all] relevant documents].

In the circumstances, unless we now hear from you to the contrary, we must proceed on the basis of your present stance which means costs, that might otherwise be saved, will need to be incurred.

If you wish to remedy this breach of the protocol, would you please do so immediately. We would remind you that we will refer the court to relevant correspondence, with particular reference to the exercise of case management powers and to costs, should you not do so.

Yours faithfully

FURTHER DEFENDANTS

5.16 Letter – to Further Defendant

We are instructed [by] [on behalf of] [*name of client*] in connection with a claim for personal injuries [suffered in an accident on [*date*]]/[as a result of [disease]].

We have exchanged correspondence with the insurers of [*name of opponent*], who blame you for our client's injuries.

Accordingly, we enclose copies of the correspondence exchanged with the insurers of [*name of opponent*], together with a copy of this letter for you to send to your own insurers. Please refer the copy letters to the appropriate insurers as soon as possible as, if you do not, this may affect insurance cover and/or the conduct of any subsequent legal proceedings.

We are, as you will see from the enclosed correspondence, dealing with this matter on the basis of the Pre-action Protocol for [Personal Injury] [Disease and Illness] Claims, as we believe that will help to resolve the matter as expediently and proportionately as possible.

May we refer you to the letter dated [*date*], which deals with relevant matters under the protocol, and ask you, through your insurers, to consider the content of that letter in the light of the comments made by the insurers of [*name of opponent*]. Please respond to this claim in accordance with the protocol subject to the time limits, so far as you are concerned, running from the date of this letter.

We would ask for an acknowledgment of this letter, from you or the relevant insurers, by [*date*] and a decision on liability by [*date*] at the latest.

[The claim is funded by a conditional fee agreement dated [*date*], which provides for a success fee, supported by an insurance policy issued on [*date*] by [insurer] (policy number [*number*]).

We enclose Notice of Funding, in Form N251, to confirm.]

Yours faithfully

5.17   Letter to Client – Advising of Claim against Further Defendant

[*Name of opponent*] ('the Defendant') denied any liability for the injuries suffered and has suggested that any responsibility for the injuries must rest with [*name of third party*].

Accordingly, I should like to confirm the further action I am taking on your behalf to pursue the claim, given the stance the Defendant has adopted.

Although the matters raised by the Defendant do not necessarily absolve the Defendant from responsibility, I think details of the claim should be put to [*name of third party*] for a response.

Essentially, therefore, we are now pursuing the claim once more through the protocol, but this time to clarify the liability of [*name of third party*].

We do now have the benefit of having investigated the background to the case already and so I have copied the correspondence already exchanged with the Defendant to [*name of third party*] and requested that [*name of third party*] respond in accordance with the protocol.

Of course, the protocol does allow [*name of third party*] time to investigate the matter and so, whilst we should have an acknowledgment of the claim from [*name of third party*] by [*date*], the time under the protocol for a decision on liability will not expire until [*date*].

I am sorry that this means that we have to wait further before clarifying the position on liability, but I am sure you will recognise it is necessary to take these steps, given the current response of the Defendant.

I will let you know when I hear again from [*name of third party*].

[Meanwhile, I will continue to press the Defendant to deal with certain outstanding matters and will let you know as and when I hear further on these.]

Because, at the outset, the claim was directed against the Defendant, arrangements for funding the claim must now be reviewed so that the claim can also be directed against [*name of third party*]. This will involve formally amending the conditional fee agreement so that a claim against [*name of third party*] is included and also ensuring that the insurance cover taken out will protect your position so far as the claim against [*name of third party*] is concerned. Accordingly, I shall be grateful if you would contact [me]/[*name*] to arrange a meeting.

I hope this letter brings you up to date and explains why it is necessary to investigate, and obtain a response to, a claim against [*name of third party*].

Yours sincerely

MOTOR INSURERS' BUREAU

5.18   Letter to Opponent – Request for Information under section 154(1) of the Road Traffic Act 1988

[client's title, initials and surname]

[client's address]

[date]

[opponent's title, initials and surname]

[opponent's address]

Dear *[Sir or Madam]*

Accident on: *[date of accident]*

[Vehicle Registration: *[registration number]*]]

This letter is a request under s 154 of the Road Traffic Act 1988 that, within the next 3 days, you give me the following information:

(1)   whether you were, at the time of the accident, insured by a policy having effect for the purposes of the Road Traffic Act 1988 or had in force a security having effect for those purposes or would have been so insured, or would have had in force such a security, if the insurers, or giver of the security, had not avoided or cancelled the policy or security; and

(2)   (if so) particulars of the policy or security in any certificate delivered; or

(3)   (if not) the following:
  (i)   the registration mark or other identifying particulars of the vehicle concerned;
  (ii) the number or other identifying particulars of the insurance policy issued in respect of the vehicle;
  (iii) the name of the insurer; and
  (iv) the period of insurance cover.

An offence may be committed under s 154(2) of the Act if you fail to reply to this letter, fail to give the particulars requested or make a false statement.

Yours faithfully

5.19   Letter to the Motor Insurers' Bureau – Claim under Uninsured Drivers' Agreement

[We are instructed [by] [on behalf of] [*name of client*] in connection with a claim for personal injuries suffered in an accident on [*date*].]

Our client considers the accident occurred through the negligence of [*name of opponent*] ('the Motorist').

Either

[We understand that, at the material time, the Motorist was uninsured in respect of our client's claim. Accordingly, we think it appropriate to write to you here and now under the terms of the Uninsured Drivers' Agreement.]

Or

[We enclose copy correspondence sent to the Motorist which, as you will see, includes a demand for information under the terms of s 154 of the Road Traffic Act 1988. Unfortunately, this has not resulted in confirmation of cover from any insurer. In these circumstances, we must treat the Motorist as uninsured in respect of our client's claim and think it appropriate to write to you, at this stage, under the terms of the Uninsured Drivers' Agreement.]

Please let us know if you consider it is necessary for our client to take any further action in relation to the insurance position of the Motorist and, if so, advise what action you consider to be appropriate. We confirm you have our client's authority to seek the particulars specified in s 154 of the Road Traffic Act 1988.

Either

[We enclose an application form, duly signed by our client, and shall be grateful if you would confirm this complies with the requirements of clause 7 of the Uninsured Drivers' Agreement or, if not, anything further that is required.]

Or

[Would you please let us have any formal application form for our client required under clause 7 of the Uninsured Drivers' Agreement.]

We should like to deal with this matter, so far as possible, within the spirit of the Pre-action Protocol for Personal Injury Claims, as we believe that will help to resolve the matter as expediently and proportionately as possible. Accordingly, we will endeavour to deal with relevant matters and hope you will be able to reciprocate.

We should, in particular, like to deal with liability as quickly as possible. We hope that will then allow us to enter negotiations on quantum and explore the possibilities of outright settlement at the earliest opportunity.

1.   Liability

Please confirm your position on liability as soon as possible. If liability is not accepted and/or you blame anyone for our client's injuries, please give full reasons now so that we may consider what you have to say.

2.   Summary of the claim

This letter gives a summary of the factual background and the reasons why it is considered the Motorist is liable for our client's injuries.

However, this summary should not be taken to be comprehensive and we reserve the right to plead such particulars as may be appropriate when we have a response to this letter and when any further investigations that may then be required have been concluded.

We are instructed that [*factual background*].

Our client contends injuries, losses and expenses were caused by the matters already outlined and that, for the following reasons, the Motorist is liable for these.

(1)   [*allegation*].

(2)   [*allegation*].

(3)   [*allegation*].

[Furthermore, our client considers that the accident is of a kind which should not occur, in the ordinary course of events. Accordingly, it is alleged the very fact of the accident is evidence of your negligence. If you contend otherwise please explain why.]

[Our client also relies on the conviction by [*name*] Court on [*date*] of [*details of conviction*] which is considered relevant. If you contend otherwise please give full reasons when replying.]

3.   Police report

Either

[We are establishing the availability of a Police Report. Please let us know, if a report is available, whether you would like a copy.]

Or

[We have obtained a copy of the Police Report and enclose a further copy.]

4.   Documents

Unless liability is fully admitted we will expect disclosure of documents, as would apply under the protocol.

Given the background to the matter, as already set out in this letter, we consider documents within the following categories are relevant and that, accordingly, copies should be supplied to us which, in accordance with the protocol, should be provided without making a charge.

[*List documents required – examples are given in 5.2.*]

We recognise that, of course, these documents will, presently, be in the possession of the Motorist. However, on the basis that you will need to make contact with the Motorist, we think it reasonable to expect that you will make enquires concerning these documents with a view to giving disclosure.

We will, if necessary, draw the content of this letter to the court's attention at a later stage should any document not be preserved on the basis that, having specifically requested the same at this stage, any disposal of documents would be a deliberate non-compliance with the obligations to the court under the Civil Procedure Rules.

5.   Injuries and loss

We should like to get liability dealt with as quickly as possible, hence the request for information already made in this letter, so that we may move on, we hope, to negotiations on quantum.

Presently, we can only summarise, under broad heads, the nature of our client's claim.

(1)   *General damages*

Our client has suffered [*details of injury*]. This is, however, just a summary and should not be regarded as a comprehensive description of the injuries pending receipt of expert medical opinion. We wish to obtain medical evidence and would suggest, as suitable experts to instruct, [*name*], Consultant [*speciality*], [*name*], Consultant [*speciality*], and [*name*], Consultant [*speciality*].
[We propose to submit instructions through [*agency*] as we anticipate that will assist in making the necessary arrangements for obtaining medical evidence.]
Please let us know if you have any objections.

(2)   *Expenses and losses*
We expect the claim for expenses and losses will include the following heads.
(i)   [*details*]
(ii)   [*details*]
We will provide further details in due course and meanwhile it may be helpful if we indicate our preliminary view is that this claim will be suitable for the [multi-track]/[fast track].

6.   Compensation Recovery Unit

We hope the following information assists in giving appropriate notification to the Compensation Recovery Unit.

(1)   Our client's full name is [*client's full name*].

(2)   Our client's address is [*client's address*].

(3)   Our client's date of birth is [*client's date of birth*].

(4)   Our client's National Insurance number is [*client's National Insurance number*].

(5)   At the material time, our client was [not employed]/[employed by you [*if the opponent is also the employer*]]/[employed by [*name of claimant's employer*]].

(6)   Our client did [not] receive hospital treatment for the injuries [at [*name of hospital*]].

No doubt you will now report the claim and confirm your interest on behalf of the compensator to the Compensation Recovery Unit.

7.   Identity

Please confirm the correct identity of the Motorist for the purpose of any proceedings.

Please also confirm the address for service of any proceedings on the Motorist. We invite you to give the Bureau's address as the address for service.

8. Alternative Dispute Resolution (ADR)

We should like to see if it is possible to resolve, or at least narrow, any issues. We consider the appropriate means of ADR to be negotiation, though please let us know if you contend any other method to be suitable. Accordingly, we hope you will comply with your obligations under the pre-action protocol and act on our invitation to negotiate within its framework. Should you decline to do so we do reserve the right to refer to this, and further relevant, correspondence when seeking any orders that may be necessary from the court, on case management, and also in connection with the costs of any specific application and, indeed, the matter generally.

9. Funding

The claim is funded by a conditional fee agreement dated [*date*], which provides for a success fee, supported by an insurance policy issued on [*date*] by [*insurer*] (policy number [*number*]).

We enclose Notice of Funding, in Form N251, to confirm.

10. The Uninsured Drivers' Agreement

We should like, if possible, to agree a framework which, by protecting the position of the Bureau, will allow some provisions of the Agreement to be waived or relaxed. We should also like to confirm a number of matters relating to that Agreement.

(1) Please confirm that it is accepted that our client has made application as required by clause 7 or, if not, what is required.

(2) Please confirm that, in consideration of the Claimant endeavouring to comply with the pre-action protocol, joining in the Bureau as an additional Defendant in any proceedings against the Motorist and giving 35 days' notice of any application for judgment, the Bureau will waive any entitlement it may have had or will have under clauses 9(1), 9(2)(a), 9(2)(b), 9(2)(e), 9(2)(f), 9(2)(g), 9(3), 10(1), 10(2), 10(3), 11(1)(a), 11(1)(b), 11(1)(c) and 12(1) of the Agreement.

(3) Please confirm whether the Bureau will be dealing with the claim or let us have details of any insurers nominated.

We look forward to hearing from you and would hope, again in the spirit of the protocol, to have an acknowledgment of this letter by [*date 21 days ahead*] and a decision on liability by [*date which is 3 calendar months after 21 days*].

In accordance with the notes for guidance issued by the Bureau, we are sending this letter by fax and by recorded delivery post.

Yours faithfully

5.20　Letter to Client – Enclosing Motor Insurers' Bureau Application Form

[*Name of opponent*] ('the Defendant') appears to have been an uninsured motorist at the date of the accident.

Accordingly, I have notified the claim to the Motor Insurers' Bureau who deal with claims against uninsured motorists.

The Bureau has issued a standard application form, which is usual practice. I have completed that application form on your behalf and shall be grateful if you would check the details and, assuming these are correct, kindly sign the application on the back page between the marked crosses, date it and return it to me in the pre-paid envelope enclosed. It is important the information given to the Bureau is accurate so please make any amendments, before signature, if necessary.

The Bureau will nominate an insurance company to deal with the claim on its behalf. That insurance company will then deal with the claim as though it had been the Defendant's motor insurer at the time of the accident although, of course, it will have to refer back to the Bureau from time to time for authority.

In most respects, the claim, once referred to insurers, will proceed in exactly the same way as if the Defendant had been insured at the time of the accident with those insurers.

However, the Bureau is entitled to request information which would not normally be provided to an insurer. In particular, it is necessary to disclose a copy, or details, of any insurance policy providing benefits in the case of death, injury or damage to property. This could be any cover you have for employer's liability, union benefits, personal accident cover, motor insurance, private medical insurance, household cover, legal expenses insurance and cover available under credit cards. Please could you let me have copies of any such cover, or if this is not possible, a summary of relevant details.

I hope this letter helps to explain the involvement of the Motor Insurers' Bureau and reassures you that the Defendant's insurance position should not make any significant difference to how the claim proceeds except for certain procedural steps I will need to take on your behalf and that, if proceedings are commenced, the Bureau will probably need to be involved in those proceedings.

I look forward to receiving the application form back from you, duly signed and dated, in due course.

Yours sincerely

SECTION 6

NEGOTIATION AND QUANTUM

CONTENTS

ADVISING ON QUANTUM

6.1   Letter to Client – Advising on Quantum

I have now had the opportunity of reviewing the available evidence to make an assessment of what I consider to be the appropriate level of compensation to be claimed from [*name of opponent*] ('the Defendant')

Accordingly, I write to offer my advice on what I believe to be the potential value of the claim.

Compensation [assuming liability can be established] will be assessed by the court under two main heads.

1.   Pain, suffering and loss of amenity [with other unquantified claims]

The court will award compensation to reflect pain, suffering and loss of amenity resulting from the injuries [also for the disadvantage that might be faced on the labour market as a result of those injuries] [as well as for disappointment reflecting the loss of a job you enjoyed].

The assessment of compensation by the court will be made, to a large extent, on the medical evidence. That assessment will be based on this individual case, as each claim is unique. Nevertheless, some guidance on the appropriate level of compensation can be obtained from previous cases and that enables an estimate to be made of the likely award if the matter had to be decided by the court.

I consider the court would be likely to award damages for pain, suffering and loss of amenity in the region of £[*figure*] [to £[*figure*]]. [A further sum may well be awarded to allow for [disadvantage on the labour market] [and] [loss of congenial employment] [in the region of £[*figure*]] [and I will advise further on the likely amount when I can.]

The award of compensation under this main head is sometimes termed 'general damages'.

2.   Expenses and losses

The court will also assess compensation for quantifiable expenses and losses resulting from the injuries. The award will reflect sums which are reasonably claimed and can be shown to have been caused by the injuries.

The compensation awarded under this head is sometimes termed 'special damages'.

Either

[When the necessary information became available I made a detailed calculation of expenses and losses, which I sent to you. Please write or telephone [*name*]/[me] to advise if you have incurred any further expenses and losses since that calculation was prepared.

With an award of general damages I consider, on the information presently available, that the potential value of the claim as a whole is in the region of £[*figure*].]

Or

[When I prepared your statement, I included a summary of the financial losses and expenses incurred as a result of the injuries and mentioned that, once further information was available, I might want to prepare a more detailed and up-to-date calculation of those expenses and losses.

On the basis of the information which is now available I have been able to make a further calculation of the financial expenses and losses resulting from the injuries. Accordingly, I am pleased to enclose a copy of that calculation.

May I ask you to bear in mind that the calculation of expenses and losses I have prepared puts forward your case on the most reasonably optimistic basis possible at this stage. Whilst it is right to put the case at its best it is likely that the Defendant will argue lower figures are appropriate on certain aspects of the claim. Accordingly, you do need to keep an open mind on the level at which a settlement might be achieved should sensible proposals be put forward by the Defendant. I will advise further on this as and when the Defendant responds to the calculation.

I shall be grateful if you could check the calculation, and in particular let me know if there have been any further items of expenditure or loss incurred but not yet included in it. If any amendments are required, either to include or delete items, please could you amend the calculation accordingly and then return it to me.

If the calculation is approved, as presently drafted, please would you sign it, in the space provided, and then return it to me.

I enclose a pre-paid envelope for your use in returning the calculation.

If it is not possible to let me have your instructions by returning the calculation, please telephone [*name*]/[me] to discuss matters further.

With an award of general damages I consider, on the information presently available, that the potential value of the claim as a whole is in the region of £[*figure*].]

Or

[I appreciate that, so far, it has only been possible to form a broad view of the claim for expenses and losses. I will, of course, try to provide a detailed calculation once outstanding enquiries are complete and advise on the total potential value of the claim.]

The advice given in this letter is made on the basis of the Defendant being fully liable for the injuries. An apportionment of liability means a reduction in the figures given, by an equivalent percentage, to allow for that apportionment.

Either

[The Defendant has, however, admitted liability in full.]

Or

[The Defendant has suggested that there should be an apportionment of liability and, although this remains subject to further negotiation, it is something that you should bear in mind.]

Or

[Liability has, of course, already been agreed on the basis that the Defendant will pay [*figure*]% of any compensation ultimately agreed or awarded by the court.]

Or

[Liability is present denied, although it may be that the Defendant's stance will change and some negotiations will be possible. Accordingly, despite the denial of liability, I think it right to let you have my views on the potential value of the claim.]

[Given the available evidence, I think we will have to make some allowance to reflect the risks if the case had to be decided by the court. Allowing for this, I would suggest that a settlement in the region of £[*figure*] would be worth careful consideration.]

May I remind you that the advice given so far in this letter takes no account of State benefits received as a result of the injuries. You will recall that if corresponding benefits have been received the Defendant can offset those benefits against relevant parts of the claim.

Either

[It may be necessary to give an allowance, in round terms, of £[*approximate figure of corresponding benefit*] against the claim for expenses and losses, for deductible benefits, which would bring the potential settlement figure down to approximately £[*figure*].]

Or

[However, the information received from the Compensation Recovery Unit indicates that no recoverable benefits have been paid as a result of the injuries. If that remains the position recoupment of benefits will not have any impact on the value of the claim.]

[May I also remind you that you have received interim provision of £[*interim payments to date*]. I have ignored that when giving the figures already set out in this letter but, of course, allowance will have to be made for all such monies received if and when any settlement is achieved.]

I hope it is useful for you to have the advice in this letter. That is purely for your information to help assess any offers made by the Defendant and the level at which any offers should be put to the Defendant.

Yours sincerely

DISCLOSURE OF INFORMATION ON QUANTUM

6.2   Letter to Opponent – Disclosing Quantum Information

We write to provide further information relating to quantum.

We hope this will allow us[, despite your present stance on liability,] to enter negotiations and explore the possibility of [agreeing an interim payment]/[achieving an early resolution of this claim] [without the need for court proceedings].

1.   Pain, suffering and loss of amenity [with other unquantified claims]

We enclose a medical report prepared by [*name of medical expert*].

[The medical evidence has been prepared, as you would expect, on the basis of a review of medical records. We do not think inspection of [all] those records would be appropriate or proportionate [though we do enclose those records of particular relevance]. That is because the expert, whose overriding duty is to the court, has had access to the records and will have been able to take account of all relevant matters when writing that report and also because of the importance that should be attached to the confidentiality of documents such as medical records. We think it right to make our position on this aspect of the matter clear now and for disclosure of the enclosed evidence to be given expressly on this basis.]

Please let us know if the enclosed evidence can be agreed (by which we mean that no part will be directly or indirectly challenged). If you do intend to challenge or disagree with any part of the evidence, please identify, as precisely as possible, points of disagreement and your reasons.

May we remind you that if you choose to put any questions on the enclosed evidence to the expert copies of those questions should be sent to us.

Either

[We ask you to put forward proposals for an interim payment as we do not think a final view can yet be formed on the appropriate level of damages for pain, suffering and loss of amenity.]

Or

[We invite you to put your proposals for damages in respect of pain, suffering and loss of amenity [along with [disadvantage on the labour market] [and] [loss of congenial employment]].]

[Given the terms of the enclosed evidence we wish to obtain a report from [*name of expert and speciality of expert*] and would suggest, as suitable, [*name of expert(s)*]. Please let us know if you have any objection or suggestions.]

2. *Expenses and losses*

Either

[We enclose a schedule of expenses and losses.

Now you have details of the Claimant's claim for expenses and losses, we shall be grateful if you would respond, by counter-schedule, identifying which items are agreed and which are not agreed. Please give reasons for any items which are not agreed and the Defendant's calculation of each such item. This will ensure that the issues relating to expenses and losses are narrowed, so far as possible at this stage, and should help to save costs being incurred on matters that are either agreed or on which we are not far apart.

In any event, having given a detailed breakdown of the Claimant's claim, we will need to have an equally detailed response from the Defendant in order properly to assess any offers that may be made.]

Or

[We have already summarised the claim for expenses and losses. Fuller and further details will follow once a more detailed schedule can be prepared.]

[The documentary evidence comprises [*details*] copies of which we enclose.]

It is a condition precedent to our client agreeing any final figure for damages that costs will be paid in addition to[, on the predictable basis provided for in Part 45 Civil Procedure Rules, and at the same time as] the damages.

The enclosed documentation on quantum is submitted to you at this stage on the basis that, if there are to be negotiations towards settlement, prompt proposals [for at least an interim payment] will be made. Accordingly, we look forward to hearing from you within the next 21 days.

[By disclosing this information we consider you have the opportunity, if you wish to do so, of promptly settling the claim on reasonable terms as envisaged by the protocol.]

We look forward to hearing from you.

Yours faithfully

6.3   Letter to Client – Advising on Disclosure of Quantum Information

I now have available [some of] the evidence necessary for negotiations to proceed with the representatives of [*name of opponent*] ('the Defendant').

Either

[Before this information was received the Defendant indicated that it was intended to enter negotiations towards settlement of the claim once this evidence was available.]

Or

[It seems unlikely , as matters stand, that the Defendant will make any proposals for settlement of the claim but, as the evidence now available will have to be disclosed when any court proceedings are commenced, it seems sensible to let the Defendant have this information now in case the Defendant should be prepared to enter negotiations.]

Accordingly, I am now sending the evidence of [*name of author(s) of evidence disclosed*] to the Defendant [together with details of expenses and losses].

Either

[I hope this will result in suitable proposals being put forward by the Defendant in the reasonably near future for settlement of the claim. I have already advised you on what I consider to be the value of the claim. I am not giving that information to the Defendant, but hope it will help you to assess any offer that may be made.]

Or

[Given the nature of the injuries, and that all the evidence to assess fully the implications of these is not available, an outright settlement of the claim cannot yet be negotiated but it may, at least, be possible to get the evidence already disclosed agreed by the Defendant.]

I hope this letter brings you up to date for the moment and I will advise further once I can.

Yours sincerely

6.4 Letter to Opponent – Following up Disclosure of Information on Quantum

We do not appear to have heard from you with any proposals, following our letter of [*date*], enclosing information on quantum.

We wished, as indicated in earlier correspondence, to receive proposals[, at least for an interim payment,] promptly if there are to be any negotiations.

[We should, in any event, like to hear from you with confirmation that the evidence disclosed is agreed or, if not, points of disagreement and your reasons.]

[We do, of course, recognise that liability is denied. However, given our invitation to try and resolve matters by negotiation, we must take the absence of any proposals, or willingness to take up our invitation at all, as confirmation that you have no intention of entering any form of ADR or attempting, whatever your formal position on liability, to try and achieve a settlement, or narrow the issues, without the need for court proceedings.]

[We must assume that[, despite your admission,] there is an issue between us preventing progress which the court may need to deal with, though we would welcome hearing from you if that is not the case.]

If you do wish to make progress[, which at this stage would mean at least proposals for an interim payment,] may we hear from you within the next 7 days, failing which we will need to take further action. That will, of course, incur costs which might otherwise be avoided.

Yours faithfully

6.5   Letter to Opponent – Enclosing Photographs

We now have available photographs illustrating the [continuing cosmetic effect of the injuries]/[scene of the accident].

We enclose copies of the photographs and confirm that these were taken of [our client]/[the locus] on [*date*] by [*name of photographer*].

Kindly acknowledge safe receipt and confirm that these photographs are agreed. If you are not able to give this confirmation, please explain why not.

We look forward to hearing from you.

Yours faithfully

ADVISING ON ADR

6.6 Letter to Client – Advising Generally on ADR

The courts expect efforts to be made, at the earliest appropriate stage, to find ways of resolving claims or, if that cannot be achieved, for agreement to be reached on as many issues as possible. This approach is reflected in the protocol which parties are expected to follow.

There are various ways in which progress towards settlement, without matters having to be decided by the court, can be made. These are collectively often referred to as 'Alternative Dispute Resolution' (ADR).

I hope it will be possible to engage [*name of opponent*] ('the Defendant') in ADR and it is, in any event, important to keep in mind, throughout the case, the prospect of agreeing reasonable terms to resolve particular issues or the claim as a whole.

At this stage, given the information now available, I think it is appropriate to advise on ADR. I hope that will allow a decision to be reached on what may be appropriate at this stage and also be a useful introduction to further steps that may be taken regarding ADR as the case progresses.

The most effective method of ADR for this type of claim, and the usual starting point, is negotiation. I will, therefore, outline the options for negotiation in some detail before looking, more briefly, at other methods which, if negotiation is not successful, may have to be considered. I will then offer my advice on how I think it best to approach ADR at this stage.

1. Negotiation

Negotiation will usually take place by offers to settle being made, either dealing with the whole claim or a particular issue.

If an offer made by one party is accepted by another there will be a legally binding agreement on the issue to which the offer relates and if the offer is of outright settlement there would be a legally binding agreement finalising the whole claim.

Offers to settle can be made in a way that has potential costs consequences if the outcome of the claim, or relevant issue in the claim, is less advantageous to the party receiving that offer than the terms proposed.

If an offer to settle is made in accordance with Part 36 of the Civil Procedure Rules ('a Part 36 offer') that offer will, unless to do so would be unjust, carry specific costs consequences.

I will deal both with offers made to the Defendant and offers received from the Defendant in turn, as well as outlining the costs consequences that apply where such an offer is made under Part 36.

(1)   Offers made

An offer of settlement may be made to the Defendant at any time on any issue. For example, you might offer [to accept a proportion of liability on the part of the Defendant (so that, ultimately, the Defendant would pay a corresponding proportion of the compensation assessed by the court or agreed upon); and/or] to reach agreement on any particular issue; and/or to accept a figure as compensation in final settlement of the claim as a whole.

To be a valid Part 36 offer the proposal would have to be in writing and give the Defendant at least 21 days to accept the offer within which, unless the court gave permission, that offer could not be withdrawn or the terms changed to be less advantageous to the Defendant.

If the Defendant did not accept the offer within 21 days the consequences of that offer would be likely to depend upon whether the outcome is eventually more advantageous to the Defendant.

(1)   If the claim, or a relevant issue in the claim, had to be decided by the court and judgment was more advantageous to the Defendant than the offer, or offer on the relevant issue, such an offer would not usually be relevant.

(2)   If the claim, or a relevant issue in the claim, had to be decided by the court and judgment was not more advantageous to the Defendant than the offer, or offer on the relevant issue, such an offer is likely to have important costs consequences. These consequences, for the time from 21 days after the offer, are that:
   (i)   the Defendant can be required to pay more of the costs of the claim (if it was an offer of outright settlement) or costs of dealing with the relevant issue (otherwise); and/or
   (ii)   a higher rate of interest can be awarded on any compensation the Defendant is ordered to pay; and/or
   (iii)   interest can be awarded on costs the Defendant is ordered to pay.

Meanwhile, and provided you did not withdraw or change it, the Defendant could still accept the offer after 21 days, at any time until a final court hearing begins, but with the same consequences, though only up to the date of acceptance, as if a court judgment was not more advantageous to the Defendant than the offer.

In certain circumstances an offer which is not made as a Part 36 offer may still carry costs consequences.

(2)   *Offers received*

The Defendant can, similarly, make an offer of settlement on any issue at any stage. For example, a Defendant might offer [to accept a proportion of liability (so, again, the Defendant would pay a corresponding proportion of the compensation assessed by the court or agreed upon): and/or] to reach agreement on any particular issue; and/or to pay a figure as compensation in final settlement of the whole claim.

Once again, to be a valid Part 36 offer, the proposal would have to be in writing and give you at least 21 days to accept the offer within which, unless the court gave permission, that offer could not be withdrawn or the terms changed to be less advantageous to you.

If not accepted the costs consequences of the offer are likely to depend upon whether the outcome is eventually more advantageous to you.

(1)   If the claim, or a relevant issue in the claim, had to be decided by the court and judgment was more advantageous to you than the offer, or offer on the relevant issue, such an offer would not usually be relevant to costs.

(2)   If the claim, or a relevant issue in the claim, had to be decided by the court and judgment was not more advantageous to you than the offer, or offer on the relevant issue, such an offer is likely to have important costs consequences. These consequences are that:
   (i)   whilst the Defendant would still have to pay costs of the claim (if it was an offer of outright settlement) or the costs of the relevant issue (otherwise) up to [*date*];
   (ii)   the Defendant would not have to pay costs of the claim, or costs of the relevant issue, after [*date*];
   (iii) and you would be expected to pay costs of the claim, or of the relevant issue, incurred by the Defendant after [*date*] and interest on those costs.

(3)   Meanwhile, and provided the Defendant did not withdraw or change it, that offer could still be accepted after 21 days, in certain circumstances if the court gave permission, at any time until a final court hearing begins but with the same cost consequences, though only up to the date the offer was accepted, as if the claim, or relevant issue in the claim, had been decided by the court and judgment was not more advantageous to you than the offer, or offer on the relevant issue.

However, it is important to note that after 21 days the Defendant might, any time until acceptance, withdraw the offer or change the terms to be less advantageous to you. If withdrawn the offer would no longer be open for acceptance. If changed the offer would only be open on the new terms.

In certain circumstances an offer which is not made as a Part 36 offer may still carry costs consequences.

2. Other methods of ADR

If negotiation is not successful it might be necessary to consider other methods of ADR though, in many cases, these will not be applicable.

(1) Settlement conference

This, really, is a form of negotiation but in the format of a meeting, arranged for the specific purpose of trying to achieve a settlement, when all concerned can get together.

A settlement conference will usually be more appropriate at a later stage of the claim, if efforts to achieve settlement meanwhile have not been successful.

(2) Mediation

This is a process in which someone independent, a mediator, tries to help the parties find a resolution.

Mediation might perhaps be appropriate if there seems no prospect of any negotiation or perhaps if negotiations take place but there remains a difference between the parties which the negotiations are unlikely to bridge.

(3) Early neutral evaluation

This is rather like mediation except that the independent person involved in the process is able to help assess the strengths and weaknesses of each case.

3. Advice

Either

[I do not think it is appropriate, at this stage, to put forward an offer to settle but should an offer be received from the Defendant efforts should be made to pursue negotiations.]

Or

[I think it is appropriate to get negotiations underway by making an offer to settle [on the issue of [*details*]] of [*details*]. [I would suggest, given the potential costs consequences, this be made as a Part 36 offer.]]

If this letter enables you to reach a decision on the advice given would you please sign, in the space provided, the enclosed confirmation. This can be completed either to confirm that you accept the advice given in this letter or to let me have any other specific instructions. I also enclose a pre-paid envelope for your use in returning this authority.

If you would prefer not to accept the advice given and are unable to give any specific instructions, or would like to discuss the matter with me before deciding how to proceed, please telephone [me]/[*name*].

I look forward to hearing from you.

Yours sincerely

ACKNOWLEDGING AND ADVISING ON OFFERS

6.7   Letter to Opponent – Acknowledging Offer

We thank you for your letter of [*date*] making an offer to settle [the whole of the claim] [and] [an issue in the claim].

Either

[We [acknowledge safe receipt of the notice of offer to settle [the whole of the claim] [and] [an issue in the claim] and note the offer is intended to have the consequences of Part 36 Civil Procedure Rules. We do, therefore, rely upon the provisions in that rule, in particular Part 36.10, as applying. Please let us know, straightaway, if you disagree.

Or

[We note the offer is made with reference to Part 36 Civil Procedure Rules. However, and given the duty of the parties to co-operate, we think it right to advise you now of the reasons why we do not consider the offer does accord with Part 36. That is because [*reasons*].]

Or

[We note the offer does not state that it is intended to have the consequences of Part 36 Civil Procedure Rules [but is made without prejudice [except as to costs]].]

[Given the nature of the claim, and that court proceedings have not yet been commenced, we take the offer, if it is accepted, to be made on the basis that fixed recoverable costs, calculated on the predictable basis provided for in Part 45 Civil Procedure Rules, will be paid at the same time as, and in addition to, the damages.

Predictable costs should be exactly that and, for the avoidance of doubt, we take your proposal as an offer to enter an entire agreement concluding all aspects of the claim including damages and costs, those costs being calculated in accordance with Part 45 on the following basis:

Base profit costs [with London weighting]	£[figure]
[Counsel's fees (for approval purposes)]	£[figure]
[Success fee at 12.5% (you are already aware our client has entered a conditional fee agreement which provides for a success fee)]	£[*figure*]
VAT on the above	£[*figure*]

Police Accident report	£[*figure*]
Engineer's report	£[*figure*]
DVLA search	£[*figure*]
Medical report	£[*figure*]
Copy medical records	£[*figure*]
[Court fees (for approval)]	£[*figure*]
VAT on disbursements	£[*figure*]
[Insurance premium]	£[*figure*]
Total	£[*figure*]

[We enclose copy vouchers, where applicable, for disbursements.]

Accordingly, we understand your proposal as an offer to pay a total of £[*figure*] and that such sum, if the offer is accepted, will be paid within 14 days of the date of [acceptance] [approval]. If that is not what you intend by the offer please clarify that offer, within the next 7 days, by confirming the figures and your reasons.]

[We seek clarification of the following matters relating to the offer so that our client has information we consider reasonably necessary to help properly consider it. In particular please clarify [*clarification requested*].]

[The offer has been made at a time when our client awaits information which we consider is necessary to properly assess that offer. In the circumstances we invite you to agree that time for accepting the offer be extended until [*date*].]

We will [, subject to clarification,] take our client's instructions.

Yours faithfully

6.8 Letter to Client – Advising on Offer to Settle

I write to advise that I have received an offer to settle from [*name*] ('the Defendant').

I would like to outline the terms and the implications of the offer before confirming the options open to you and giving my advice on the response I think it is appropriate to make.

1.   The offer

[The offer is to accept [*figure*]% of liability, in other words to meet [*figure*]% of the compensation for injuries, losses and expenses that would be payable if the Defendant was fully liable.]

[The offer is [also] to reach agreement on the issue of [*details*] by [*details*].]

[The offer is [also] to pay compensation totalling £[*figure*] [as a lump sum together with periodical payments of [*details*] in settlement of the whole claim [with [no] [provisional damages] [of [*details*]]].

[I hope it is helpful if I now deal with some matters that may help explain the offer of settlement.

(1)   Liability

Either

[The offer of settlement takes account of the proportion of liability the Defendant has also offered to accept.]

Or

[Whilst the Defendant has [made no admissions on liability] [denied liability, and this offer does not prevent the Defendant maintaining that stance,] the making of an offer, whilst not an admission, suggests the Defendant recognises the risk of being found liable for the injuries.]

Or

[The Defendant has already admitted [primary] liability for the injuries.]

Or

[Liability has, of course, already been agreed on the basis that the Defendant will pay [*figure*]% of any damages ultimately awarded by the court. The Defendant has allowed for this apportionment on liability when making the offer.]

(2)   Quantum

Either

[(i)   For pain, suffering and loss of amenity the Defendant proposes
£[*figure*].

(ii)   For expenses and losses the Defendant proposes:
(a)   £[*figure*] for [*head*];
(b)   £[*figure*] for [*head*].]

Or

[The Defendant has offered a global sum, rather than a total made up of individual figures identified for each part of the claim.]

(3)   Recoupment of state benefits

The Defendant must, as and when any compensation is paid, refund to the Government any state benefits that have been paid as a result of the injuries. Such benefits are termed 'recoverable benefits'.

If any of those recoverable benefits correspond to claims made for expenses and losses the Defendant is entitled, provided the amount of that benefit does not exceed the sum being paid by the Defendant on that part of the claim, to reduce the compensation paid accordingly. Recoverable benefits which can be deducted from the compensation payable on this basis are termed 'deductible benefits'.

This method of recoupment reflects the receipt of any benefits, which would not have been paid but for the injuries, whilst ensuring the Defendant has to reimburse public funds.

Either

[There are, however, no recoverable benefits and hence there are no deductible benefits to be recouped out of the offer.]

Or

[Whilst there are recoverable benefits none of these are deductible and hence there are no benefits to be recouped out of the offer.]

Or

[The Defendant has, however, made the offer without regard to any liability for recoverable benefits so there are no deductible benefits to be recouped out of the offer.]

Or

[The Defendant does, therefore, include in the total offer of £[*figure*]
deductible benefits of £[*figure*] to be recouped out of the offer on the basis
that this sum reflects benefits that correspond to, and therefore can be
used to reduce, appropriate heads of the claim.]

Or

[As the Defendant presently awaits an up-to-date certificate from the
Compensation Recovery Unit, it is not possible to state, with certainty,
whether there are any deductible benefits to be recouped out of the offer.]

[(4)   Interim payments

There have been interim payments of £[figure] which are treated, for
present purposes, as being part of the total offer.]

[(5)   Refunds

Please bear in mind that, out of any compensation paid by the Defendant,
there will need to be refunded to [*employer*] [£[*figure*] being] monies paid
during the absence from work] [and to] [[*insurer*] [£[*figure*] as] outlays
incurred for treatment].]

(6)   Summary

All of this means that the offer, if accepted now, is to pay £[*total figure
less any CRU deduction and/or interim payments*] [subject to any deduction
for benefits that may be appropriate once the Defendant has heard from
the Compensation Recovery Unit].

2.   Consequences of the offer

Either

[The Defendant has not made the offer in a way that, if the outcome is
less advantageous to you than its terms, there are likely to be costs
consequences.]

If the offer is accepted [there would be a legally binding agreement on the
issue to which it relates and finalise this aspect of the claim] [and if the
offer of outright settlement was accepted] [that would make a legally
binding agreement finalising the claim on the terms proposed] [whatever
might happen in the future] [except if [*details*] when it would be possible
to invite the court to consider awarding further compensation but only in
respect of [*details*].

The Defendant has [not] imposed a specific time limit for acceptance of the offer [which is until [*date*] and after that date the offer cannot be accepted unless the Defendant agrees].

It is important to note that the Defendant may, any time until it is accepted, withdraw the offer or change the terms so that these are less advantageous to you. If withdrawn the offer would no longer be open for acceptance. If changed the offer would only be open on the new terms.

Unless the offer is accepted now the claim will continue and there is nothing to stop the parties entering further negotiations, perhaps continuing to exchange offers, and reaching agreement on any issue or even outright settlement on satisfactory terms.

If agreement could not be reached and the court had to decide the claim, or any issues, details of the offer would not be disclosed to the judge who would reach a decision which could, if appropriate, be less advantageous to you than the terms of the offer now made.]

Or

[The Defendant has made the offer in a way that, if the outcome is less advantageous to you than its terms, there may be costs consequences.

It is important I set out the potential implications of the offer and that if in any doubt as to the effect of these you discuss the matter with me.

(1) If the offer is accepted [there would be a legally binding agreement on the issue to which it relates and finalise this aspect of the claim] [and if the offer of outright settlement was accepted] [that would make a legally binding agreement finalising the claim on the terms proposed] [whatever might happen in the future] [except if [*details*] when it would be possible to invite the court to consider awarding further compensation but only in respect of [*details*].

(2) If the offer is not accepted at this stage the cost consequences of that offer are likely to depend upon whether the outcome is eventually more advantageous to you.
    (i)   If the claim, or a relevant issue in the claim, had to be decided by the court and judgment was more advantageous to you than the offer, or offer on the relevant issue, such an offer would not usually be relevant to costs.
    (ii) If the claim, or a relevant issue in the claim, had to be decided by the court and judgment was not more advantageous to you than the offer, or offer on the relevant issue, such an offer may have important costs consequences which, if these follow, are likely to be that:

(a) whilst the Defendant would still have to pay costs of the claim (if it was an offer of outright settlement) or the costs of the relevant issue (otherwise) up to now;

(b) the Defendant would not have to pay costs of the claim, or costs of the relevant issue, from now;

(c) and you would be expected to pay costs of the claim, or of the relevant issue, incurred by the Defendant from now.

The Defendant has [not] imposed a specific time limit for acceptance of the offer [which is until [date] and after that date the offer cannot be accepted unless the Defendant agrees].

It is important to note that the Defendant may, at any time until it is accepted, withdraw the offer or change the terms so that these are less advantageous to you.

[After [date], provided the Defendant agreed and did not withdraw or change it, you might still be able to accept that offer but that would probably involve the same costs consequences, though only up to the date the offer was accepted, as if the claim, or relevant issue in the claim, had been decided by the court and judgment was not more advantageous to you than the offer, or offer on the relevant issue.]

If withdrawn the offer would no longer be open for acceptance. If changed the offer would only be open on the new terms.

Unless the offer is accepted now the claim will continue and there is nothing to stop the parties entering further negotiations, perhaps continuing to exchange offers, and reaching agreement on any issue or even outright settlement on satisfactory terms.

If agreement could not be reached and the court had to decide the claim, or any issues, details of the offer would not be disclosed to the judge who would reach a decision which could, if appropriate, be less advantageous to you than the terms of the offer now made.]

Or

[The Defendant has made the offer under Part 36 of the court rules so, if the outcome is less advantageous to you than its terms, there are likely to be costs consequences.

It is important I set out the potential implications of the offer and that if in any doubt as to the effect of these you discuss the matter with me.

(1) If the offer is accepted before [date] [there would be a legally binding agreement on the issue to which it relates finalising this aspect of the claim] [and if the offer of outright settlement was accepted] [that

would make a legally binding agreement finalising the claim on the terms proposed] [whatever might happen in the future] [except if [*details*] when it would be possible to invite the court to consider awarding further compensation but only in respect of [*details*].

(2) If the offer is not accepted before [*date*] the costs consequences of that offer are likely to depend upon whether the outcome is eventually more advantageous to you.

    (i)   If the claim, or a relevant issue in the claim, had to be decided by the court and judgment was more advantageous to you than the offer, or offer on the relevant issue, such an offer would not usually be relevant to costs.

    (ii)   If the claim, or a relevant issue in the claim, had to be decided by the court and judgment was not more advantageous to you than the offer, or offer on the relevant issue, such an offer is likely to have important costs consequences (and the same consequences will probably follow, up to the date of acceptance, if the offer was accepted after [*date*]). These consequences are that:

        (a)   whilst the Defendant would still have to pay costs of the claim (if it was an offer of outright settlement) or the costs of the relevant issue (otherwise) up to [date];

        (b)   the Defendant would not have to pay costs of the claim, or costs of the relevant issue, after [*date*];

        (c)   and you would be expected to pay costs of the claim, or of the relevant issue, incurred by the Defendant after [*date*] and interest on those costs.

    (iii)   Meanwhile, and provided the Defendant did not withdraw or change it, that offer could still be accepted after [*date*] [if the Court gave permission] at any time until a final court hearing begins but with the same cost consequences, though only up to the date the offer was accepted, as if the claim, or relevant issue in the claim, had been decided by the court and judgment was not more advantageous to you than the offer, or offer on the relevant issue.

Unless the offer is accepted the claim will continue and there is nothing to stop the parties entering further negotiations, perhaps continuing to exchange offers, and reaching agreement on any issue or even outright settlement on satisfactory terms.

However, it is important to note that after [*date*] the Defendant may, any time until it is accepted, withdraw the offer or change the terms so that these are less advantageous to you.

If withdrawn the offer would no longer be open for acceptance. If changed the offer would only be open on the new terms.

Until [*date*] the offer might still be withdrawn or changed, prior to acceptance, but only if the court gives the Defendant permission to do so.

If the offer is withdrawn the costs consequences I have outlined would cease to apply. If the offer is changed, so that the terms are less advantageous to you, the costs consequences I have outlined would only apply if the outcome is less advantageous to you than the terms of the offer as changed.

If agreement could not be reached and the court had to decide the claim, or any issues, details of the offer would not be disclosed to the judge who would reach a decision which could, if appropriate, be less advantageous to you than the terms of the offer now made.]

[These consequences apply individually to that part of the offer dealing with [*details*] and that part of the offer dealing with the claim as a whole.]

[Whilst it is important to explain the costs consequences of the offer, the effect of the conditional fee agreement you have entered with my firm, coupled with your insurance policy, protects your position in certain circumstances. If, on my advice, you do not accept an offer, and then subsequently fail to beat that offer, then, under the terms of the agreement, you will not be required to pay any costs to my firm after [*date*] (although you will still have to pay costs, with a success fee on those costs, up to that time). Furthermore, the insurance cover you have for the claim will meet costs you might be required to pay to the Defendant after [*date*] should the offer not be beaten.

If, against my advice, you decide not to accept the offer my firm does have the right to review the terms on which we are dealing with the claim but if the current agreement remains in place will be entitled to paid costs, and a success fee on those costs, for all work carried out. Furthermore, you will not have the protection of insurance cover, so far as the Defendant's costs are concerned, should the offer not be beaten.

I will give my advice on the offer next.]

3.   *Advice*

[It may be useful if I summarise my advice on what I believe to be the value of the claim. I consider the total, potential, value is in the region of £[*figure*].]

[To advise on what I believe to be the value of the claim it would be helpful to have [details]. Once this information is available I will let you have my further advice.]

[It may [also] be useful if I summarise my advice on liability which is [*details*].]

[When considering whether to accept the offer it is also appropriate to take account of the risk that the court would not decide the matter in your favour, or not entirely in your favour. To allow for this risk I consider it is appropriate to look at settlement in the region of £[*figure*].]

[Allowance must also be made for the apportionment of liability on the basis the Defendant should pay [*figure*]% of any damages ultimately awarded by the court. Taking that into account I consider it is appropriate to look at settlement in the region of £[*figure*].]

[Furthermore, on the basis the Defendant is entitled to reduce the claim for [*details*] by [*details*] , it does seem appropriate to accept a deduction in respect of these benefits of £[*figure*] leaving a balance of £[*figure*].]

[These figures are inclusive of the interim payments already made.]

Either

[Accordingly, my advice is that you should accept the offer. Whilst there may be the chance of a more advantageous outcome I do not think the prospect of you doing better than the present offer outweighs the risk of doing worse.]

Or

[Accordingly, my advice is that the offer should not be accepted. I consider the prospect of a more advantageous outcome than the present offer outweighs the risk of doing worse. However, the offer is there to accept here and now if you wish.]

Or

[Accordingly, my advice is that the offer should not, for the moment, be accepted but that you should keep an open mind on the possibility of accepting the offer once an accurate assessment is possible. Having said as much the offer is there to accept here and now if you wish.]

[You may, irrespective of how the offer in settlement of the whole claim is dealt with, accept the offer on [liability] [and/or] [*issue*]. My advice is that you should [not] accept this offer [at least for the time being].]

[I do think further negotiations should be pursued with the Defendant to see if reasonable terms can be agreed.]

[I think it would be appropriate to make an offer that you would accept £[*figure*] [which includes] [benefits to be deducted of £[*figure*] [and] [the interim payments already made of £[*figure*]] [and] [monies paid during the absence from work which are to be recouped by [*details*] of [*figure*] [as a lump sum and periodical payments of [*details*] [with no award of provisional damages] [with an award of provisional damages if [*details*]] [without deduction of any benefits paid] in settlement of the whole claim [on the basis this has taken account of, and reflects, the apportionment on liability] [and on the basis that this takes account of the counterclaim] with a view to achieving, if possible, [settlement in these terms] [an offer in the region of £[*figure*]] [settlement on the basis of some improvement on the offer made].]

[I think it would [also] be appropriate to make an offer that you would accept [*figure*] [% liability on the part of the Defendant with a view to achieving, if possible,] [agreement in these terms] [an offer in the region of [*figure*]] [agreement on the basis of some improvement on the offer made].]

[I think it would [additionally] be appropriate to make an offer that you would be prepared to reach agreement on the issue of [*details*] by [*details*] with a view to achieving, if possible, [agreement in these terms] [an offer in the region of [*details*]] [agreement on the basis of some improvement on the offer made].]

If the Defendant accepted such an offer then [there would be a legally binding agreement on the issue to which it relates and finalise this aspect of the claim] [and if the offer of outright settlement was accepted] [that would make a legally binding agreement finalising the claim on the terms proposed] [whatever might happen in the future [except if [*details*] when it would be possible to invite the court to consider awarding further compensation but only in respect of [*details*]].

Either

[I would suggest any such offer be open for [*number*] days only so that it is possible to establish quickly whether or not terms can be agreed. However, such an offer is unlikely to have the costs consequences for the Defendant which would apply if the offer was made under Part 36 of the court rules should you later obtain judgment in more advantageous terms from the court.]

Or

[I would suggest any such offer be made in accordance with Part 36 of the court rules, so that this has potential costs consequences for the Defendant.

To comply with Part 36 the offer must be in writing and give the Defendant at least 21 days to accept the offer within which, unless the court gave permission, that offer could not be withdrawn or the terms changed to be less advantageous to the Defendant.

If the Defendant did not accept the offer within 21 days the consequences of that offer are likely to depend upon whether the outcome is eventually more advantageous to the Defendant.

It would be helpful if I remind you of the implications of such an offer.

(1) If the claim, or a relevant issue in the claim, had to be decided by the court and judgment was more advantageous to the Defendant than the offer, or offer on the relevant issue, such an offer would not usually be relevant.

(2) If the claim, or a relevant issue in the claim, had to be decided by the court and judgment was not more advantageous to the Defendant than the offer, or offer on the relevant issue, such an offer is likely to have important costs consequences (and the same consequences will probably follow, up to the date of acceptance, if the offer was accepted after 21 days). These consequences, for the time from 21 days after the offer, are that:
   (i)   the Defendant can be required to pay more of the costs of the claim (if it was an offer of outright settlement) or costs of dealing with the relevant issue (otherwise); and/or
   (ii)   a higher rate of interest can be awarded on any compensation the Defendant is ordered to pay; and/or
   (iii) interest can be awarded on costs the Defendant is ordered to pay.

Meanwhile, and provided you did not withdraw or change it, the Defendant could still accept the offer after 21 days at any time until a final court hearing begins but with the same consequences, though only up to the date of acceptance, as if a court judgment was not more advantageous to the Defendant than the offer.

Accordingly, if the offer were, at any future stage, to no longer represent satisfactory terms for settlement of the claim, or agreeing the relevant issue, it is important to note that the offer would need to be withdrawn or changed. Please let me know, straightaway, if such a step should become necessary.

If the offer is withdrawn it is likely to cease having the cost consequences I have outlined. If the offer is changed, so that the terms are less advantageous to the Defendant, it is unlikely to continue having cost consequences unless the Defendant failed to beat the new, less advantageous, offer.]]

[4.   Approval

If an agreement is reached it will be necessary to have that agreement approved by the court because [*name*] is a [child] [protected party].

Court approval has the advantage of making the settlement binding once and for all, though it does require an application for a hearing when the court can decide whether any proposed terms for settlement are appropriate.

[You can, as an alternative to formal court approval, give the Defendant a parental indemnity. However, that does not achieve a settlement which is binding once and for all. Accordingly, whilst this might finalise matters a little quicker than approval by the court, it leaves open the possibility of [*name*] contending subsequently that a higher sum should have been paid and you having to reimburse the Defendant for any sums subsequently paid out. In these circumstances my advice is that any settlement should be approved by the court.]

I shall be grateful if you would let me have your instructions on the offer made by the Defendant.

If this letter enables you to reach a decision please would you sign, in the space provided, the enclosed confirmation. This can be completed either to confirm you accept the advice given in this letter or to let me have any other specific instructions. I also enclose a pre-paid envelope for your use in returning this authority.

If you would prefer not to accept the advice given and are unable to give any specific instructions or would like to discuss the matter with me before deciding how to proceed please telephone [me]/[*name*].

[I need to notify your insurers of the offer as this may have an effect on the extent to which cover for further costs is continued.]

[I [also] need to notify Counsel, your Barrister, under the terms of the conditional fee agreement entered with Counsel.]

I look forward to hearing from you.

Yours sincerely

6.9 Letter to Client – Confirming Instructions to Make Offer

I write to confirm the negotiations now taking place with [*opponent*] ('the Defendant').

Thank you for your instructions that [, whilst not accepting the present offer of settlement,] you would be prepared to accept £[*counter-offer*], [including benefits to be deducted of £[*figure*]] [and] [including the interim provision already made of £[*figure*],] together with payment of costs in settlement of the claim at this stage [which it is hoped will allow a settlement to be reached in the region of £[*figure*]].

[Thank you [also] for confirming that you would be prepared to reach agreement on the issue of liability on the basis that the Defendant accepts [*figure*]% of liability.]

[Thank you [also] for confirming that you would be prepared to reach agreement on the issue of [*details*] by [*details*].]

I have advised the Defendant's representatives accordingly and will let you know when I hear further. A copy of the letter is enclosed.

[I also confirm that I have put forward this proposal as an offer made under Part 36 of the court rules, given the potential consequences this has for the Defendant.]

The claim will continue until such time as negotiations result in a settlement or a final court hearing takes place. In the event of there being a final court hearing, the judge will not know about any of the offers exchanged between the parties (at least not until the issues have been decided and the judge is considering the costs); it is, therefore, important that nothing should be said to the judge during any hearing which would reveal the fact there have been offers of settlement.

Yours sincerely

MAKING OFFERS

6.10 Letter to Opponent – Making Non-Part 36 Offer

[We have now taken our client's instructions on the offer to settle.]

[Our client is prepared, subject to reaching overall agreement on the terms set out in this letter, to accept damages of £[*figure*] [inclusive of [interest] [and] [deductible benefits of £[figure]] [and] [interim provision already made of £[*figure*]] [and] [net of any recoverable benefits] [on the basis that this has taken account of, and reflects, the apportionment on liability] [and on the basis that this takes account of the counterclaim] with costs to be paid in addition.]

Either

[This offer is made on the condition precedent that, if accepted, those costs will be the subject of a detailed assessment if not agreed.]

Or

[Given the nature of the claim, and as court proceedings have not yet been commenced, we would expect costs to be calculated on the predictable basis of fixed recoverable costs provided for in Part 45 Civil Procedure Rules.

Predictable costs should be exactly that and, accordingly, it is a condition precedent to any agreement being reached at this stage that there be an entire agreement concluding all aspects of the claim under which costs, as set out in this letter, and damages will be paid together promptly on settlement.

We calculate costs, in accordance with Part 45, on the following basis:

Base profit costs [with London weighting]	£[*figure*]
[Counsel's fees (for approval purposes)]	£[*figure*]
[Success fee at 12.5% (you are already aware our client has entered a conditional fee agreement which provides for a success fee)]	£[*figure*]
VAT on the above	£[*figure*]
Police Accident report	£[*figure*]
Engineer's report	£[*figure*]

DVLA search	£[*figure*]
Medical report	£[*figure*]
Copy medical records	£[*figure*]
[Court fees (for approval)]	£[*figure*]
VAT on disbursements	£[*figure*]
[Insurance premium]	£[*figure*]
Total	£[*figure*]

[We enclose copy vouchers, where applicable, for disbursements.]

Accordingly, our client offers to settle the whole of the claim (inclusive of damages and costs) for £[*figure*] on the basis that, if the offer is accepted, such sum will be paid within 14 days of the date of [acceptance] [approval].

Please note that this offer is only open for acceptance until 4 pm on [*date*].

In the event this matter is not resolved in circumstances where the scheme for predictable costs will apply then, of course, the figures for costs set out in this letter will not be applicable and costs will have to be dealt with by detailed assessment if not agreed.]

[Our client is [also] prepared to agree the issue of [liability, so far as this claim is concerned, on the basis our client will receive [*figure*]% of the damages and interest that would be awarded on full liability] [the issue of [*details*] by [*details*]. Please note that the offer is only open for acceptance until 4 pm on [*date*].]

This is an offer to settle by our client which our client reserves the right to draw to the attention of the court when necessary, but in particular if and when the court exercises discretion as to costs under Part 44 Civil Procedure Rules.

If you need any longer in which to respond to this letter and consider that might allow the claim to be resolved before further steps are taken, please let us know, with your reasons, within the timescale stipulated.

[If terms are agreed it will, of course, be necessary to obtain court approval of the settlement.]

Yours faithfully

NOTE: This letter should be headed 'Without Prejudice Except as to Costs'

6.11   Letter to Opponent – Making Part 36 Offer

[We have now taken our client's instructions on the offer to settle.]

We enclose, by way of service [notice of offer to settle the whole of the claim] [and] [notice of offer to settle an issue in the claim,] in Form N242A, intended to have the consequences of Part 36.

[We should like to clarify that the offer of £[*figure*] is to accept this as [a lump sum for] damages [inclusive of] [interest] [and] [deductible benefits of £[*figure*] [and] [interim provision already made of £[*figure*]] [net of any recoverable benefits] in settlement of the [whole] claim [for [*details*]] [on the basis that this has taken account of, and reflects, the apportionment on liability] [and on the basis that this takes account of the counterclaim] [together with periodical payments as stated in the enclosed notice] [and] [with provisional damages as stated in the enclosed notice] [with no award of provisional damages].]

Kindly acknowledge safe receipt of the enclosed Notice[s]. Given the duties of the parties to co-operate under the Civil Procedure Rules please tell us now, with your reasons, if you are to contend that there is any non-compliance with the requirements of Part 36 by our client at this stage.

[If terms are agreed it will, of course, be necessary to obtain court approval of the settlement.]

Yours faithfully

NOTE: This letter should be headed 'Part 36 Offer – Without Prejudice Except as to Costs'

6.12   Letter to Opponent – on Defendant's Rejection of Offer/Failure to Negotiate Further

[We thank you for your letter of [*date*] but are disappointed to note the content.]

[We note that we do not appear to have heard from you in response to the recent offer by our client and that the timescale referred to at the time of that offer has now elapsed.]

We consider the parties should be making every effort to resolve matters without the need for determination of issues by the court and we would suggest that the appropriate method of resolution remains negotiation.

[In the circumstances we cannot do more than confirm that our client is willing to enter further negotiations with a view to reaching agreement. If that is not reciprocated we consider that would be a disproportionate approach which is relevant to conduct, and therefore costs, whatever the outcome may be.]

We renew our invitation to pursue negotiations and hope to hear from you accordingly.

Yours faithfully

WITHDRAWING/CHANGING OFFER

6.13   Letter to Opponent – Withdrawing (Part 36) Offer

On [*date*] our client made an offer to settle that [*details*].

Please note that this offer is hereby withdrawn.

[This does not affect other offers to settle made by our client.]

Yours faithfully

6.14   Letter to Opponent – Changing Terms of (Part 36) Offer to be Less Advantageous to the Defendant

On [*date*] our client made an offer to settle that [*details*].

Please note that the Claimant hereby changes the terms of that offer.

That offer should now be read as though it contained [*details*] for [*details*].

Yours faithfully

6.15   Letter to Client – Advising on Withdrawal/Change of Offer

I write to advise that [*name*] ('the Defendant') has [withdrawn] [changed so this is less advantageous to you] the offer of [*details*].

This means the [original terms of the] offer can no longer be accepted.

[The new terms are that [*details*]. Please let me know if this causes you to change the instructions given when the offer was originally made, otherwise I will assume those instructions have not changed.]

Yours sincerely

SECTION 7

STOCKTAKE PRIOR TO ISSUE OF PROCEEDINGS

CONTENTS

STOCKTAKE

7.1   Letter to Client – Recommending Issue of Proceedings Following Stocktake

After preparation of your statement, I wrote to you giving the best view I could, at that stage, on the strength of the case against [*name of opponent*] ('the Defendant').

I also outlined the enquiries which were being made to pursue the claim and also to put me in a better position to advise on the strength of the case.

I have, meanwhile, brought you up to date with the information that has become available from those enquiries and now write to offer my advice on the basis of all the information now obtained.

[I have also been able to obtain the opinion of Counsel, your Barrister, on the case.]

I will deal, as I did initially, with both liability and quantum before moving on to summarise the current status of the claim, the action I think is now appropriate and the costs implications of that.

1.   Liability

Either

[The Defendant has admitted liability. Whilst the Defendant could still try to dispute liability I consider the information obtained suggests the Court would hold the Defendant responsible for the injuries in any event.]

Or

[The Defendant has not admitted liability. On the information now available my advice is that I would hope to establish that the Defendant is liable. It is, however, right to point out that the case on liability may still have to be reassessed once further information relating to the Defendant's stance is available.]

Or

[The Defendant has not admitted liability. On the information now available my advice is that you may succeed in showing the Defendant is liable but, equally, the Defendant may be able to defend the claim successfully. Much depends upon how a court would, ultimately, view the evidence. Nevertheless it does seem appropriate to proceed with the claim, although it is right to warn you of the potential difficulties.]

Or

[The Defendant has not admitted liability. I have, as you know, encountered some difficulty in completing enquiries that would help me to advise on whether the Defendant will be liable.

As, on the information available, I consider that the Defendant may be liable I think it is appropriate to proceed. Once proceedings are under way I should be able, by court order if necessary, to complete investigations which will allow me to advise further on liability.

It is, however, right to point out that the case on liability may have to be reassessed, if necessary, once further information is available.]

2. *Quantum*

Either

[My advice on quantum, as set out in earlier correspondence, is that the potential value of the claim is in the region of £[*net value of claim*].]

Or

[Some information I need to advise on quantum is still awaited so I am not yet able to give you a firm view on the value of the claim, although I will do so when I can.]

[I should remind you that any valuation of the claim is subject to allowances for the risks of litigation and arguments that the Defendant can advance on how the level of compensation should be assessed.]

3. *Current status*

The claim has not been resolved as [the Defendant has not dealt with liability] [the Defendant has maintained a denial of liability and not put forward any offers]/[, whilst progress has been made on liability, the Defendant has not put forward an acceptable offer of settlement]/ [although the case is not yet capable of final settlement, I think it is reasonable for there to be some interim provision, but no suitable proposals for this have been put forward by the Defendant.]

4. *My advice*

Given the merits of the case, and the potential level of compensation, my advice is that[, unless a satisfactory settlement can now be achieved,] it is appropriate to pursue the claim by court action against the Defendant.

Unless I hear from you to the contrary I shall assume that you are prepared to commence court proceedings against the Defendant at this stage if necessary.

[I should like, however, to make a final effort at negotiation before court proceedings are commenced. So, whilst I will, with your approval, move on to prepare the court papers I will also, again subject to your instructions, pursue some further negotiations and will be writing, in the near future, to explain what form I think these should take.]

5.   Costs

I should, at this stage, advise you that once court proceedings have been issued, there will be a change in the position on costs.

Either

[I have, as you know from earlier correspondence, attempted to give you an estimate of the costs on a stage by stage basis. At this stage I need to bring that information up to date.

(1)   By issuing proceedings you will be committing yourself to a further liability for costs. I now require your authority to incur costs, including for work done to date, up to a total of £[*figure*]. I would expect to take the case through the early stages of the court action within that estimate, but this estimate does not include the latter stages of preparation or the cost of a final hearing. I hope that the Defendant would be prepared to make an acceptable offer before we reach the stage of having to decide whether to take the case to a final hearing but there can, of course, be no guarantee of this.

(2)   Once court proceedings have been issued, should the claim not succeed, the Defendant would be entitled to ask the court that you pay the Defendant's own legal costs. I cannot give you any assurance about what those costs could, potentially, be, but I think it reasonable to suppose they would be at least as great as your own costs. Of course, you would only be responsible for the costs of the Defendant if your claim were to fail[, if an offer of settlement by the Defendant was not beaten] or if you were to drop the claim after the issue of court proceedings. If your claim succeeded, you would not usually have any significant liability for the costs of the Defendant and, moreover, the Defendant would have to pay most, though probably not all, of your legal costs.

As confirmation that you wish me to proceed further, I shall be grateful if you would let my firm have, say, a further £[*figure*] on account of costs.]

Or

[It is right to advise you on the usual rules relating to costs, following issue of court proceedings, although those rules are modified under the terms of the conditional fee agreement you have entered.

(1)   The issue of proceedings does not affect the conditional fee agreement we have already made in respect of your own costs.

(2)   Once court proceedings have been issued, you have, potentially, a liability for the Defendant's own legal costs. However, you should only have any responsibility for the costs of the Defendant if your claim were to fail[, if an offer of settlement by the Defendant was not beaten] or if the claim was dropped after the issue of proceedings. If any such liability arises this should be met under the terms of the insurance policy you took out at the time of entering the conditional fee agreement.

(3)   If the claim succeeds the Defendant will have to pay the costs of the claim, which would mean the Defendant paying most, but probably not all, of the costs.]

Or

[It is right to advise you on the usual rules relating to costs, following issue of court proceedings, although your legal expenses insurance cover should continue to provide costs protection.

(1)   The issue of proceedings does not affect the cover for your own costs.

(2)   Once court proceedings have been issued, you have, potentially, a liability for the Defendant's own legal costs. However, you should only have any responsibility for the costs of the Defendant if the claim were to fail[, if an offer of settlement by the Defendant was not beaten] or if the claim was dropped after issue of proceedings. If any such liability arises this should be met under the terms of the insurance policy you have for legal expenses.

(3)   If the claim succeeds the Defendant will have to pay the costs of the claim, which would mean the Defendant paying most but probably not all, of the costs.]

I hope that the summary in this letter brings you fully up to date and usefully confirms the further action I think is appropriate.

I am now going to work further on the court documents ready for the issue of proceedings and will write again as soon as these are ready.

Yours sincerely

7.2   Letter to Client – Recommending Discontinuance after Stock-take/on Failure of Negotiations

After preparation of your statement, I wrote to you giving the best view I could, at that stage, on the strength of the case against [*name of opponent*] ('the Defendant').

I also outlined the enquiries which were being made to pursue the claim and also to put me in a better position to advise on the strength of the case.

I have, meanwhile, brought you up to date with the information that has become available from those enquiries and now write to offer my advice on the basis of all the information now obtained.

[I have also been able to obtain the opinion of Counsel, your Barrister, on the case.]

I will deal, as I did initially, with both liability and quantum before moving on to summarise the current status of the claim, the action I think is now appropriate and the costs implications of that.

1.   *Liability*

The Defendant has [denied liability] [not admitted liability, or given any indication that liability is likely to be admitted].

The Defendant has also [at least substantially] complied with the protocol in explaining why liability is not admitted and producing [at least some of] the documents that support this view and, accordingly, this considered response must be taken seriously.

2.   *Quantum*

My advice on quantum, as set out in earlier correspondence, is that the potential value of the claim is in the region of £[*net value*].

3.   *Current status*

We have [a denial] [no admission] of liability and no offers of settlement.

[Given the efforts we have already made to see if any settlement can be achieved,] I am concerned that there is no realistic prospect of pursuing negotiations that might lead to settlement.

[I explained, at an earlier stage, that it was open to any party to put forward a formal offer of settlement, on any issue, which could have certain consequences if the party making the offer subsequently received a more favourable decision from the court on that issue.

Whilst, as you know, I would generally prefer the Defendant to make an opening offer on any issue I think we have reached the stage at which the possible disadvantages in opening relevant negotiations are outweighed by the possible advantages which may follow from Part 36 of the Court Rules by you making an offer.

I remind you of the effect of a formal Part 36 offer made by you.

(1) You can, at any stage, make an offer of settlement to the Defendant on any issue. So, you might offer:
     (i)   to accept a proportion of liability on the part of the Defendant (so that, ultimately, the Defendant would pay a corresponding proportion of the compensation assessed by the court or agreed upon);
     (ii) to reach agreement on any particular issue;
     (iii) to accept a figure you would be prepared to take as compensation in final settlement of the claim.

(2) Any such offer must be made in writing and must be open for acceptance by the Defendant for at least 21 days.

(3) If the Defendant accepted such an offer then:
     (i)   that would become a binding agreement on the issue to which the offer related and finalise that aspect of the claim;
     (ii) if that agreement finalised the amount of compensation to be paid by the Defendant then the claim would be concluded, the compensation would have to be paid by the Defendant within a reasonable timescale and the Defendant would also have to pay most, though probably not all, of the costs of the claim.

(4) If the Defendant did not accept such an offer then:
     (i)   further action would be taken to pursue the claim. Of course, the parties could still enter further negotiations, perhaps exchange further formal Part 36 offers and reach agreement on any issue, or even outright settlement of the claim, on appropriate terms;

      (ii)   if any issue, which had been the subject of a formal Part 36 offer by you, had to be decided by the court and you failed to do better than the offer on that issue, then the offer would effectively be irrelevant.

(5)   If, however, any issue which had been the subject of a Part 36 offer by you was decided by the court and you did better than the offer on that issue, this would imply that the Defendant should have accepted that offer. Accordingly, the court might, if it considered that was appropriate, then impose a financial penalty on the Defendant by:

      (i)   requiring the Defendant to pay all, or virtually all, of the costs of the claim (if it was an offer of outright settlement) or costs of dealing with the relevant issue (otherwise); and/or

      (ii)   awarding a higher rate of interest then would normally be given on any compensation the Defendant is ordered to pay.

Therefore, the making of an offer at this stage will inevitably clarify whether the Defendant has any intention of pursuing negotiations.

I think it would be appropriate to make an offer to the Defendant that you would settle the claim at £*[figure]* with a view to negotiating the best offer that can be obtained, should this prompt any proposal.]

4. My advice

I must [in the event that any final effort to get negotiations under way should be unsuccessful] advise you on my current view of the case overall.

It has not to date been possible to resolve the claim by negotiation with the Defendant. Accordingly, [and unless negotiations should now be prompted,] I consider it would be necessary to issue court proceedings for the claim to be pursued.

Unfortunately, for the reasons already set out when considering liability, I must conclude that the claim is more likely to fail than succeed if it had to be decided by a court.

In these circumstances, my firm's risk assessment panel has to review the case and has concluded that these risks outweigh the benefits that might be gained in the event of proceedings succeeding.

Whilst it has been quite right for the matter to be investigated[, and my firm has been happy to do that whilst running the risk of not being paid if the claim could not be successfully concluded,] we have reached the point at which it does not seem appropriate for the firm to incur further costs, which will probably not be recovered, or for you to have to spend further time and energy when a successful recovery of compensation seems unlikely.

It is for these reasons that, regrettably, I must advise that[, unless it does prove possible to initiate negotiations now,] it seems appropriate not to proceed further with the claim.

5. *Summary*

Either

[Accordingly, I consider that the claim cannot be pursued in accordance with the conditional fee agreement.

You may, of course, give instructions to proceed on a private basis if you wish, although I would be reluctant to recommend that you incur the costs of this given the assessment of the case already set out in this letter. However, if you do wish to have an estimate of the costs that would be incurred on a private basis, please let me know.

By dropping the claim at this stage you do not incur any responsibility for costs because my firm will not be paid for the work undertaken, as we agreed at the outset by entering the conditional fee agreement, and any other outlays will be met by the insurance policy you took out.]

Or

[Accordingly, I do not think it is appropriate to recommend that any further costs be incurred although this does, of course, mean that costs, in accordance with earlier estimates, have been incurred.]

Or

[Accordingly, I consider the claim cannot be pursued in accordance with the legal expenses insurance as that cover depends upon the claim still being assessed as likely to succeed.

You may, of course, give instructions to proceed on a private basis if you wish, although I would be reluctant to recommend that you incur the costs of this given the assessment of the case already set out in this letter. However, if you do wish to have an estimate of the costs that would be incurred on a private basis, please let me know.

By dropping the claim at this stage you do not incur any responsibility for costs as my firm will be paid for the work undertaken by the cover you have for legal expenses.]

If you are prepared to accept the advice in this letter, I shall be grateful if you would kindly sign and return the enclosed acknowledgment to confirm as much. If, before reaching your decision, you would like to review matters, please telephone [*name*] to arrange for a discussion with me.

I look forward to hearing from you.

Yours sincerely

7.3   Letter to Opponent – Prior to Issue of Proceedings

We note, on reviewing our file, that this matter is not yet resolved. In these circumstances we write to assess the current position, to try and identify the matters in issue and to outline how these might be resolved.

[We note that you have made a decision not to admit liability. However, having considered what you have to say, our client considers that liability will be established, for the reasons set out in earlier correspondence.]

[We note that we do not appear to have a decision from you on liability despite the time for you to reach that decision, under the protocol, having elapsed.]

[You have failed to clarify the allegations of contributory negligence so that we may properly assess these allegations and respond more specifically.]

[Furthermore, you have failed to give full disclosure of documents, as requested in earlier correspondence, despite the requirements imposed on you by the protocol given your present stance on liability.]

[We consider that we have complied, so far as possible, with the pre-action protocol and that you are in breach of that protocol.]

[We have indicated, in earlier correspondence, that we believe the appropriate method of ADR to be negotiation. If you are prepared to enter further negotiations or to admit liability, so that this issue is disposed of, we urge you to do so now with a view to narrowing the issues and saving costs.]

[In all the circumstances, to resolve the issue of liability, it would seem that litigation is now inevitable.]

[We are pleased to note that negotiation has resulted in an admission of liability. We have, of course, relied on that admission in order to save costs. We have indicated, in earlier correspondence, that we believe the appropriate method of ADR to be negotiation. If you are prepared to enter further negotiation towards outright settlement please let us know at once but, if not, it would seem that litigation will be inevitable.]

[Whilst, given the current prognosis, we do not consider that an outright settlement of the claim can be achieved now, we do consider that, having disclosed details on quantum to you, it is reasonable to seek satisfactory interim provision. Unfortunately, we have not heard from you with suitable proposals and so it would seem necessary for our client to seek such provision from the court.]

Accordingly, we are now instructed to issue proceedings on our client's behalf.

[In the circumstances, please would you accept this letter as formal notice, pursuant to s 152(1) of the Road Traffic Act 1988, of our client's intention to issue proceedings against [*name of opponent*].]

[In the circumstances, we will join the Motor Insurers' Bureau as an additional Defendant.]

Our understanding is that the correct identity of the Defendant is [*name*]. Please let us know if it is not. In the event of any application being required, at a later stage, to amend or substitute the name of the Defendant, we reserve the right to refer to this correspondence to confirm both that you have had the opportunity to clarify the identity of the Defendant and in support of any application for costs occasioned by the amendment.

We should like to confirm arrangements for service of proceedings.

Either

[Thank you for advising that the Defendant's address for service is [*name of solicitors*] [*address*]. We will effect service accordingly at that address.]

Or

[Please let us know, straight away, if you wish to give an address for service on the Defendant. Unless we hear accordingly we will send the court papers direct to [*name of opponent*] at [*address at which proceedings are to be served*], which we understand to be the appropriate address. Please let us know, again straight away, if it is otherwise.]

[We think it is appropriate, at this stage, to provide you with an estimate of costs. We calculate costs of £[*amount*] have been incurred to date with disbursements of £[*amount*] (all exclusive of VAT).

[Please note that the figure given is for base costs only. We consider there will be an additional liability as we are acting for our client under a conditional fee agreement which provides for a success fee. Consequently, a success fee will be sought as part of the additional liability. Furthermore, the premium for the insurance policy supporting the conditional fee agreement will be claimed though it is not appropriate for that to be included in the figure given for disbursements at this stage.]

Costs will, of course, need to be agreed or assessed by the Court at the appropriate stage but we hope it is helpful to have, along with the details of the claim we have already provided, this information now.]

[Finally, on the basis of information presently available and in order to keep court fees to a minimum, we propose to provisionally assess quantum provisionally so as not to exceed £[*upper limit on damages*]. This is on the strict understanding that we reserve the right to claim such sums as may be appropriate in due course. Unless we hear from you to the contrary, we shall assume this is agreed. If, however, you do formally object, we shall be required to pay a higher court fee and will produce this letter to the court on assessment, if necessary, in support of a claim to recover court fees at that higher level.]

Yours faithfully

PRE-ACTION APPLICATIONS

7.4 Letter to Client – Recommending Pre-action Application

After preparation of your statement, I wrote to you giving the best view I could, at that stage, on the strength of the case against [*name of opponent*] ('the Defendant').

I also outlined the enquiries which were being made to pursue the claim and also to put me in a better position to advise on the strength of the case.

I have, meanwhile, brought you up to date with the information that has become available from those enquiries and now write to offer my advice on the basis of all the information now obtained.

[I have also been able to obtain the opinion of Counsel, your Barrister, on the case.]

I will deal, as I did initially, with both liability and quantum before moving on to summarise the current status of the claim, the action I think is now appropriate and the costs implications of that.

1. Liability

The Defendant has not admitted liability. On the information now available, my advice is that you may succeed in showing that the Defendant is liable but, equally, the Defendant may be able to defend the claim successfully. Much depends upon how a court would, ultimately, view the evidence.

Furthermore, the Defendant has not [fully] complied with the protocol which the parties are encouraged to adopt in [explaining why liability is not admitted] [and] [producing relevant documents]. I consider that this failure to comply with the protocol is an important matter as the information the Defendant ought to be providing would be of great assistance in assessing the prospects of success the claim has.

For the moment, therefore, I can still only advise that there appear to be reasonable grounds for pursuing a claim but we do not yet know whether this can be successfully answered by the Defendant.

2. Quantum

Either

My advice on quantum, as set out in earlier correspondence, is that the potential value of the claim is in the region of £[*net value of claim*].

Or

[As some information on quantum is still awaited, I am not yet able to give you a firm view on the value of the claim, although I will do so when I can.]

3.   Current status

The claim has not been resolved as the Defendant has [maintained a denial of liability]/[not been prepared to make a full admission of liability].

4.   My advice

I consider, given the grounds that exist for pursuing a claim and the potential value of that claim, it is appropriate to continue pressing the Defendant into compliance with the protocol so that the further information, which I consider you are entitled to, can be obtained and a definitive assessment of the case, and whether it is strong enough to proceed, can be made.

The Court Rules allow for an application to be made before the formal issue of proceedings, in certain circumstances. One of those circumstances is, in effect, to enforce the protocol that the parties are expected to comply with.

Accordingly, I consider it is appropriate for you to make a specific application to the court for an order that the Defendant deal with these outstanding matters as, if such an order can be obtained, the information gained should be extremely useful in making a proper assessment of the case.

5.   Further action

Subject to giving the Defendant a final opportunity to deal with outstanding matters, I will, unless you have any objection, now prepare the appropriate court documentation and send this through to you, for approval, as soon as I can.

I hope the summary in this letter brings you up to date and usefully confirms the action I now think appropriate.

I am now going to work further on the case and will write to outline the steps I shall then be taking.

Yours sincerely

7.5   Letter to Opponent – Prior to Issue of Pre-action Application

We note, on reviewing our file, that this matter is not yet resolved. We therefore write to assess the current position, to try and identify the matters in issue and to outline how these might be resolved.

[We note that you have made a decision not to admit liability.]

[We note that we do not appear to have a decision from you on liability despite the time for you to reach that decision, under the protocol, having elapsed.]

[You have failed to clarify the allegations of contributory negligence so that we may properly assess these allegations and respond any more specifically.]

You have [furthermore] failed to give full disclosure of documents, as requested in earlier correspondence, despite the requirements imposed on you by the protocol given your present stance on liability.

We consider that we have complied, so far as possible, with the pre-action protocol and that you are in breach of that protocol.

In these circumstances, we are now instructed to make a pre-action application to the court seeking, so far as possible at this stage, orders relating to these outstanding matters.

If an application to the court is necessary, we shall be obliged to produce this, and earlier, correspondence to confirm that you have had the opportunity of dealing with the matter on a voluntary basis and in support of a request that the court include in the order provision that you pay the costs of the application.

Our understanding is that the correct identity of the Defendant, for the purposes of this application, is [*name*]. Please let us know if it is not.

We should like to confirm arrangements for service of the application.

Either

[Thank you for advising that [*name of solicitors*] are authorised to accept service on behalf of [*name of opponent*]. We will effect service, accordingly, on the Solicitors at [*address*]]

Or

[Please let us know, straight away, if solicitors are authorised to accept service on behalf of [*name of opponent*] confirming the name of the firm, any reference and the address of the office to which papers should be sent by way of service. Unless we hear accordingly we will send the court papers direct to [*name of opponent*] at [*address at which proceedings are to be served*], which we understand to be the appropriate address. Please let us know, again straight away, if it is otherwise.]

If you do wish to deal with outstanding matters on a voluntary basis, please ensure this is done no later than 4 pm on [*date*] (although this does not amount to any waiver of existing breaches of the protocol).

Yours faithfully

SECTION 8

ISSUE AND SERVICE OF PROCEEDINGS

CONTENTS

ISSUE

8.1   Letter to Client – Sending Claim Form and Particulars of Claim for Approval

I have now prepared the court papers setting out details of your claim against [*name of opponent*] ('the Defendant').

These papers comprise:

(1)   *Claim Form*
      This is the document used to start court proceedings which gives details of the parties and a summary of the claim. [You will note that, in order to calculate the appropriate court fee, it is necessary to give the court an indication of the value of the claim. I should stress that this means completing the form with the top figure from the relevant band and that figure is purely for this purpose and does not supersede the advice previously given on the estimated value of the claim.]

(2)   *Particulars of Claim*
      These give, in concise form, the factual background, the reasons why the Defendant is considered responsible for the injuries caused and the compensation claimed as a result.

(3)   *Schedule of Expenses and Losses*
      This [sets out in some detail] [summarises] the financial losses and expenses claimed.

[(4)   *Certificate of Suitability of Litigation Friend*
      As [*name*] is [under 18] [a protected party] the Court Rules require that the proceedings, whilst taken in [*name*]'s name, must be supported by a person who is known as the 'litigation friend'. I believe you are the most suitable person to be the litigation friend and hope, therefore, that you are happy to act in this role. The Court Rules also provide that you must agree, in writing, to act and give the court certain assurances. It may be useful if I summarise what signature of this form means.
      (a)   You are agreeing to act as the litigation friend of [*name*].
      (b)   You are confirming that you have no interests which conflict with those of [*name*] in the claim.
      (c)   You are accepting responsibility for any liability [*name*] may have for the legal costs of the Defendant in dealing with the claim. Whilst it is right to make this clear, I do not think giving this assurance should lead to any liability on your part to pay costs as:

(i) this concerns only the legal costs of the Defendant, as the costs of [*name*] in pursuing the claim will continue to be [covered by the conditional fee agreement] [indemnified by legal expenses insurance];

(ii) [*name*] would only have liability for the legal costs of the Defendant if the claim were unsuccessful and I would hope the claim will succeed;

(iii) even if the claim were unsuccessful the [insurance policy, in support of the conditional fee agreement, should cover the liability] [legal expenses insurance will indemnify the liability] [*name*] might have to pay the costs of the Defendant.

Accordingly, I hope this reassures you about the reference to costs in the form and that you are happy to give these assurances to the court.

These documents, subject to approval by you, will be sent to the court and then, in turn, to the Defendant. The documents will be accompanied by the evidence of [*name of expert(s) whose reports are to be filed and served on issue of proceedings*] in written report form.

It is important that the facts stated in these documents are correct and so the court expects you to sign the forms confirming as much. Accordingly, would you please carefully check the enclosed documents. If any amendments are required, please can you show these on the document concerned or, if you prefer, in a covering letter. Alternatively, if it would be easier to explain or discuss any amendments, please contact [me] [*name*]. If the facts in the documents are correct as presently drafted, please sign the statement to this effect on each document (in the space provided between the marked crosses) and then return these to me.

It is my duty to remind you that if the court took the view that facts were stated without an honest belief in the truth of those facts, proceedings for contempt of court could be taken by the court against you. I am sorry, once again, to give such a strict warning but I am sure you can see the sense of the court insisting the information given is accurate as that is likely to lead to a speedier, and more economic, resolution of the case. For this reason, the court will expect the Defendant, similarly, to confirm the truth of any response to the claim.

I enclose a pre-paid envelope and look forward to receiving the documents back, either signed and approved or with appropriate amendments, as soon as possible.

Once the documents are signed and approved, I will be able to commence court proceedings and outline to you how the matter will then proceed.

Yours sincerely

8.2   Letter to Court – Issue of Proceedings

We are instructed by [*name of client*].

We enclose, for your kind attention, the following documents for the issue of proceedings.

(1)   Claim Form for filing together with copies for service and for our file.

(2)   Particulars of Claim for filing together with copy for service.

(3)   Medical evidence for filing together with copy for service.

(4)   Schedule of Expenses and Losses for filing together with copy for service.

(5)   Notice of Funding together with copy for service.

[(6)   Certificate of suitability of litigation friend.]

(7)   Cheque for the court fee of £[*figure*].

[We have calculated the court fee on the basis of the band exceeding £[*figure*] [but not exceeding £[*figure*]]. We tender the cheque on the basis that our client reserves the right, on payment of a further fee if so requested, to amend the value of the claim to whatever level may be appropriate. [As the claim form states that the Claimant expects to recover more than £50,000 we consider the claim can properly be started in the High Court.]

[This is a case in which we are required to send copies of the court documents to the Motor Insurers' Bureau (or to insurers acting on behalf of the Bureau), under the terms of the Uninsured Drivers' Agreement, within 14 days of issue of proceedings. Accordingly, we shall be grateful if the papers could be returned to us as soon as possible after issue and, in any event, within sufficient time for us to comply with the requirements of the Uninsured Drivers' Agreement.]

Either

[We should like to effect service of the claim form upon the Defendant ourselves and, accordingly, shall be grateful if you would return to us, after issue, the claim form duly sealed together with all copy papers intended for service and a response pack along with the sealed copy claim form for our file and notice of issue.]

Or

[We shall be grateful if the court can serve the claim form and accompanying papers on the Defendant and let us have notice of issue, confirming details of service, along with sealed copy claim form for our file.]

Yours faithfully

8.3   Letter to Motor Insurers' Bureau – Following Issue of Proceedings

Our Client: [*name*]

Uninsured Motorist: [*name of motorist*]

Date of Accident: [*date of accident*]

We write to advise that proceedings have now been issued on behalf of our client against the above motorist in the [*name*] County Court under Claim Number [*claim number*].

In accordance with clause 9 of the Uninsured Drivers' Agreement we now enclose copies of the following documents:

(1)   Claim Form sealed by the Court;

(2)   Particulars of Claim;

(3)   Medical evidence filed on issue of proceedings;

(4)   Schedule of Expenses and Losses;

(5)   Notice of Funding;

(6)   Form for Acknowledging Service;

(7)   Form for Defending the Claim;

(8)   Form for Admitting the Claim.

Kindly acknowledge safe receipt and confirm that we have complied with this aspect of the Uninsured Drivers' Agreement.

To facilitate service of proceedings upon the uninsured motorist, please let us know if the address for service is other than as shown on the claim form. [Please also let us know, within the next 14 days, if you wish to give an address for service on the Defendant [and/or you].]

[We are sending a copy of this letter to [*name and address of nominated insurers*] who have been acting on behalf of the Bureau in this matter.]

In accordance with clause 8 of the Agreement, we are sending this letter and enclosures by fax and by recorded delivery post.

Yours faithfully

SERVICE

8.4   Letter to Opponent – Serving County Court Proceedings

We now enclose, by way of service, the following documents:

(1)   Sealed copy Claim Form (and attached notes);

(2)   Particulars of Claim;

(3)   Medical evidence filed on issue of proceedings;

(4)   Schedule of Expenses and Losses;

(5)   Notice of Funding;

(6)   Form for Acknowledging Service;

(7)   Form for Defending the Claim;

(8)   Form for Admitting the Claim.

Either

[We have been in correspondence with your insurers [*name of insurance company*] of [*address*] (under reference [*reference number of insurance company*]) to whom you may care to refer these papers straight away. We shall be grateful if your insurers, or their solicitors, would acknowledge safe receipt.]

Or

[On the basis of the confirmation in earlier correspondence, you are authorised to accept service on behalf of the Defendant and we shall be grateful if you would acknowledge safe receipt.]

Yours faithfully

8.5   Letter to Opponent – Advising Insurers of Service of Proceedings

We write to advise that we have today sent the appropriate court papers [to your Insured at [*address per letter to Defendant effecting service*]]/[to *name of solicitors*] at [*address of solicitors*] on the basis that is the address given for service.

Please accept this letter as notice of our intention to apply to the court for default judgment unless the acknowledgment of service and/or Defence are filed within the appropriate timescales. Initially, we calculate that, unless we reach agreement granting a suitable extension of time for the Defence meanwhile, either the acknowledgment or Defence must be at court by [*date*].

Finally, if, under your Insured's policy, any further information should be supplied to you at this stage, please let us know without delay. If we do not hear from you with any such request, we shall assume that the terms of the policy have been complied with for the purposes, if necessary, of the Third Parties (Rights Against Insurers) Act 1930.

Yours faithfully

8.6   Letter to Motor Insurers' Bureau – Advising of Service of Proceedings

Our Client: [*name of client*]

Uninsured Motorist: [*name of motorist*]

Date of Accident: [*date of accident*]

We write to confirm that we have served proceedings on [*name*] [by post]/[personally] on [*date*].

Please accept this letter as any notice required pursuant to clause 10 of the Uninsured Drivers' Agreement. If you do not accept this letter as appropriate notice please advise us forthwith, giving your reasons.

Please would you also accept this letter as notice that, in accordance with clause 12 of the Uninsured Drivers' Agreement, after 35 days from service, we shall apply to the court for judgment unless, within that time, we receive a Defence or agree to a suitable request that there be an extension of time for the filing of service of a Defence.

[We are sending a copy of this letter to [*name and address of nominated insurers*] who have been acting on behalf of the Bureau in this matter.]

In accordance with clause 8 of the Agreement, we are sending this letter and enclosures by fax and by recorded delivery post.

Yours faithfully

8.7 Letter to Client – Summarising Personal Injury Proceedings

I write to confirm that court proceedings have now been issued on your behalf and, in the near future, copies of the formal court documents detailing your claim will be received by [*name of opponent*] ('the Defendant').

I think this is a convenient point to outline the way in which the court case will proceed and to remind you of the costs implications of court action.

I hope this will give you a clear picture of the action I will be taking on your behalf and usefully confirm some aspects of my earlier advice.

1. *Stages of the court process*

The court process will follow a number of stages which I will explain in turn.

(1) *Details of the case*
The court papers sent to the Defendant include the Particulars of Claim which set out what happened, the effect of that and why the Defendant is considered responsible.
The Defendant has 14 days, from receiving the court papers, to indicate whether the claim is to be defended.

(2) *The Defence*
The Defendant must respond to the claim by a Defence within 14 days, or 28 days if the Defendant first indicates the claim will be defended, from receipt of the court papers.
The Defence must confirm which parts of your claim are admitted, which parts are not admitted but not denied, and which parts are denied. The Defendant must give reasons for the matters that are denied. In this way the Defence will define which aspects of the case have to be proved at a later stage and should help to narrow, to some extent, those issues.

If the Defendant fails to indicate whether the claim is to be defended or fails to provide a Defence I can ask the court to enter judgment in your favour. Any such judgment would finalise the question of liability in your favour, leaving only the amount of compensation to be decided by the court. The amount of compensation would be fixed at a court hearing if terms could not be agreed meanwhile.

It is quite likely, however, that the Defendant will ask for further time, over and above 28 days, to prepare the Defence. The Defendant should not, generally, have more than 42 days from receipt of the court papers to send out a Defence, although, in appropriate circumstances, the court may allow longer. I will let you know if this timescale is extended.

(3)   *Exchange of further detail on the case*
Once I have the Defence I will:
(i)   write to outline the issues that have emerged;
(ii)   consider whether I need to reply on your behalf (a reply is not normally required, but sometimes fresh points can be raised in the Defence which do require comment);
(iii)   consider whether any questions need to be put to the Defendant to obtain further information on matters arising out of the Defence.

The Defendant may send, with the Defence, a request for some further information on your case and I will let you know if I need further information from you to deal with any such request.

(4)   *Allocation and case management directions*
When the defence has been received (or judgment entered in the absence of a defence) the court will ask the solicitors acting for each party to file a report. That report will detail the background to the proceedings, the issues that have arisen, the evidence that will be necessary to deal with those issues and any other information that the court might need to ensure that the issues which remain in dispute, at that stage, can be resolved as justly as possible. For these purposes, the court is particularly concerned to ensure that the matter is dealt with expeditiously, economically and proportionately. The court may, at that stage, direct any specific issue, such as liability, to be determined ahead of other issues as this sometimes helps in resolving the whole case.

When the court has considered the reports, a decision will be made:
(i)   allocating the case to a particular 'track'. I will explain in more detail what this involves when the allocation has taken place but, briefly, there are particular tracks suited to particular types of case, designed to achieve the overall objective of a just outcome;
(ii)   giving appropriate directions, which I will explain in more detail once made, to help guide the case, again as justly as possible, through the remaining stages towards a final hearing;

(iii) fixing a trial window which will be a period of time, usually 3 weeks, within which the court will subsequently fix a final hearing date if a settlement cannot be achieved meanwhile.

(5) *Disclosure of documents*

The directions given by the court will normally direct all parties to give disclosure of documents.

This involves the preparation of a list containing all documents which that party has, or has had, possession of relating to the issues in the case, as these have been defined by the Particulars of Claim and the Defence. That list must also contain written confirmation that the list is complete and that it has been prepared after an appropriate search for any documents that might be relevant.

Sometimes, particularly if the issues are narrowed or there is unlikely to be any relevant documentation, the court may dispense with the need for a formal list from one or more parties but, meanwhile, I think it best to assume that disclosure will take place and to give this advance warning of what that will involve.

I may well already have all relevant documents from you but, to ensure that I will be ready to deal with this stage of the case promptly, it would be helpful if you could give the matter some thought, and if necessary search for any further relevant documents, so that, as and when we reach this stage of the process, I will be able to ask you for:

(i) any further documents still in your possession (except for the letters and documents I have sent you as, of course, I already have these), including documents that have come into existence or into your possession since the claim started (if, at that stage, you are in doubt as to the relevance of any documents it would be best to let me have them);

(ii) a list of any documents you once had, but no longer have, relating to the case in any way, stating the identity of those documents and, if known, when you last had them and what became of them.

As disclosure of documents is such an important stage of the case, I will write to you again confirming what is required, when we reach it.

(6) *Dealing with the documents disclosed*

Any party is entitled to ask for copies of documents disclosed in another's list.

Either

[Of course, in accordance with the protocol, documents have already been obtained from the Defendant but I will, nevertheless, be reviewing the matter, once we have the Defence, to see if there are any further documents which the Defendant should be disclosing. If so, I will check the Defendant's list to ensure that disclosure has been given and seek copies of such documents so that I can send further copies to you for your information and comment.]

Or

[Strictly, to comply with the protocol, the Defendant should have effectively dealt with this stage of the case already but, unfortunately, the Defendant has failed to deal fully with this obligation. Accordingly, unless appropriate admissions are now made, I will be checking the Defendant's list to ensure that disclosure of all relevant documents is given and seeking copies so that I can send further copies to you for your information and comment.]

If there are any further specific documents you expect the Defendant to have concerning the issues that have emerged, it would be helpful to have a list from you, when we reach this stage of the case, identifying either particular documents or, if necessary, categories of document.

(7) *Exchange of witness statements*

The court will also usually give a direction that each party must disclose to any other party the statements of any witness of fact on whose evidence it is intended to rely.

The court will generally stipulate that this exchange should take place on the same day, so that no party has the advantage of seeing the other's statements first.

As I mentioned, when preparing your statement, that statement is not necessarily intended for disclosure to the Defendant and, before dealing with this stage of the action, I shall most likely be preparing an up-to-date statement concentrating on the main issues of the case and covering any further points that may arise out of the earlier stages. Once any up-to-date statement is completed, or I have decided we can rely on the existing statement this, together with any statements from other witnesses on whose evidence you rely, will be sent to the Defendant. I will let you have copies of statements produced by the Defendant.

(8) *Exchange of expert evidence*

To assist the court in making a decision on the case it is helpful to have expert evidence; that is guidance from a suitably qualified expert to help the court in deciding any issues arising in the case.

However, the court's permission is required for any party to rely on any expert evidence at a hearing. Permission to rely on expert evidence is one of the matters the court will deal with when giving case management directions (although initially the court may simply direct the arrangements for disclosure of evidence, with permission to rely on the evidence being considered once that disclosure has taken place).

There are some further specific points to deal with concerning expert evidence.

(i) Expert medical evidence

I have sent to the Defendant, with the court papers, the medical evidence obtained from [*name of medical expert(s) whose evidence is served on the Defendant now*].

The Defendant must decide whether to agree that evidence (and medical evidence is very often agreed) or, if it is not agreed, to try and identify points of disagreement.

Either

[I hope that the medical evidence already obtained and disclosed should be all we need to confirm the injuries suffered and the effect of these, although I will let you know, at the appropriate stage, if I think anything further is required.]

Or

[I anticipate reliance on further medical evidence as the matter progresses and I will, of course, keep you advised of the arrangements for this.]

Either

[As the Defendant did not object to [*name of expert*], I hope that the court will take the view that it would not be appropriate for this evidence to be duplicated by any further expert in the same field nominated by the Defendant. However, it is possible that the Defendant may be able to show that it is reasonable for a further opinion to be obtained in the same or some different field of expertise and I will, of course, advise further if this should happen.]

Or

[The Defendant has, of course, been given facilities to obtain medical evidence from [*name of Defendant's medical expert(s)*]. If this evidence is to be relied on, the Defence should make that clear and ought to have copies of relevant reports attached as confirmation.]

(ii) Other expert evidence

Any other expert evidence will be exchanged at or soon after the time when witness statements are exchanged. Like witness statements, it may be appropriate for reports to be exchanged, if the Defendant has corresponding evidence, on the same day.

Once the Defence has clarified the issues, I will advise you on whether I think it is necessary to rely on further expert evidence.

(iii) Questions

Questions may be put to any experts for the purposes of clarifying the opinion set out in any written reports relied upon. The court is likely to allow for questions once exchange of expert evidence is complete and give a timescale in which any such questions must be answered.

(iv) Agreement of expert evidence

If there should be more than one expert in any particular field, the court, with a view to encouraging agreement, will normally direct the experts to confer and prepare a joint statement either confirming agreement or identifying points of disagreement. This is very useful in helping to narrow the issues and can often help promote a settlement of the case.

It may be possible for the expert evidence to be agreed, or at least the issues narrowed, as that should avoid the need for any experts concerned to attend court and give evidence which, in turn, will make any final hearing date easier to arrange.

(v)   Permission to rely on expert evidence

As already mentioned the court needs to give permission before any party can rely on expert evidence at a hearing. I will ask the court for permission to rely on the expert evidence disclosed to the Defendant when the court reviews progress, although it may be that the court will not be able to deal with this or give a final decision about whether the evidence in written form should suffice until after exchange of evidence.

Once further expert evidence has been exchanged, or I can confirm we are content to rely on the evidence already obtained, most of the preparatory stages of the case will have been dealt with and each party will have a very clear idea about the case of the other.

(9)   *Review*

After all these preparatory stages have been dealt with, the court will expect further reports from the solicitors for the parties, confirming all the directions previously given by the court have been complied with. This is a further opportunity for the court to give any further directions that may be appropriate to ensure the case reaches a just conclusion as soon as possible.

I would hope that, at or soon after this review, the court will arrange a final hearing date or, if appropriate, arrange a hearing to decide any issue, such as liability, to be dealt with as a preliminary to any other issues in the case.

Accordingly, at this stage the court will aim to arrange that hearing within the 'trial window' scheduled at the stage of the initial review by the court and, to facilitate that, I will need, when reporting on progress, to advise the court of any dates that would not be convenient to those involved in the hearing.

(10) *The final hearing*

Once a final hearing date has been arranged I will carefully review the case to ensure that it is ready to be heard.

The hearing will often deal with all the issues in the case, so that the matter reaches a conclusion there and then. However, as already indicated, it may be appropriate for a particular issue to be dealt with as a preliminary, in which case some of the stages already outlined will be confined to that issue, and the final hearing will be on that issue only. I will explain, in more detail, how issues can be dealt with separately, if this seems appropriate, when we receive the Defence, or if the court directs issues to be dealt with separately.

At the final hearing, a judge will read the statements of case and consider the documents, witness statements and expert evidence disclosed. The judge will then reach a decision on the issues the hearing is concerned with, so this may involve a ruling on liability, an assessment of the appropriate level of compensation, or both.

Should a final hearing be necessary I will arrange for you to be represented, usually by a barrister.

I think it best to summarise all the stages in the case as I hope this overview will assist when I write to report as we deal with each stage. It may, however, be possible to avoid some of the stages, if the issues in the case can be narrowed or a settlement of the case achieved. Settlement can be reached at any stage in the proceedings and the court then asked to make a final order in the terms without the need for a hearing exploring the background.

2. *Timescale*

I am, at this stage, able to give only a very broad indication of the likely timescale for dealing with all of these stages in the court proceedings.

You will gather, from the stages in the court process, that it is likely to be about a month before the Defence is received and it may be a further 2 or 3 months after that before the court can deal with allocation and case management directions. However, once case management directions have been given we should have a much better idea of when the case is likely to reach a conclusion, as the court will normally aim to ensure any final hearing date takes place within 6 to 9 months of those directions being given, although the actual timescale must depend on the circumstances of each case and the time by which the evidence required by the court to make any final decision will become available.

I will provide a more detailed timetable for you once the court has had the opportunity of giving appropriate directions.

3. *Negotiations and settlement*

Most cases of this kind do reach settlement without the need for a hearing which you would need to attend and give evidence. As I have already mentioned the issue of court proceedings does not prevent the parties reaching agreement at any stage. The exchange of offers (either informally or on the more formal Part 36 basis) which I explained to you at an earlier stage is just as applicable after the issue of proceedings as prior to those proceedings being commenced.

Accordingly, although court proceedings have been issued, it is unlikely that you will have to give evidence at any court hearing, although you would need to attend any final hearing if the case got that far. The reason for issuing proceedings now is, essentially, to try and force a settlement of the claim sooner rather than later.

4.   Costs

Now that proceedings have been issued may I remind you that there is a change in the position on costs which I should like to confirm.

(1)   *Your own costs*
    The issue of proceedings does not affect the [conditional fee agreement]/[arrangements] we have already made in respect of your own costs.

(2)   *Recovery of costs from the Defendant*
    If the claim succeeds you would not usually have any significant liability for the costs of the Defendant and, moreover, the Defendant would have to pay most, though probably not all, of your legal costs.

(3)   *The Defendant's costs*
    If the claim is unsuccessful, or dropped by you, the Defendant would be entitled to ask the court to order that you pay the Defendant's own legal costs. Should you have any such liability then this should be met under the terms of the insurance policy you took out [at the time of entering the conditional fee agreement]/[for legal expenses].

I will, of course, write to you further at each stage of the case, but hope this letter brings you fully up to date meanwhile, usefully summarises the action I will need to take on your behalf to deal with the stages of the court process and gives an idea of likely timescale.

Yours sincerely

SECTION 9

THE DEFENCE

CONTENTS

ACKNOWLEDGMENT OF SERVICE AND EXTENSION OF TIME

9.1   Letter to Opponent – Dealing with Request for an Extension of Time for the Defence

We thank you for your [letter]/[telephone call] of [*date*].

[We confirm we have noted your interest on behalf of the Defendant.]

[We note you have filed an Acknowledgment of Service on behalf of the Defendant so that a Defence is due on [*date*].]

Either

[We note your request for an extension of time for filing a Defence and, confirm that we are prepared to give you the additional time you seek. We confirm that this means the Defence must now be filed by [*date*].]

Or

[We note your request for an extension of time for filing a Defence. Whilst we try to adopt a reasonable approach to timescale, we do not think, in all the circumstances, the extension of time sought is necessary or appropriate. [However, we would be prepared to extend time until [*date*]].]

Yours faithfully

9.2   Letter to Client – Confirming Extension of Time for the Defence

Following service of the court papers, I have now heard from solicitors instructed by [*name of opponent*] ('the Defendant').

[The Defendant has, at this stage, just acknowledged receiving the court papers which means the Defendant now has an extra 14 days to prepare a Defence.]

[Furthermore, the Defendant has, as I expected, asked for some extra time to complete the Defence. I have, as I previously indicated I would, allowed the extra time and we should now have that Defence by [*date*].]

I will advise further as and when the Defence has been received.

Yours sincerely

RECEIPT AND REVIEW OF DEFENCE

9.3 Letter to Opponent – Acknowledging Safe Receipt of and Reviewing Defence and Accompanying Documents

We thank you for your letter of [*date*].

We will deal with the matters arising in turn.

[1. *Your interest*

We confirm that we have noted your interest on behalf of the Defendant in this matter.]

2. *The Defence*

We acknowledge safe receipt of the Defence.

[3. *Admissions*

We are concerned that the terms of the Defence do not appear to be consistent with the Defendant's stance prior to the issue of proceedings.

[We consider a binding compromise was reached on the issue of [liability] [*details*] and that, accordingly, the Defendant is not entitled to defend this issue.]

[We consider the Defendant made a pre-action admission, for the purposes of CPR Part 14.1A and, accordingly, is not entitled to defend this issue without the permission of the court.]

[We consider [in any event] that, as this is a fast track claim, there is a presumption the admission is binding and, certainly as matters stand, the Defendant is not entitled to defend the issue of [liability] [*details*]. However, so that we may consider the matter further would you please:

(1) explain, precisely, why the Defendant seeks to resile from the stance taken previously;

(2) advise when and in what circumstances the decision to resile was made;

(3) produce, insofar as this is disclosable under the protocol, any further evidence taken account of in the decision to resile;

(4) produce, forthwith, all documents which would have been disclosable under the protocol if the Defendant had then adopted the stance which the Defence seeks to take; and

(5)   either confirm that there are no documents the Defendant did have, but no longer has, which would have been disclosable under the protocol or identify such documents with details of when, and in what circumstances, the Defendant parted with those documents and what, to the best of the Defendant's knowledge, has now become of those documents.

Please would you respond to these questions as soon as possible given that, if the stance the Defendant now seeks to take had been adopted all along, much of this information should have been provided already.]

[In the circumstances, we consider relevant parts of the Defence are susceptible to being struck out under CPR Part 3.4 and so our client reserves the right to apply to the court for an appropriate order [including judgment on the issue of [liability] [*details*]]. We invite you, before the costs of an application are incurred, to amend the Defence, or confirm that the Defendant abandons those parts of the Defence which are inconsistent with the stance previously taken.]

[4.   The protocol

We consider the Defendant has not complied with the pre-action protocol by [*details*].

The failure to comply with the protocol does prejudice the Claimant who has not had made known the full nature of the Defendant's case, despite the Claimant's case having been set out in detail in the letter of claim. This may have a bearing on the directions that are appropriate and, of course, in relation to costs.

Please let us know if you contend that the Defendant has complied with the protocol, giving reasons, or let us have any explanation there may be for the failure to deal with matters at the appropriate stage in accordance with the protocol.]

[5.   Statement of truth

We note that the Defence does not contain an appropriate statement of truth. Please remedy this promptly, failing which we reserve the right to ask the court to strike out the Defence.]

[6.   Defendant's request for further information

Either

[We acknowledge safe receipt of the request for further information sought from the Claimant. The information you are entitled to will be given without the need for you to obtain a court order.]

Or

[We acknowledge safe receipt of the request for further information sought from the Claimant.

The information sought is not, in our view, confined to matters which are reasonably necessary for the Defendant's case to be prepared or for the Defendant to understand the case which has to be met. Accordingly, we do not think that this information is required as a preliminary to disclosure and exchange of evidence.

If, after disclosure and exchange of evidence, you consider that any matters remain outstanding, you will remain able to renew your request for any such information, although we think it unlikely this will be required.

Accordingly, our client objects to complying with the request at this stage as it is considered disproportionate.]]

[7.   Claimant's request for further information

We enclose, by way of service, a request for further information. [We are serving this request as we do not consider that the Defence complies with the requirements of CPR Part 16.5, and accompanying Practice Direction, and we wish to be made aware of the nature of the Defendant's case now.]

If you do not provide further information and/or particulars and/or relevant documents and/or factual evidence, we will assume that you intend to raise only those affirmative allegations which you have already pleaded.]

[8.   Counter-schedule

[We are grateful for the counter-schedule [included in] [served with] the Defence.]

[We do not appear [, however,] to have a counter-schedule which complies with the terms of paragraph 12 of the Practice Direction to CPR Part 16. We shall be grateful if you would forward this to us as soon as possible [in accordance with the Request for Further Information].]

We are now moving on to prepare for allocation and case management which we will write to you about in due course. [Meanwhile, we look forward to hearing from you in response to the matters raised in this letter.]

Yours faithfully

9.4   Letter to Client – Advising on Defence

I write to report that I have now received the Defence of [*name of opponent*] ('the Defendant'), setting out exactly which aspects of the claim are disputed.

I enclose a copy of the Defence. As you will see, this sets out the Defendant's response to the Particulars of Claim which gave details of your case. However, it may be useful if I summarise the points taken by the Defendant and the way in which the Defence defines the issues.

(1)   The role of the Defendant is [denied]/[neither admitted nor denied]/[admitted].

(2)   Your role is [denied]/[neither admitted nor denied]/[admitted].

(3)   The fact of the accident is [denied]/[neither admitted nor denied]/[admitted].

(4)   The cause and circumstances of the injures are [denied]/[neither admitted nor denied]/[admitted].

(5)   The allegations that the injuries were caused by the Defendant's fault are [denied]/[neither admitted nor denied]/[admitted].

(6)   The injuries suffered are [denied]/[neither admitted nor denied]/[admitted].

(7)   The expenses and losses claimed as a result of the injuries are [denied]/[neither admitted nor denied]/[admitted].

Either

[Although liability for the injuries is denied it will not be until a later stage, after evidence is exchanged, that a proper assessment can be made about whether the stance taken by the Defendant can be justified by that evidence. A Defendant may often deny, or not admit, liability in the Defence even though the Defendant recognises the court may well find in your favour on this issue.]

Or

[It is encouraging that the Defence formally accepts [at least partial] responsibility for the injuries. I would not expect a Defendant to admit the extent of the injuries, losses and expenses so the terms of the Defence are the best you could expect at this stage.]

The Defence is intended to set out, precisely, the Defendant's response to the claim and supersedes any earlier admissions or denials. Usually, the Defence sets out the Defendant's final position, although the court can subsequently allow any part of the Defence to be amended. If there should be an amendment to the Defence at a later stage I will let you know.

[The Defence does, therefore, supersede the admission previously made by the Defendant. It is regrettable that, after making this admission, the Defendant now seeks to withdraw it. I have, in the circumstances, asked the Defendant to explain why the earlier admission is to be withdrawn. Once I have a response I will be able to advise whether I think the court will allow the Defendant to withdraw that admission or if it may be possible to ask the court to rule that the Defendant must stand by it. For the moment, I must advise on the basis of the Defendant's case as set out in the Defence.]

[The Defendant has sent, with the Defence, a request for some further information concerning the background to the claim. Whilst I have much of the information necessary to respond to the request there are some points upon which I should like to obtain your further instructions.

So that you can think the matter over, I confirm that the particular points upon which I require your further instructions are [*details*].

It may not be appropriate to give answers to all the questions at this stage and, in any event, you may not be able to be specific about some of the points raised. However, I shall be grateful if you can consider what information it is possible to give above and beyond that which I already have from you and telephone [me]/[*name*].]

Now that we know the Defendant's exact position on the claim I am reviewing the case generally to ensure all evidence will be ready for exchange, at the appropriate time, to deal with the matters that are in dispute.

I will let you know when we are ready to move on to the exchange of evidence with the Defendant. Meanwhile, I anticipate that the court will require reports from the parties suggesting how the case should best proceed. I will advise further once I am ready to make this report to the court.

Yours sincerely

SECTION 10

ALLOCATION AND CASE MANAGEMENT

CONTENTS

ALLOCATION QUESTIONNAIRES

10.1   Letter to Client – Explaining the Allocation Questionnaire

Following receipt of the Defence of [*name of opponent*] ('the Defendant')
I have received a request from the court for a report on the case. The
Defendant's solicitors will have received a similar request.

Accordingly, I am giving that report and inviting the court to give suitable
directions which I hope will help to manage the case and ensure that it is
progressed as quickly as possible towards a resolution.

[I anticipate that when giving directions the court will want to identify the
time during which a hearing date will be arranged. Once this 'trial
window' is known, we will have a good idea of when the [final] hearing [to
deal with liability] will take place, if a settlement cannot be agreed
meanwhile.]

I enclose a copy of the report made to the court on your behalf, in the
format of the court's own questionnaire. The questionnaire includes a
costs estimate and so it is right to let you have sight of this.

I confirm the main purpose of this estimate is to appraise the Defendant
of the costs that are likely to be claimed following a settlement or
successful conclusion of the case and this does not affect in any way the
funding arrangements already made to pursue the claim.

I hope to hear back from the court within the next few weeks and will
then let you have a further report with, I hope, a timescale for detailing
the remaining stages of the claim.

Yours sincerely

10.2   Letter to Court – Filing Allocation Questionnaire

We enclose, for filing, the following:

(1)   allocation questionnaire, duly completed;

[(2)   costs estimate;]

[(3)   draft case management directions;]

[(4)   case summary;]

(5) cheque for the court fee on filing the allocation questionnaire of £[*figure*].

[We shall be grateful if you could send us copies of the Defendant's allocation questionnaire together with any accompanying information or documentation.]

We look forward to receiving, in due course, either notice confirming the date of the case management conference or notice of allocation and case management directions.

Yours faithfully

10.3   Letter to Opponent – Enclosing Completed Allocation Questionnaire

We enclose, for your information, a copy of the allocation questionnaire, duly completed, as filed at court.

[We also enclose documentation filed at court with the allocation questionnaire.]

[We shall be grateful if you could let us have a copy of the Defendant's allocation questionnaire together with any accompanying documentation that you ask the court to consider with the questionnaire.]

Yours faithfully

10.4   Letter to Opponent – Dealing with Defendant's Listing Questionnaire

[Thank you for your letter enclosing] [We have received from the court] the Defendant's Allocation Questionnaire [and accompanying documentation].

[We are surprised that the Defendant contends, in the questionnaire, compliance with the pre-action protocol. Please would you either explain how you contend the Defendant has complied with the protocol or acknowledge that this part of the questionnaire has been completed incorrectly, failing which we reserve the right to raise the matter with the court.]

[The Defendant's Allocation Questionnaire indicates that the Defendant wishes to rely on evidence corresponding to expert evidence upon which the Claimant relies [though please identify any experts you have in mind]. We are not, as matters stand, persuaded such evidence is reasonably required to resolve the issues, as required by Part 35, and that it is not therefore appropriate for you to seek permission to rely on such evidence. Accordingly, please confirm whether the Defendant intends to seek permission to rely on such expert evidence and the reasons.] [This clearly has relevance as to whether it is reasonable for you to seek facilities to obtain such evidence. If you do intend to seek such permission please confirm whether or not you wish to have facilities for our client to be [examined]/[interviewed] so that we can seek instructions.]

[The Defendant does not appear to have given a costs estimate. Section 6 of the Practice Direction About Costs requires a costs estimate at this stage and we shall be grateful, therefore, if you would provide such an estimate failing which we reserve the right to seek an appropriate order from the court.]

[We enclose revised draft case management directions, with calendar dates, which we hope takes account of the matters raised on behalf of the Defendant. If this draft can now be agreed please let us know so that we can invite the court to give directions in these terms.]

Yours faithfully

10.5   Letter to Client – Advising of Case Management Conference

The court has now considered the written reports which were recently made by me and by the solicitors acting for [*name of opponent*] ('the Defendant').

Because there is some difference between the suggestions made by each party as to how the case should best proceed the court has decided, rather than just giving directions on the written reports, to arrange a hearing when the issues arising can be considered more fully.

The hearing will not make any final decision on the issues in the case but will determine what directions are necessary from the court to help best progress the case towards a resolution.

The hearing is scheduled to take place on [*date of hearing*]. [This hearing will be dealt with by telephone.] [You may attend the hearing if you wish but it will not be necessary for you to do so.]

I will report to you again, as soon as I can after the hearing, with confirmation of the directions, and timetable for dealing with these, given by the court.

Yours sincerely

INITIAL CASE MANAGEMENT

10.6   Letter to Opponent – Dealing with Case Management Conference

We have received notice from the court that, following the filing of Allocation Questionnaires, there is to be a case management conference at [*time*] on [*date*].

[We consider it would be appropriate to invite the court to deal with the hearing by telephone. If you are agreeable perhaps you could write to confirm so that we can make the appropriate request to the court and, if this is granted, organise arrangements accordingly.]

[The court has directed the hearing be dealt with by telephone. We will, therefore, make the appropriate arrangements for a conference call. It would be helpful if you could confirm the name, and telephone number to use, of the person who will be dealing with the hearing.]

We have indicated to you the directions the Claimant considers appropriate, so we consider you have ample notice of these without the need for the Claimant to issue any further specific application (though please let us know if you disagree). We assume any case management issues to be raised on behalf of the Defendant will be limited to matters covered in the Defendant's Questionnaire [and accompanying draft order] or will be matters that can properly be regarded as core case management business, set out for example in paragraph 5.3 of the Practice Direction to CPR Part 29. If there are any further matters you will want to raise at the hearing please give us advance notice so that we can properly prepare for those issues, without spending unnecessary time anticipating issues which are not going to arise.

Please let us know if we can now agree, or work towards agreement on, case management directions the court can be invited to make. We are mindful that if we reach agreement the court can be asked to approve a consent order which may allow the hearing to be vacated and costs saved.

Yours faithfully

10.7 Letter to Court – Ahead of Case Management Conference/Directions

We enclose, for filing, draft order, incorporating calendar dates, setting out [the Claimant's] [the parties'] proposed case management directions [together with [supplemental] case summary].

[We are pleased to confirm that consultations have allowed the parties to reach agreement on the case management directions the court is invited to make, which are as set out in the enclosed draft. In the circumstances it is hoped that the court is able to deal with allocation and case management directions in, or along the lines of, the draft [and to vacate the date fixed for the case management conference].]

Yours faithfully

10.8 Letter to Client – Advising of Allocation and Case Management Directions

Either

The Court has now considered the written reports which were made by me and by the solicitors acting for [*name of opponent*] ('the Defendant') giving suggestions as to how the case should proceed.

Or

[I write to report on the hearing which took place when the court considered how the claim against [*name of opponent*] ('the Defendant') should proceed.]

Having considered the case the court has been able to assess [the most suitable track and] the directions that are appropriate to ensure the case can be heard, if a settlement cannot be agreed meanwhile, as soon as possible.

I will deal, in turn, with the various matters on which the court has given directions at this stage.

[(1) The court has entered judgment in your favour on the question of liability. This confirms that there is no dispute about responsibility for the injuries and the only remaining issue concerns the amount of compensation that should be paid for those injuries [though the court will still need to determine whether, and if so to what extent, you contributed to those injuries as any final award of compensation will be reduced by a percentage equivalent to any such contribution].]

[(2) Liability has been dealt with on the basis the Defendant will pay [*figure*]% of the compensation that would have been payable if the Defendant had been held fully liable for the injuries by the court.]

Either

[(3) The court has allocated the case to the fast track, which is the track specifically designed to get the majority of claims to a final hearing as quickly as possible.]

Or

[(3) The court has allocated the case to the multi-track, which is the track designed to ensure that larger value claims, or those which have complexities for other reasons, get to a hearing as quickly as possible, whilst ensuring that cases of this type are properly managed.]

[(4) The court has directed that the dispute about the Defendant's liability be tried as a preliminary issue, ahead of any final hearing to determine the appropriate level of compensation. This is an encouraging development as it means:
   (i)   the claim can move straight ahead to a hearing when the court can determine liability, if this issue cannot be agreed meanwhile, as it will not be necessary to finalise all the evidence concerning the appropriate level of compensation before that hearing, if this issue cannot be agreed meanwhile;
   (ii)   if liability should be determined against you, although I hope that will not happen, there is nothing to be gained by undertaking further work to help assess the appropriate level of compensation;
   (iii) if liability is found in your favour that will leave only the amount of compensation to be determined, which should improve the prospects of agreeing an outright settlement.]

(5) The court has directed that there be disclosure of documents [by both parties] [which will be limited to disclosure, by you, of documents relating to the claim for compensation] to be completed by [*date*].

(6) The court has directed that the statements of witnesses [on the issue of liability] be exchanged [simultaneously] by [*date*] [so far as the statements you rely on are concerned and by [*date*] so far as the statements the Defendant relies on are concerned].

(7) The court's permission is required before any expert evidence can be relied on by any party so the need for such evidence has been considered at this stage.

    (i)   You have been given permission to rely on the evidence of [*name(s) of witness(es) or appropriate specialist field(s)*].

    [(ii) You have been given permission to rely on further expert evidence from [*name(s) of witness(es) or appropriate specialist field*] [on the basis that this is arranged jointly with the Defendant].]

    [(iii) The Defendant has been given permission to put questions on the expert evidence any time up to [*date*].]

    [(iv) The Defendant has not been given permission to rely on corresponding expert evidence.]

    [(v) The Defendant has been given permission to rely on the evidence of [*name(s) of witness(es) or appropriate specialist field(s)*] to be relied on.]

    Either

    [It was, of course, agreed at an earlier stage that the Defendant would have facilities to obtain this evidence.]

    Or

    [As the court has now given the Defendant permission to rely on this evidence, I need to advise further in relation to this.]

    I anticipate the expert will write to you direct suggesting an appointment.

    If you are not able to attend the appointment suggested, I would recommend that you telephone the expert's secretary (there is likely to be a telephone number on the appointment card or letter) to arrange an alternative time. If you encounter any further difficulty, please let [*me*]/[*name*] know.

    If the report of the expert instructed by the Defendant is to be relied on, then a copy of the report must be disclosed to me so that I can, in turn, forward this to you. If the Defendant chooses not to produce the report, we can assume that it does not help the Defendant and the matter will have to go forward without that evidence.]

    (vi) The court will make a final assessment of the need for expert evidence when arrangements are being made to list the case for a final hearing.

[(8) The court has directed that the reports of further experts be exchanged [simultaneously] by [*date*].]

[(9) The court has directed that a final, up-to-date, calculation of the financial losses and expenses resulting from the injuries should be sent to the Defendant by [*date*].]

[(10) The Defendant must respond to the [final] calculation of financial losses and expenses by [*date*].]

Either

[(11) The court expects further written reports, again from both me and from the Defendant's Solicitors, dealing with progress by [*date for filing of pre-trial checklists*]. The court will, once these further reports are available, undertake a further review of the case, perhaps at a hearing, so as to be sure that the case is then ready to proceed to a [final] hearing [to deal with liability].]

Or

[(11) The court has directed that there should be a [further] hearing, scheduled to take place in [*month and, if necessary, year*]. The court can then consider up-to-date reports on progress made, assess whether any further directions will be necessary and if it is then appropriate to identify the period during which the [final] hearing [to deal with liability] can be arranged.]

[(12) The court expects a [final] hearing [to deal with liability] to be arranged, on a date yet to be fixed, between [*first date of trial window*] and [*last date of trial window*]. I will be able to confirm when after the court has reviewed the case again. Meanwhile, I shall be grateful if you could keep these dates free or let me know as soon as possible if those dates would present a difficulty for you in attending court.]

I am pleased to report on these directions from the court which give a better idea of the likely timescale for bringing the case to a hearing if a settlement is not achieved meanwhile.

Yours sincerely

10.9   Letter to Opponent – Confirming Allocation and Case Management Directions

We have now received from the court a copy of the order made on [*date of order*] dealing with [allocation and] case management.

We trust you have also received a copy of the order from the court though please let us know if you have not.

[We wish the court to reconsider directions and, as these were given without a hearing, have filed an Application Notice a copy of which we enclose.]

[The court has directed that there be an interim payment of £[*figure*] to be paid by [*date*] which we look forward to receiving from you by then.]

We are preparing the Claimant's list of documents and look forward to receiving the Defendant's list by [*date*].

Witness statements are to be mutually exchanged by [*date*]. Please let us know if you wish to suggest a date meanwhile when each party will send to the other copies of the statements of witnesses of fact to be relied on [concerning liability]. Otherwise on [*date which is 2 working days before the date for exchange of witness statements in case management directions*] the statements of the Claimant's witnesses of fact [concerning liability] will be submitted to you in a sealed envelope on the basis that the envelope will be unopened until such time as you have sent to us statements of the Defendant's witnesses of fact [concerning liability] or confirmed that the Defendant will not be relying on the evidence of any witnesses of fact [concerning liability], provided that you shall be deemed to have opened the envelope and for the Claimant's evidence to have been disclosed to the Defendant on [*date for exchange of witness statements in case management directions*].

If the Defendant does not rely on the evidence of any witnesses of fact, please could you let us have confirmation of that as soon as you are able, as this should simplify, and speed up, exchange of the evidence of witnesses of fact.

[Expert evidence [on the issue of liability] [from [*field of expertise*]] should be mutually exchanged by [*date*]. Accordingly, unless other arrangements are made meanwhile, we will, on [*date*], send relevant evidence in a sealed envelope on the basis that the envelope will be unopened until such time as you have sent to us corresponding evidence to be relied on by the Defendant or confirmed that the Defendant will not be relying on any such evidence, provided that you shall be deemed to have opened the envelope and for the Claimant's evidence to have been disclosed to the Defendant on [*date*].]

[We anticipate, as the Court has given permission for the Defendant to rely on expert evidence, our client will give facilities for an [examination]/[interview]. Accordingly, we will[, subject to you confirming the identity of the expert concerned,] check whether our client has any objection.

Any facilities will be on condition that you promptly meet our client's reasonable expenses in attending any appointment (calculated on the basis of [first]/[standard] class rail fares, taxis to and from railway stations at each end of the journey or mileage of £[*figure*] per mile); advance notice of any tests or investigations the expert wishes to carry out; and any correspondence sent direct to our client concerning these facilities being copied to us.

We shall be grateful if you would please confirm these points are agreed and that the expert is aware of, and also agrees to, these terms. We look forward to hearing from you so that we can check with our client and confirm.]

If the timetable presents any particular difficulties please let us know as soon as possible though we hope the case will be able to proceed in accordance with the directions given so that pre-trial checklists can be promptly filed by [date].

Yours faithfully

SECTION 11

DISCLOSURE

CONTENTS

Videos

DISCLOSURE BY THE CLAIMANT

11.1 Letter to Client – Prior to Disclosure

I am now about to deal with the stage in the court case known as 'disclosure'.

You will know, from my letter summarising the steps in the court proceedings, that this stage of the case involves disclosure of relevant documents [by each party].

Accordingly, I must now prepare a list of all documents you have, or have had, relating to the claim. This list must be filed at court and sent to [*name of opponent*] ('the Defendant').

Disclosure is a very important part of the preparation of the case for any final hearing. Accordingly, it is essential that the list of documents sent out on your behalf complies with the requirements of the court rules. As you will need to sign the list, confirming that you have complied with these requirements, it is important that I explain, in some detail, exactly what the court expects.

1. *The documents to be disclosed*

(1) The court expects disclosure of:
  (i) documents on which you rely; and
  (ii) documents which adversely affect your case; and
  (iii) documents which adversely affect the Defendant's case; and
  (iv) documents which support the Defendant's case.
  Either
  [If you refer back to the letter I sent you detailing points raised in the Defence, you will know the main issues in the case, which should help identify documents which support or adversely affect the case of each party.]
  Or
  [In this case the court will only expect disclosure of documents which relate to the claims for financial losses and expenses resulting from the injuries.]

(2) The term 'documents' includes any:
  (i) written documents;
  (ii) photographs;
  (iii) video recordings;
  (iv) tape recordings;
  (v) computer records;
  (vi) e-mails;
  (vii) other permanent, semi-permanent or electronic records.

(3)   Only documents in your control have to be disclosed. The court regards a document as being in your control if:
      (i)   it is in your physical possession; or
      (ii)   you have, or have had, a right to physical possession of the document; or
      (iii) you have, or have had, a right to see or take copies of the document.

(4)   In a case of this kind documents I would expect you to disclose will include:
      (i)   receipts for any property lost or damaged as a result of the circumstances leading to the injuries;
      (ii)   receipts for any expenditure incurred as a result of the injuries;
      [(iii) health and safety documentation;
      (iv)   any other documentation concerning the background to, or responsibility for, the injuries that occurred;]
      [(v)   tax documentation;
      (vi)   state benefit documentation;
      (vii) pay slips or pay advices.]

2.   *The duty of search*

(1)   The court expects a reasonable search to be made for documents, though the list may state that this search has been limited to exclude documents pre-dating a specific date, documents elsewhere than a particular location, documents in specific categories or electronic documents.

(2)   I have assumed, though please let me know if this is wrong, that the search has not been limited [except for [electronic documents] [*details*]].

3.   *The format of the list*

(1)   The list must disclose any documents in your control, including any that have come into existence since the case began. Accordingly, if you do have any further documents please could you let me have them as soon as possible.

(2)   The list must also disclose any documents you have had, but no longer have, with details of:
      (i)   a description of any such documents; and
      (ii)   what has happened to those documents.
      If there are any such documents please can you let me have the necessary details. Unless I hear from you with those details I shall assume there are no such documents.

I hope this information assists in ensuring this important stage of the case will be dealt with properly.

Based on the documentation already available to me I have prepared, and enclose, a draft list of documents for your approval.

Once you have read this letter please would you check the draft list to ensure that all relevant documents are disclosed. If you are content that the list is complete please sign it, in the space provided on the front page between the marked crosses, and then return it to me in the pre-paid envelope also enclosed. If there are any further documents that ought to be disclosed in the list please could you return the draft list, either amended or with a separate note attached detailing those documents, so that the list can be amended ready for final approval.

If you are not sure whether further documents ought to be disclosed in the list, please telephone [me]/[*name*].

I look forward to hearing from you.

Yours sincerely

11.2   Letter to Opponent – Dealing with Disclosure

We enclose, by way of service, the Claimant's list of documents.

Either

[In anticipation of a request for inspection we enclose copies of the documents numbered [*relevant document numbers*] in the first part of the Claimant's list.]

Or

[Copies of [other] relevant documents from the first part of the Claimant's list have, of course, already been provided by way of inspection.]

Kindly acknowledge safe receipt.

Yours faithfully

11.3   Letter to Client – Confirming Disclosure Given

I write to confirm that I have now completed, and sent to the Solicitors acting for [*name of opponent*] ('the Defendant'), the list of documents you have, or have had, in your possession concerning the claim.

May I remind you that, although the list of documents has now been prepared, you should let me have as soon as you are able any further documents that become available, and which relate to the claim, as these will need to be disclosed to the Defendant.

Yours sincerely

11.4   Letter to Court – Filing Claimant's List of Documents

We enclose for filing the Claimant's list of documents and confirm that a copy has been served upon the Defendant's Solicitors.

Yours faithfully

DISCLOSURE BY THE DEFENDANT

11.5 Letter to Opponent – On Failure to Give Disclosure

We note that the Defendant has failed to comply with the case management directions which provided that disclosure be given by [*date for disclosure per court order*].

Unless the Defendant does now comply with this aspect of the order, it will be necessary for our client to seek a further order from the court.

We think it appropriate to warn you of our intentions, before applying to the Court, but must reserve the right to make appropriate application, without further notice, unless the order has been complied with by 4.00 pm on [*date*]. If it has not we are likely to ask the court to make an order striking out the Defence and, especially as we will then have given ample opportunity to put matters right, for the application to proceed without a hearing.

If you face any particular difficulties, or otherwise have grounds for seeking relief from sanctions, please let us know no later than the deadline imposed in this letter.

Yours faithfully

11.6 Letter to Opponent – Acknowledging Receipt of List of Documents (and Seeking Inspection and/or Further Disclosure)

We thank you for your letter of [*date*] and acknowledge safe receipt of the list of documents.

[Please would you let us have, by way of inspection, copies of the documents numbered [*number(s)*] in the first part of the Defendant's list.]

[We shall be grateful if you would take further instructions and provide full details of any documents which are, or have been, in the control of the Defendant within the following categories:

(1) [*details*]

(2) [*details*]

Please identify all documents, within each category, by date and with sufficient detail for us to establish which we will need to inspect.

If the Defendant no longer has control of any such documents, please state when the Defendant parted with them, in what circumstances the documents were parted with and what has become of them.

We do not anticipate that any privilege will attach to documents within the categories listed but, if you contend otherwise, please specify the precise grounds for claiming privilege and identify the relevant documents with sufficient particularity for the merits of that claim to be assessed.

We reserve the right to seek further disclosure of specific documents, pending completion of disclosure.]

[We enclose, by way of service, Notice Refusing to Admit Documents.]

[We note that the list does not disclose any videos although these are 'documents' and we consider any there may be should be disclosed now.

If there is any video please do not send this to any experts involved in the case until it has been disclosed to us and admissibility agreed or established. If you do we reserve the right, notwithstanding the costs that may be wasted as a result, to object to the admissibility of the evidence of such experts having put you on clear notice of the potential difficulties that would arise if you were to ignore this request.]

[We look forward to hearing from you.]

Yours faithfully

11.7   Letter to Client – Advising on Disclosure/Inspection by Defendant

I write to advise that I have received the list of documents that [*name of opponent*] ('the Defendant') has, or has had, relating to your claim.

The Defendant has disclosed, in the list, a number of documents relating to the issues in the claim.

Either

[The list, essentially, confirms the documentation disclosed at an earlier stage by the Defendant, which I sent on to you with my comments at that stage.]

Or

[The Defendant has disclosed some further documentation relating to the claim. I enclose copies.

Unless I hear from you to the contrary, within the next 7 days, I shall assume that you accept that the copies are of genuine documents, even though you may not necessarily agree with the content of those documents. If you do not accept the copies are of genuine documents as described please let me know as soon as possible as if I do not, promptly, deny the authenticity of the copies you will be taken to admit that they are copies of genuine documents.

[My observations on the enclosed documents are [*details*]. Please let me know if you have any further observations.]

I should remind you at this stage that all documents sent by one party to another, during the course of litigation, are disclosed on the basis that the party receiving the document will treat the document itself, and any information contained in the document, confidentially. This will remain the position unless and until the document is read out at any court hearing. Accordingly, you need to bear this duty of confidentiality in mind in respect of the documents now available and any further documents that may become available as this case progresses. Of course, the Defendant has exactly the same duty in relation to any documents you disclose.]

[I am not satisfied that the Defendant has given full disclosure of all documents relating to the issues in the claim. Accordingly, I have asked the Defendant's Solicitors to check and confirm whether the Defendant has, or has had, any documents within the following categories:

(1)   [*details*]

(2)   [*details*]

Given your instructions, and the general background to the case, I would expect the Defendant to have, or have had, such documents. If, however, you disagree please let me know.

Unless I receive a satisfactory response from the Defendant to this enquiry, I shall consider making an application to the court for an order that the Defendant do disclose any further documents and will advise further if this is necessary.]

I hope this letter brings you up to date for the moment.

Yours sincerely

DISCLOSURE BY OTHER PARTIES

11.8 Letter to Non-party – Warning of Application for Disclosure

Our Client: [*name of client*]

We refer to our earlier correspondence requesting disclosure of documents relating to our client and note that we do not appear to have received the documents requested from you.

These documents are required so that [a medical report, in final form, can be completed]/[a full and complete calculation of lost earnings can be prepared].

Our client blames [*name of opponent*] for those injuries, proceedings [are to be]/[have been] commenced against [*name of opponent*] and we confirm no claim is envisaged against you.

Unless the documents requested are disclosed within the next 28 days we must advise our client to make application to the court, in the proceedings against [*name of opponent*], for an order that you disclose to us the documents requested in our earlier correspondence. Assuming the documents are produced voluntarily we confirm that we will meet your reasonable costs in providing copies. If an application to the court is necessary we reserve the right to ask that the court make an order for the costs of and occasioned by the application be paid by you.

Should application to the court be necessary we understand that the proper party against whom the application should be made is [*addressee*] and that the address for service of any application is [*name of non-party*]. Please let us know if the details are otherwise.

We hope, of course, that it will not be necessary to make any application to the court and look forward to hearing from you. If the timescale presents any particular difficulty please respond to us, before then, with a view to reaching agreement on a mutually agreeable timescale for disclosure of the documents requested.

Yours faithfully

11.9   Letter to Client – Recommending Agreement to Disclosure by Non-party

The Solicitors acting for [*name of opponent*] ('the Defendant') have asked for access to [*description of documents*] held by [*name of non-party*] relating to you.

Each party is, as you know, required to disclose relevant documents to the other. Documents which are relevant to the claim may not be in the possession of any party. In such circumstances the Defendant can apply to the court for an order that anyone in possession of relevant documents be required to produce these. It seems to me that the documentation sought is likely to be available and relevant. Accordingly, if the Defendant had to make an application to the court, I think it likely that the application would succeed. Whilst I can oppose any such application, if you wish me to do so, the disadvantages are that this will only delay matters and there is also the risk that the court might make an order for costs against you if the application were to succeed.

In the circumstances, I think the best course is for you to sign an authority which will allow the Defendant access to the documents requested on the basis that copies are also disclosed to me. Accordingly, I enclose an appropriate form of authority.

Please let me know if you consider that the documents are likely to contain anything which is not likely to be relevant or which you think would be unhelpful. Please also let me know if you have any particular objection to disclosure of the documents.

As you know any documents disclosed by one party to the other, even if these originate from some other source, must be treated as confidential by the party receiving them unless and until those documents are referred to at a final court hearing.

If you are happy to proceed on the basis of this letter, please sign and return the enclosed authority, in the pre-paid envelope. If you have any reservations about proceeding, please write, or telephone [me]/[*name*].

I look forward to hearing from you.

Yours sincerely

11.10   Letter to Opponent – Enclosing Authority for Disclosure by Non-party

We enclose authority signed by our client for you to obtain relevant documents from the [*name of non-party*].

This authority is sent on the condition that you will forthwith on receipt disclose to us any documents obtained by you under the terms of the authority.

Yours faithfully

11.11   Letter to Client – Advising on Request for Disclosure of Medical Records

A request has been made by the representatives of [*name of opponent*] ('the Defendant') for production of medical records.

As a general rule one party should disclose to any other party all relevant documentation concerning the claim. When considering disclosure of medical records it is necessary to decide, first of all, which records are relevant which is likely to depend upon the nature and extent of the injuries. Even if records are relevant, and potentially disclosable, it is then necessary, with sensitive documents of this nature, to balance the right of privacy, associated with such documents, against the right to a fair trial, which partly depends upon all relevant documentation being disclosed. This approach reflects the European Convention on Human Rights, which is incorporated, by the Human Rights Act 1998, into English law.

Either

[Given the nature of the injuries, and hence the potential relevance of all records, I propose, unless you have any objection, to make copies of those records available to the Defendant's representatives.

The records are, of course, confidential documents and I should stress that, like all documents produced by one party to the other party during the progress of the claim, the party receiving the notes is under a duty to keep the content confidential unless and until referred to at a court hearing. Again, this reflects the requirements of the Human Rights Act 1998.

If, at any stage, you should receive forms of authority direct from the Defendant, please send those authorities to me and do not return them direct to the Defendant.]

Or

[Whilst I do not think it is appropriate for all records to be produced to the Defendant I do consider that the entries which relate directly to the treatment received for the injuries are relevant and ought to be provided to the Defendant's representatives.

The records are, of course, confidential documents and I should stress that, like all documents produced by one party to the other party during the progress of the claim, the party receiving the notes is under a duty to keep the content confidential unless and until referred to at a court hearing. Again, this reflects the requirements of the Human Rights Act 1998.

If, at any stage, you should receive forms of authority direct from the Defendant, please send those authorities to me and do not return them direct to the Defendant.]

Or

[A medical expert instructed by the Defendant is to prepare a report and, especially as corresponding evidence obtained at an earlier stage was based on a review of all records, I think it is appropriate for the records to be made available, direct to the expert, for these purposes. Accordingly, unless you have any objection, I propose to send copies of the records to the Defendant's expert.

The records are, of course, confidential documents and I should stress that, like all documents produced by one party to the other party during the progress of the claim, the party receiving the notes is under a duty to keep the content confidential unless and until referred to at a court hearing. Again, this reflects the requirements of the Human Rights Act 1998.

If, at any stage, you should receive forms of authority direct from the Defendant, please send those authorities to me and do not return them direct to the Defendant.]

Or

[I ensured, at an earlier stage, the records were reviewed, and taken account of, when the medical evidence on which you rely was prepared.

Given the primary duty of all experts is to the court I think the Defendant can safely assume that any relevant matters in the records will have been dealt with and that it is not necessary for the Defendant's representatives to undertake a further review of the records.]

In summary, my advice is that it is [not] appropriate to produce [all] medical records [except to the Defendant's expert].

If this letter enables you to reach a decision on the request made by the Defendant, please would you sign the enclosed confirmation in the space provided. This can be completed either to confirm that you accept the advice given in this letter or to let me have any other specific instructions. I also enclose a pre-paid envelope for your use in returning this authority.

If you wish to discuss the matter before reaching a decision, or would like any matters clarifying, please telephone [me]/[*name*].

I look forward to hearing from you.

Yours sincerely

11.12   Letter to Opponent – Dealing with Request for Disclosure of Claimant's Medical Records

We thank you for your letter of [*date*].

We note your request for production of medical records relating to our client.

Either

[We enclose, as requested, [relevant] records relating to our client.]

Or

[We accept it is appropriate for the records to be disclosed to any medical expert instructed on behalf of the Defendant, on the basis the expert will refer only to relevant entries and otherwise not give any further disclosure of the records. We consider that, to ensure our client controls disclosure of such confidential documents, this should be by the provision of copies direct to any expert concerned. Please confirm all of this is agreed.]

Or

[Whilst recognising your need to carry out reasonable enquiries, we must also be mindful of our client's rights under Article 8 of the European Convention on Human Rights. We consider we have best achieved the balance of these rights by having had relevant records reviewed when the medical evidence relied on was prepared. Given the primary duty of experts to the court, we think you can be assured that all relevant matters in the records will have been dealt with. Accordingly, we do not think it would be appropriate or proportionate for our client to agree the request for disclosure to you of all medical records. [We do not accept the records are required for the purpose of formulating questions, given that the purpose of such questions is only clarification of the expert opinion given rather than provision of further information.]]

Yours faithfully

INSPECTION OF DOCUMENTS

11.13   Letter to Client – Advising on Disclosure/Inspection by Defendant

You will recall that, when dealing with disclosure of documents, I was not satisfied that [*name*] ('the Defendant') had disclosed all documents relating to the claim.

Accordingly, I wrote to the Defendant's Solicitors requesting confirmation whether the Defendant has, or has had, any documents within the categories which I detailed to you at the time.

I have now heard in reply to that request. Dealing with the further categories of document in the same order as before, I am told by the Defendant's Solicitors that:

[(1)   [*description of relevant category of document*]: Copies of documents have been produced and I enclose further copies herewith.]

[(2)   [*description of relevant category of document*]: I am told that there are no such documents within this category.]

If you consider there are further documents, in the categories of documents already produced, or that documents do exist in those categories where the Defendant says there are none, please let me know.

I shall assume, unless I hear from you to the contrary within the next 7 days, you accept that the documents produced are copies of genuine documents, even though you may not necessarily agree with the content of those documents. If, however, you do not accept that the copies are of genuine documents that purport to be what they are described as please let me know as, if authenticity of the copies is not disputed now, you will be taken to admit that they are copies of genuine documents.

May I remind you that all documents sent by one party to another during the course of litigation are disclosed on the basis that the party receiving the document will treat the document itself, and any information contained in the document, confidentially unless and until it is referred to at any court hearing.

I welcome any comments you may have on the documents now produced and also whether you accept that there are no further relevant documents the Defendant should produce.

Yours sincerely

11.14   Letter to Opponent – Giving Inspection of Further Documents

We enclose further documentation, by way of disclosure, comprising [*details*].

Either

[Please would you treat the enclosed documentation as having been added to the relevant part of the Claimant's list of documents (although if this is not agreed, please advise and we will either amend the list or serve a Notice to Admit).]

Or

[We also enclose Notice to Admit the documents.]

Kindly acknowledge safe receipt.

Yours faithfully

VIDEOS

11.15   Letter to Client – Advising in Relation to Surveillance

In your claim against [*name of opponent*] ('the Defendant') you are contending that the injuries are having a significant effect on many aspects of life.

It is not unusual, where such claims are made, for the Defendant to arrange for surveillance to be carried out by enquiry agents. Usually, the surveillance will involve the agents preparing a video showing you coming and going from your home and any activities undertaken while you are out. The Defendant's object is to see whether, in your day-to-day life, you do face restrictions of the kind claimed.

Whilst I appreciate it is not very pleasant to think that you may be being observed, I am sure you will accept that, if carried out in a reasonable manner, this type of surveillance is an appropriate enquiry to be made on the Defendant's behalf.

I think it right to explain the possibility of this surveillance as, from time to time, clients become alarmed that they may be being observed. I hope that knowing this may happen, and the reasons why, may reassure you that there is nothing more sinister involved.

I would add that such surveillance will normally only be undertaken over a very short period of time, although there may be such a period of surveillance followed by another period of surveillance at a later date. It would be unusual for you to be observed for days on end, let alone weeks or months. Surveillance is most likely to be carried out at times when the Defendant will know your whereabouts, for example when travelling to or from appointments with experts nominated by the Defendant.

From time to time, enquiry agents have been known to do more than simply make observations. For example agents may use the pretext of a consumer or political survey to obtain information from you or even access to your home.

If in doubt you should ask to see, and make a note of, formal identification from anyone making such enquires.

Video evidence, like other evidence, will need to be disclosed by the Defendant if it is to be relied on at a later stage. I will send to you any video evidence the Defendant does disclose.

Generally, evidence of this kind is only of any use to the Defendant where claims are exaggerated. Where, as sometimes happens, any evidence confirms the restrictions on day-to-day life, it can be useful to the claimant. Furthermore, if no video evidence is produced, when it seems likely that surveillance has taken place, this, too, tends to suggest that the video simply confirms that the disabilities claimed are genuine. Accordingly, the fact of surveillance may assist the claim.

I have no wish to alarm you about the possibility of surveillance and hope this letter puts the matter in proper context.

Yours sincerely

11.16 Letter to Opponent – Acknowledging Receipt of Video Evidence

We thank you for your letter of [*date of letter received from opponent*] and acknowledge safe receipt of the enclosed video [and accompanying documentation].

[We enclose a Notice Refusing to Admit. Kindly acknowledge safe receipt.]

So that we can assess if, or to what extent, the enclosures with your letter may be admitted, we shall be grateful if you would:

(1) confirm whether the video supplied to us is an original;

(2) confirm (if the video supplied is not an original):
   (i) whether the original is in digital or analogue form;
   (ii) that the original has not been altered in any way and that the copy supplied is a complete and faithful copy of all original video footage taken of our client;
   (iii) that we may have facilities to view the original (ideally by letting us have this on loan);
   [(iv) whether the original has a sound track;]

[(3) provide a copy of the video showing data relating to both the date and time of the recording;]

[(4) confirm when, and by whom, the video was taken;]

(5) disclose all notes made by those taking the video relating to the surveillance in any way;

(6)   confirm that the evidence disclosed is the totality of the video surveillance carried out or, if not, produce promptly all further video footage taken as a result of surveillance of our client;

[(7)   explain, so far as the footage was taken in circumstances when privacy might have been expected, why you consider that this does not infringe rights of privacy under the Human Rights Act 1998;]

We look forward to hearing from you.

Yours faithfully

11.17   Letter to Client – on Receipt of Video Evidence/ Surveillance Report

It appears that the representatives of [*name of opponent*] ('the Defendant') have carried out some surveillance as a video has now been disclosed [together with an accompanying surveillance report].

I enclose a copy of the video for you to view [along with the accompanying report].

If you have any comments on the video [and accompanying report] please can you telephone [me]/[*name*].

Yours sincerely

SECTION 12

EXCHANGE OF FACTUAL EVIDENCE

CONTENTS

PREPARING FOR EXCHANGE OF WITNESS STATEMENTS

12.1   Letter to Client – Sending Statement for Exchange

We are now approaching the stage of the case against [*name of opponent*] ('the Defendant') at which each party must [disclose]/[complete disclosure of] the evidence, which will be relied on at any [final] hearing [on the issue of liability].

Like most of the other stages in the case, this is intended to avoid either party being taken by surprise at the hearing and to ensure that the parties are ready to deal with all issues likely to arise. Furthermore, the disclosure of evidence allows a more accurate assessment of the other party's case to be made and will, I hope, make a settlement more likely.

The next step is, therefore, for each party to [disclose]/[complete disclosure of] the statements of witnesses who will need to give evidence at any [final] hearing [relating to liability].

At this stage, I need to bring your earlier statement up to date.

Either

[Whilst I have prepared a draft of the revised statement, I think it would be sensible if we could discuss this so that I can ensure I have your full and up-to-date instructions on all relevant matters. Accordingly, I shall be grateful if you could contact [me]/[*name*].]

Or

[I have redrafted your statement so that this is up to date and ready for disclosure to the Defendant. I enclose that revised statement for your approval. Like your earlier statement, I shall be grateful if you would read it carefully to check the content.

I must remind you, once again, that the final paragraph of the statement is your confirmation to the court that the facts in the statement are true. Accordingly, if the court took the view that any facts were stated without an honest belief in the truth of those facts proceedings for contempt of court could be taken against you by the court.

After reading the statement, please make any amendments, on the statement itself or by a covering letter, that may be required to correct any detail or to cover points you feel have been omitted. Please return details of any amendments required to me so that I can arrange for a further version of the statement, incorporating those amendments, to be sent out to you.

If it is necessary to discuss the amendments that may be necessary please would you telephone [me]/[*name*].

Should the statement be approved in its present form, I shall be grateful if you would just sign and date it, in the space provided at the end of the statement, prior to return to me.

I enclose a pre-paid envelope for you to return the statement if approved or the details of any amendments required.]

When the evidence to be relied on is ready I will make arrangements to exchange this [simultaneously] with [any further] corresponding evidence on which the Defendant intends to rely.

I will let you know once exchange has taken place and send copies of any statements disclosed by the Defendant with my advice on any particular matters that may arise.

I look forward to hearing from you.

Yours sincerely

12.2 Letter to Witness – Sending Statement for Exchange

I am now approaching the stage in [*name of client*]'s case when statements of witnesses must be exchanged with [*name of opponent*] ('the Defendant').

As it would be helpful to rely on a statement from you, I have prepared a draft statement which I hope accurately sets out the information you are able to provide. I enclose that draft statement for your approval.

I shall be grateful if you would read the statement carefully to check the content. It is essential that the statement is full and accurate. Accordingly, I hope the statement sets out, in your words, the information you are able to provide and, as well as being accurate, includes all matters necessary to fairly reflect what you are able to say.

To comply with court rules, to which this statement will be subject, the final paragraph is your confirmation that the facts stated are true. If, at a later stage, the court took the view that facts were stated without an honest belief in the truth of those facts, proceedings for contempt of court could be taken by the court against you. I am sorry to have to issue a warning in such strict terms, but I am sure you will appreciate that it is my duty to do so.

After reading the statement, please make any amendments, on the statement itself or by a covering letter, that may be required to correct any detail or to cover points you feel have been omitted. Please return details of any amendments required to me so that I can arrange for a further version of the statement, incorporating those amendments, to be sent out to you.

If it is necessary to discuss the amendment that may be necessary, please would you telephone [me]/[*name*].

Should the statement be approved in its present form I shall be grateful if you would just sign and date it, in the space provided at the end of the statement, prior to return to me.

I confirm that, once disclosed, it will be my intention to rely on your evidence in that written form so that, even if this case does have to be heard at court, it will not, I hope, be necessary for you to attend any hearing. However, I cannot at this stage rule out the possibility you might have to give evidence at a hearing.

I enclose a pre-paid envelope for you to return the statement if approved or the details of any amendments required.

I look forward to hearing from you.

Yours faithfully

DEALING WITH EXCHANGE OF WITNESS STATEMENTS

12.3   Letter to Opponent – Exchanging Witness Statements

We now enclose, to deal with exchange, [a sealed envelope containing] the Claimant's factual witness evidence [on the issue of liability].

[The enclosed envelope is sent to you on the basis that:

(1)   you are sending to us today the statements of the Defendant's witnesses of fact [on the issue of liability]; or

(2)   you let us have confirmation, by return, that the Defendant will not rely on the evidence of any witnesses of fact [on the issue of liability]; and

(3)   the envelope will not be opened until such time as you have sent to us the statements of the Defendant's witnesses of fact [on the issue of liability] or confirmed that the Defendant will not be relying on the evidence of any witnesses of fact [on the issue of liability]; provided that you will, in any event, be deemed to have opened the envelope, and for the Claimant's evidence to have been disclosed to the Defendant, on [*date for exchange in case management directions*].]

Kindly acknowledge safe receipt.

Yours faithfully

12.4   Letter to Opponent – Following Exchange of Witness Statements

Either

[We thank you for your letter of [*date*] and [acknowledge safe receipt of the enclosed factual witness evidence]/[are grateful for the confirmation the Defendant does not rely on any factual witness evidence].]

Or

[We note that we have not received from you, in exchange for the evidence sent out on our client's behalf, factual witness evidence on which the Defendant may intend to rely.

We must assume, therefore, that the Defendant has no such evidence but shall, as requested in previous correspondence, be grateful if you would please confirm.

We anticipate that you will have opened the envelope containing the Claimant's evidence and will, in any event, treat the Claimant's evidence as having been disclosed. The Claimant will rely, if necessary, on the sanctions that now automatically apply. We would, of course, have to object if the Defendant subsequently sought leave to introduce factual evidence, having then gained the advantage of unilateral disclosure by the Claimant. Accordingly, if the Defendant does intend to seek any relief from this sanction, may we suggest you make application here and now, although we must tell you that any such application will be opposed, unless you can provide cogent reasons why it should not.]

Yours faithfully

12.5   Letter to Client – Following Exchange of Witness Statements

Thank you for letting me have back the statement I prepared for you in readiness for the exchange of witness statements with [*name*] ('the Defendant'). I enclose a copy of the factual evidence disclosed on your behalf to the Defendant.

Either

[I have, in turn, received the factual evidence on which the Defendant intends to rely and I also enclose a copy of this.]

Or

[The Defendant has confirmed no corresponding factual evidence is to be relied upon.]

Or

[The Defendant has failed to send, in return, any factual evidence upon which the Defendant intends to rely or to confirm that there is no such evidence.]

Strictly, the evidence disclosed at this stage should contain all factual matters to be confirmed by witnesses on which each party will rely in support of the relevant statement of case if and when a final hearing takes place. Accordingly, we are now in a better position to assess the extent to which the Defendant is able to support the matters set out in the Defence which I summarised for you at an earlier stage.

[My observations on the evidence available to deal with the main issues in the case are that [*details*]. It is not necessary for me to respond to the matters contained in the Defendant's evidence at this stage. However, it is right to let you review the evidence now as questions can be put to the witnesses, on the evidence, if and when a final hearing takes place. Accordingly, if you have any particular observations on the Defendant's evidence I would welcome these.]

[In the absence of factual evidence in support it may be difficult for the Defendant to sustain all aspects of the Defence.]

[I am not particularly surprised that the Defendant has disclosed no factual evidence, given the limited issues that remain in dispute.]

I am pleased to report that we have now dealt with this important stage of the case.

Yours sincerely

SECTION 13

EXCHANGE OF EXPERT EVIDENCE

CONTENTS

REQUEST BY THE DEFENDANT FOR FACILITIES TO OBTAIN EXPERT EVIDENCE

13.1   Letter to Opponent – Dealing with Request for Facilities to Obtain Expert Evidence

We thank you for your letter of [*date*]. We note you wish to rely upon expert evidence and [assume] that you seek facilities for our client to be [examined]/[interviewed].

[Please explain why you consider the Defendant reasonably requires expert evidence, and hence facilities to obtain this, so that our client can make an informed decision about whether it is appropriate to give facilities. When considering whether expert evidence of the kind proposed is 'reasonably required' for the purposes of Part 35 CPR we consider the following matters are relevant.

[(1)   Our client has already disclosed evidence from an expert in this field. Whilst we recognise that the Defendant may not accept all aspects of the evidence disclosed, the involvement of experts in the way encouraged by the protocol and the Civil Procedure Rules, coupled with the primary duty of experts to the court, means that the parties may not accept the views expressed on all matters, but this does not necessarily justify a further opinion.]

[(2)   You have not taken the opportunity to clarify any matters by putting questions.]

[(3)   You have not identified specific points of disagreement, and reasons, with the evidence already disclosed.]

[(4)   The grant of facilities at this stage would seem likely to result in delay that can otherwise be avoided.]

[(5)   Our client will disclose evidence from an expert in this field and we would suggest it is premature to obtain evidence from an expert in the same field when the evidence to be disclosed may be capable of agreement.]

[(6)   We do not consider evidence from an expert in the field proposed is reasonably required to resolve the issues in the case.]

(7)   Costs should be saved, where possible, by avoiding unnecessary expert evidence [particularly where that involves duplication of evidence in a field of expertise.

We are, of course, prepared to consider, and take instructions on, your response to these points but the further comments in this letter are all subject to you satisfying us the evidence is reasonably required.]

[Whilst we note you wish to obtain evidence from an expert in the field of [*details*] please would you identify the expert in that discipline you have in mind.]

Any facilities will be on condition that: our client has no reasonable objection to the expert concerned; you promptly meet our client's reasonable expenses in attending any appointment (calculated on the basis of [first]/[standard] class rail fares, taxis to and from railway stations at each end of the journey or mileage of £[*figure*] per mile); advance notice of any tests or investigations the expert wishes to carry out; and any correspondence sent direct to our client concerning these facilities being copied to us.

We shall be grateful if you would please confirm these points are agreed and that the expert is aware of, and also agrees to, these terms.

We look forward to hearing from you so that we can seek instructions from our client accordingly.

[We also note your request for disclosure of medical records. Whilst recognising your need to carry out reasonable investigations, we must also be mindful of our client's rights under Article 8 of the European Convention on Human Rights. We consider that the balance of these rights is best achieved by us disclosing directly to the expert you wish to instruct, copies of the records on the strict understanding that only those entries and documents relevant to the claim will be referred to by the expert in any report and that further copies of those records will not be the subject of onward disclosure.]

We look forward to hearing from you.

Yours faithfully

13.2   Letter to Client – Advising on Defendant's Request for Facilities to Obtain Expert Evidence

When, at an earlier stage, expert evidence was obtained I explained that the insurers of [*name of opponent*] ('the Defendant') might ask for your co-operation in obtaining similar evidence, as a check against the opinion on which you rely.

I write to advise that a request has now been made that you agree to see an expert nominated by the Defendant.

Neither the Defendant nor the court can require you to see such an expert. However, if a reasonable request by the Defendant for appropriate facilities to obtain expert evidence is declined the court might be asked to make an order halting further steps in the court process until such time as the necessary facilities are given.

The court, if having to decide whether such facilities are reasonably required would have to balance, on the one hand, your right of privacy and the need to avoid unnecessary expert evidence with, on the other hand, the Defendant's right to obtain evidence reasonably necessary for there to be a fair trial. These rights are confirmed by the European Convention on Human Rights which is incorporated into English law by the Human Rights Act 1998.

Accordingly, if the facilities requested are not given the Defendant could make an application to the court, seeking an appropriate order, and in any event refusal to give facilities at this stage may delay progress towards settlement.

Either

[My view is that this is a case in which the court would probably take the view that the Defendant ought to have the opportunity of obtaining expert opinion corresponding to the evidence on which you rely, even though experts concerned may end up agreeing their opinions.

Consequently, I think progress is likely to be best made at this stage by viewing the Defendant's request sympathetically.

Accordingly, and subject to the terms set out subsequently in this letter, I am happy to recommend that you agree to provide the facilities now sought by the Defendant.]

Or

[Consequently, if the point had to be decided, I consider the court may be prepared to uphold a decision by you not to give those facilities. Accordingly, I think there are reasonable grounds for refusing the facilities requested but a court may view the matter otherwise and if you would prefer to avoid arguing the point, and agree to give those facilities now, please let me know.

Whilst my advice is that the facilities requested should not, at this stage, be given it does seem sensible for me to set out further details of the request, and what would be involved if these are agreed, so that you are aware of the choices.]

The Defendant would like to instruct [*name of expert*] of [*place of practice of expert*]. Please let me know if you have any objection, for example if the expert nominated has previously treated you.

If you have no objection to the arrangements proposed by the Defendant, I will advise the Defendant accordingly and suggest that the nominated expert write to you direct suggesting a suitable appointment.

You would, of course, need to attend the appointment which the expert arranges for you. If you were not able to attend the appointment suggested, I would recommend that you telephone the expert's office (there is likely to be a telephone number on the appointment card or letter) to arrange an alternative time. If you encounter any further difficulty, please let [me]/[*name*] know.

You are entitled to be reimbursed for attending any appointment. Accordingly, please keep tickets, or get receipts, for any expenses incurred. If you make the journey by car, please keep a record of the mileage involved. Please then send receipts, tickets or a note of any mileage to me so that I can arrange for reimbursement of those travel expenses by the Defendant.

The purpose of the meeting with an expert nominated by the Defendant is to assess [the medical condition, continuing complaints and interference with all aspects of life, as a result of the injuries] [*details*]. You should, of course, give the expert full details of these matters.

Whilst it is reasonable for the expert nominated by the Defendant to carry out an [examination]/[interview] I would expect that if any further tests or investigations are proposed details will be given in advance so that you can reach an informed decision, if necessary after further advice from me, on the extent to which it is reasonable to agree to any such matters. If, at the appointment, the expert does wish to carry out any tests or investigations which have not been the subject of an advance request, and that you are not comfortable with, you are entitled to object. I am, however, happy for you to agree to anything you consider reasonable and are happy with.

[I confirm that, if the evidence of the expert instructed is to be relied on, the Defendant will have to disclose a copy of the report and I can then ask the corresponding expert, on whose evidence you rely, to comment on the opinion of the Defendant's expert. Should the Defendant not disclose the report of the expert, which would suggest the opinion does not assist the Defendant, the case will proceed on the basis of just the expert evidence on which you rely from the expert in this field.]

[If facilities are to be given for the Defendant to obtain medical evidence I think it is appropriate to disclose all medical records to the expert concerned, given that these records were used when the expert evidence you rely on was obtained. Accordingly, unless you have any objection, I would propose to make copies of the records available to the expert nominated by the Defendant. Whilst the records are, of course, confidential documents, I would expect the expert will only refer to relevant entries so as to respect your privacy and the confidentiality of the records. If, at any stage, you receive any forms of authority direct, please refer these to me in the first instance.]

I shall be grateful if you could let me have your instructions on the Defendant's request by completing the enclosed confirmation. I also enclose a pre-paid envelope for your use in returning this.

If you wish to discuss the matter before reaching a decision, or would like any matters clarifying, please telephone [me]/[*name*].

I look forward to hearing from you.

Yours sincerely

13.3 Letter to Opponent – Confirming Claimant's Agreement to See Defendant's Expert

We now have our client's instructions on your request for facilities to obtain expert evidence.

We confirm that, subject to the terms set out in previous correspondence, our client has no objection to seeing [*name(s) of expert(s)*]. [Please confirm these terms are agreed.]

May we remind you any letters sent to our client suggesting or arranging appointments should be copied to us.

Yours faithfully

13.4   Letter to Opponent – Confirming Claimant's Refusal to See Defendant's Expert

We now have our client's instructions on your request for facilities to obtain expert evidence.

Our client does not consider that the expert evidence you propose to obtain is reasonably required [at this stage] or that, in these circumstances, it is appropriate to give the facilities requested.

Yours faithfully

13.5   Letter to Opponent – Following Claimant's Meeting with Defendant's Expert

We are pleased to confirm that our client has now seen [*name of expert*].

We look forward to receiving a copy of the report [in due course] [by [*date in case management directions*]].

Our client incurred travel expenses of £[*figure*] in attending the appointment [for which we enclose copy documentation] [being [*number*] miles at £[*figure*] per mile].

We shall be grateful if you could arrange for reimbursement to be made, through us, to our client as soon as possible.

Yours faithfully

13.6   Letter to Client – Following Claimant's Meeting with Defendant's Expert

Thank you for letting me know that you were able to see [*name of expert*], the expert instructed on behalf of [*name of opponent*] ('the Defendant').

[Thank you also for letting me have details of your travel expenses. I confirm that I have given details to the Defendant's solicitors and asked for you to be reimbursed as soon as possible.]

I will let you know if and when the Defendant discloses the report of [*name of expert*].

Yours sincerely

DEALING WITH EXCHANGE OF EVIDENCE

13.7   Letter to Opponent – On Exchange of Expert Evidence

We have now reached the stage at which exchange of expert evidence [on the issue of liability] should be dealt with.

Either

[We have already disclosed to you the expert evidence of [*name(s) of expert(s)*]. [That evidence is the expert evidence upon which our client intends to rely so we consider that our client has already complied with the requirement to disclose expert evidence.]]

Or

[Accordingly, we now enclose the Claimant's [further] expert evidence comprising the report of [*name(s) of expert(s)*].]

Or

[Accordingly, we now enclose a sealed envelope containing the Claimant's [further] expert evidence [on the issue of liability].

The enclosed envelope is sent to you on the basis that:

(1)   you are sending to us today the Defendant's expert evidence [on the issue of liability]; or

(2)   you let us have confirmation, by return, that the Defendant will not rely on any expert evidence [on the issue of liability]; and

(3)   the envelope will not be opened until such time as you have sent to us the Defendant's expert evidence [on the issue of liability] or confirmed that the Defendant will not be relying on any expert evidence [on the issue of liability]; provided that you will, in any event, be deemed to have opened the envelope, and for the Claimant's evidence to have been disclosed to the Defendant, on [*date for exchange in case management directions*].

If we have not received from you by [*date for exchange in case management directions*] the expert evidence relied on by the Defendant [on the issue of liability], we shall assume that the Defendant does not intend to rely on any expert evidence which has not, by then, been disclosed. The Claimant would, of course, be prejudiced in the event of the Defendant subsequently seeking to rely on further expert evidence, as the Claimant would then have effectively disclosed expert evidence unilaterally.]

It would be helpful to know, in connection with the expert evidence disclosed, if, or to what extent, such evidence is agreed and, insofar as the evidence may not be agreed, specific points of disagreement with reasons.

Following exchange, so far as experts in the same discipline are concerned, we anticipate arrangements for joint statements between those experts will be appropriate.]

[May we remind you that if you choose to put any questions on the expert evidence disclosed copies of your questions should be sent to us at the same time.]

Unless we hear from you to the contrary, within a reasonable timescale, we shall assume that, even if the expert evidence disclosed is not agreed, you accept that the opinion given is expert evidence that our client may rely on as such. Otherwise, please let us know, with reasons for your objections, as soon as possible.

Yours faithfully

13.8   Letter to Client – Confirming Disclosure of Expert Evidence

I have disclosed to [*name of opponent*] ('the Defendant') the report of [*name of expert*] [and the report of [*name of expert*]].

I have asked the Defendant to advise whether this evidence can be agreed or, if not, to identify particular points of disagreement.

[I should receive, in return, any corresponding evidence on which the Defendant intends to rely and will advise further on this at that stage.]

Yours sincerely

13.9   Letter to Opponent – Following Exchange of Expert Evidence

Either

[We thank you for your letter of [*date*] and [acknowledge safe receipt of the enclosed expert evidence]/[are grateful for the confirmation the Defendant does not rely on any [further] expert evidence].]

Or

[We note that we have not received from you, in exchange for the evidence sent out on our client's behalf, expert evidence on which the Defendant intends to rely.

We assume the Defendant has no [further] such evidence but shall be grateful if you would please confirm.

We anticipate that you will have opened the envelope containing the Claimant's evidence and will, in any event, treat the Claimant's evidence as having been disclosed. The Claimant will rely, if necessary, on the sanctions that now automatically apply. We would, of course, have to object if the Defendant sought leave to introduce corresponding expert evidence, having then gained the advantage of unilateral disclosure by the Claimant. Accordingly, if the Defendant does intend to seek any relief from this sanction, may we suggest you make application here and now, although we must tell you that any such application will be opposed, unless you can provide cogent reasons why it should not.]

Yours faithfully

13.10   Letter to Client – Enclosing Defendant's Expert Evidence

The representatives of [*name of opponent*] ('the Defendant') requested facilities to obtain expert evidence which you agreed to give and subsequently saw [*name of expert*].

The Defendant has now disclosed the evidence obtained, which suggests that the Defendant intends to rely on that evidence and I am, accordingly, able to enclose a copy of the report prepared by [*name of expert*].

The evidence disclosed is now part of the Defendant's case, which the court will consider at any final hearing, so it is right to let you review that evidence at this stage.

Either

[I have carefully considered the evidence disclosed by the Defendant and I conclude this expresses broadly the same opinion as that given in the report of [*name of expert*] on which you rely. However, it must be the experts themselves who confirm whether their opinions are the same, so that the expert evidence can be agreed or if those opinions differ on any important points.]

Or

[I have carefully considered the evidence disclosed by the Defendant. Although in many cases the experts broadly agree in their opinion there does appear to be a difference of view, between the experts, on some points. In particular:

(1) [*details*]

(2) [*details*]

However, it must be the experts themselves who confirm whether their opinions are the same, or, as I suspect, materially different.]

Any party receiving expert evidence is entitled to put questions, intended to clarify any matters in the report, to the expert concerned. I will consider whether we do need to put any questions and, if I think this necessary, will write again giving out details of any questions put to the expert.

When each party has expert evidence from corresponding experts, the court will expect there to be a discussion between those experts to confirm whether they are in agreement or to identify points of disagreement and the reasons why those different views are held. I will make appropriate arrangements, as that will confirm whether or not the experts are in agreement, and let you know once a further report, or joint statement from both experts, becomes available.

If the evidence is agreed it is likely that the parties can rely on the written reports, without the need for the experts to attend court and give oral evidence. That will simplify and speed up any hearing and, of course, also means that there is a better prospect of reaching a settlement meanwhile, as the parties can conduct negotiations on the basis of the agreed expert opinion.

If the experts are not able to reach agreement on all matters then, whilst the court might still prefer to have only written evidence, it is more likely that those experts will need to attend any final hearing to confirm the content of the written reports and each answer questions, put by the other side, on the opinions expressed in the reports. The judge, after reading the reports and hearing oral evidence, will then have to decide, on the basis of all that evidence, which opinion should be preferred.

If you have any particular comments or observations on the medical evidence disclosed by the Defendant, please write or telephone [me]/[*name*].

Yours sincerely

13.11   Letter to Client – Advising of Defendant's Failure to Disclose Expert Evidence

The representatives of [*name of opponent*] ('the Defendant') requested facilities to obtain expert evidence. You agreed to give those facilities and subsequently saw [*name of expert*].

The court set a date by which the Defendant was required to disclose expert evidence to be relied on but no report prepared by [*name of expert*] has yet been disclosed.

Accordingly, it would appear the Defendant is not going to rely on the evidence of [*name of expert*]. I assume this evidence does not assist the Defendant and that it may well express an opinion which is similar, if not identical, to that of [*name of expert*].

In these circumstances, unless the Defendant obtains permission from the court for late disclosure of evidence, or to change experts, the evidence on this aspect of the case seems likely to be only the evidence of [*name of expert*].

I hope this letter brings you up to date in relation to exchange of expert evidence.

Yours sincerely

QUESTIONS TO CLAIMANT'S EXPERTS

13.12 Letter to Opponent – Acknowledging Questions put by Defendant to Claimant's Expert

We thank you for your letter of [*date*].

We note the questions [you wish us to] put to [*name of expert*].

[You are, strictly, outside the time limit for putting these questions. [However, we would not propose to take any point on this.] [. If you wish us to consider granting an extension of time please confirm and set out your reasons for the delay in putting those questions.]]

[Questions should be confined to clarification of the expert opinion on the issues in the claim. In these circumstances, we would not have thought it appropriate for the expert to answer question[s] [*relevant question numbers*]. However, we recognise it is a matter for the expert to deal with the questions as seems appropriate.]

Yours faithfully

13.13 Letter to Claimant's Expert – Putting Questions from Defendant

You kindly prepared a report relating to our client and, as we propose to rely on your evidence, a copy of the report was disclosed to [*name of opponent*] ('the Defendant').

We mentioned, when submitting instructions to you, that the Defendant could ask questions seeking clarification of the report. The Defendant has chosen to exercise this right.

Either

[Accordingly, we enclose the questions received from the Defendant.]

Or

[The questions put by the Defendant are:

(1) [*details*]

(2) [*details*]]

Or

[The Defendant has sent to us a copy of the questions which we understand have been put to you direct.]

Either

[Our view, although of course we leave the matter to your discretion, is that the questions do seek appropriate clarification of your opinion.]

Or

[Our view, which we have set out in correspondence to the Defendant, is that we are content with questions numbered [*numbers*] but otherwise consider the questions go beyond clarification of your opinion on the matters in issue. However, we recognise it is for you to deal with the questions as you think appropriate.]

The Defendant has asked that, if possible, the questions be answered by [*date*]. If you will need longer, and would like us to relay this to the Defendant, please let us know meanwhile.

We look forward to hearing from you in due course with answers to the questions. We are happy, if you wish, to forward your answers to the Defendant, although we have no objection to you also writing direct if you wish provided we are sent a copy.

Yours faithfully

13.14   Letter to Client – Advising of Questions put to Claimant's Expert by Defendant

The expert opinion of [*name of expert*] has been relied on in support of your claim against [*name of opponent*] ('the Defendant').

Where one party relies on expert evidence the other party is entitled to put questions to the expert seeking clarification of the opinion.

I have now received details of some questions the Defendant wishes [*name of expert*] to answer.

[I am not satisfied that the questions seek only to clarify the expert opinion so, for the moment, have advised the Defendant that it does not seem appropriate for all to be answered. Nevertheless, I consider that the expert should review the questions and provide such answers as the expert thinks are appropriate.]

I hope to have answers from [*name of expert*] in the next few weeks and will let you know when these are available with any further comments that may then be appropriate.

Yours sincerely

13.15   Letter to Opponent – Enclosing Answers by Claimant's Expert to Questions

We have now received answers from [*name of expert*] to the questions put by you.

Either

[We enclose, in case you have not received answers direct, a copy of those answers.]

Or

[We understand that the answers have also been sent direct to you.]

Now you have these answers we shall be grateful if you would confirm, as soon as possible, whether the evidence of [*name of expert*] can be agreed. If not, please identify, precisely, points of disagreement and your reasons.

We look forward to hearing from you.

Yours faithfully

13.16   Letter to Client – Enclosing Answers to Questions by Claimant's Expert

The expert opinion of [*name of expert*] has, as you rely on that opinion in support of your case, been disclosed to the representatives of [*name of opponent*] ('the Defendant') with a request that either the evidence be agreed or that the Defendant identify any specific points of disagreement.

The Defendant, like any party receiving expert evidence from another party, is entitled to put questions to the expert in order to clarify the opinion, as that can help establish whether the evidence is capable of agreement.

The Defendant took the opportunity of putting some questions to the expert, who has since considered and responded to those questions.

Accordingly, I enclose a copy of the response by the expert to the Defendant's questions. The answers become part of the expert's opinion so I think it right to let you have sight of these.

[I think the answers usefully confirm the opinion already expressed in the report previously disclosed.]

[I think the answers do clarify the opinion already expressed in the report previously disclosed by [*details*].]

I will let you know as and when I hear further from the Defendant with, I hope, confirmation of whether the evidence is now agreed or, if not, any specific points of disagreement.

Yours sincerely

QUESTIONS TO DEFENDANT'S EXPERTS

13.17   Letter to Defendant's Expert – Putting Questions

We act for [*name of client*] ('the Claimant') in a claim against [*name of opponent*] ('the Defendant').

[*Name of opponent's solicitors*], who act for the Defendant, have disclosed to us a copy of a report prepared by you on [*date of report*].

You may be aware that, under the Civil Procedure Rules 1998, we may put questions to an expert whose report has been disclosed by the other party in the case.

Having carefully reviewed your report we should like to put some questions to clarify your opinion. Accordingly, we shall be grateful if you would please answer the following points:

(1)   [*details*]

(2)   [*details*]

We shall be grateful if you could let us have answers to these questions within, say, the next [*number*] days. If this presents a particular problem, please let us know meanwhile.

We understand that any fee dealing with this request should be met by [*name of opponent's solicitors*], as they originally instructed you.

We have sent a copy of this letter to [*name of opponent's solicitors*] so that they are aware of this request and they will, no doubt, wish to have a copy of your response to us.

We look forward to hearing from you.

Yours faithfully

13.18   Letter to Opponent – Confirming Questions put to Defendant's Expert

We enclose, for your information, a copy of a letter sent to [*name of expert*] putting forward some questions.

[Although it is strictly outside the time for us to put questions, we hope you will agree that it is appropriate for these to be answered, without us having to seek any further order from the court, as answers may help narrow the issues [and avoid the need for us to obtain expert opinion in reply (although for the moment we must reserve the right to do so)].]

Yours faithfully

13.19   Letter to Client – Advising of Questions put to Defendant's Expert

The solicitors acting for [*name of opponent*] ('the Defendant') obtained a report from [*name of expert*].

That report has since been disclosed, which indicates that the Defendant intends to rely on the expert opinion of [*name of expert*].

It may be possible to agree some or all of the evidence of [*name of expert*]. One way to explore the possibility of agreeing expert evidence is to put questions seeking clarification of the expert opinion given in the report which has been disclosed.

I think it is appropriate to put some questions to [*name of expert*] which I have framed as the following:

(1)   [*details*]

(2)   [*details*]

I will let you know when I receive answers to these questions. I may then be in a position to confirm whether the evidence of [*name of expert*] can be agreed.

I have asked that these questions be answered in [*number*] days, although I have indicated to the expert concerned that I recognise there may be reasons which mean a little longer will be required. I have asked for an indication of likely timescale if that is the case.

I will let you know when I hear further.

Yours sincerely

13.20   Letter to Client – Dealing with Answers to Questions Received from Defendant's Expert

I have now heard from [*name of expert*], the expert instructed on behalf of [*name of opponent*] ('the Defendant'), in response to the questions put to that expert arising out of the report disclosed by the Defendant.

I enclose a copy of the answers for your information.

My observations are [*details*].

These answers help to clarify the opinion of [*name of expert*] [which I consider can now be accepted] [but I still do not consider this can be accepted].

Yours sincerely

JOINT STATEMENTS

13.21   Letter to Expert – Instructions to Prepare Joint Statement

You kindly prepared, at an earlier stage, a report giving your expert opinion which, as it is relied upon by our client, we have since disclosed to the solicitors acting for [*name of opponent*] ('the Defendant').

The Defendant has, in turn, disclosed corresponding expert evidence. Accordingly, we enclose [*details of corresponding expert evidence*].

We shall be grateful if you would now act further on our behalf in reviewing matters on the basis of the evidence now available.

The court has directed that, following exchange of evidence, there should be a discussion between you and [*name of corresponding expert*], by [*date by which meeting is to take place*], so that there can be prepared, for filing at court by [*date*], a jointly prepared statement confirming the issues on which you are agreed, identifying the issues on which you are not agreed and setting out the reasons why you hold the opinion you do on those matters which are not agreed.

Accordingly, we shall be grateful if you could contact [*name of corresponding expert*] and make arrangements for a meeting, or telephone discussion if you prefer, so that a joint statement can be prepared.

We enclose an agenda we have prepared [and agreed with the Defendant's solicitors] which we hope will assist the discussion.

If these instructions present you with any difficulty, please let us know as soon as possible so that we can contact the Defendant's solicitors and/or seek further directions from the court.

We confirm that we shall be responsible for your reasonable fee in acting again on our behalf.

We look forward to hearing from you.

Yours faithfully

13.22   Letter to Client – Enclosing Joint Statement of Experts

I obtained on your behalf expert opinion evidence from [*name of Claimant's expert*].

I subsequently exchanged the evidence of [*name of Claimant's expert*] with corresponding evidence obtained by [*name of opponent*] ('the Defendant') from [*name of Defendant's expert*].

When I received the report of [*name of Defendant's expert*] from the Defendant, I sent a copy to you outlining what appeared to be differences of opinion between [*name of Claimant's expert*] and [*name of Defendant's expert*].

The court is concerned that, so far as possible, any points of agreement and disagreement between the experts acting for each party should be clarified. This can result in the expert opinion being agreed or, at least, ensure specific points of disagreement are identified.

Accordingly, a discussion has now taken place between the experts which has resulted in a joint statement, a copy of which I enclose for your information.

You will see that the joint statement usefully confirms that a number of points are agreed.

Either

[There remain some points of disagreement, but these are narrowed down to:

(1) [*details*]

(2) [*details*]

It may well be necessary for the experts to attend any final hearing, as these points of disagreement remain, to give evidence so that the judge can make a decision as to which opinion should be preferred.]

Or

[There do not appear to be any significant points of disagreement between the experts. It is helpful to have narrowed down the issues in this way as it is likely the judge at any final hearing can deal with the expert evidence simply by reading the written reports without the need for the experts to attend court.]

I hope this letter explains why it is helpful to have the joint statement.

Yours sincerely

13.23   Letter to Opponent – Enclosing Joint Statement of Experts

We are pleased to note that a discussion has now taken place between [*name of relevant expert*] and [*name of relevant expert*].

We enclose a copy of the joint statement (although you may well have received a copy direct).

Either

[We consider that the evidence of the experts is agreed to the extent that written reports should suffice and it would not seem necessary to call those experts to give oral evidence. However, we welcome your views.]

Or

[We think the joint statement usefully identifies some important areas of agreement. We consider the agreement reached should avoid the need to call the experts to give oral evidence on the basis the trial judge should be able to deal with the remaining issues on the written reports, including the joint statement, in the context of the evidence as a whole. However, we welcome your views.]

Or

[Although the joint statement helps to identify the issues the experts are not in agreement and, furthermore, the differences do appear to arise out of conflicting opinions as to matters within the expertise of the experts. Accordingly, we consider the experts will need to be called to give oral evidence so that the trial judge can decide which view is to be preferred. However, we welcome your views.]

We confirm we have filed a copy of the joint statement at court.

We look forward to hearing from you.

Yours faithfully

13.24   Letter to Court – Enclosing Joint Statement of Experts

We enclose, for filing, the joint statement of [*name of expert*] and [*name of expert*].

Yours faithfully

SECTION 14

APPLICATIONS AND ENFORCEMENT OF CASE MANAGEMENT DIRECTIONS

CONTENTS

NON-COMPLIANCE WITH CASE MANAGEMENT DIRECTIONS

14.1   Letter to Opponent – On Failure to Comply with Court Order

The Defendant does not appear to have complied with the terms of the order requiring [*details*], which should have been dealt with by 4 pm on [*date*].

Either

[In these circumstances our client relies on the sanctions that will now apply. If you wish to seek relief from such sanctions please explain why now, so that we may consider those reasons. Please note that, in the absence of such an indication, the claim will be pursued on the basis that those sanctions will apply and we consider our client will be further prejudiced by delay in any application for relief.]

Or

[Unless the Defendant does now comply it will be necessary for our client to seek further order from the court.

We think it appropriate to warn you of our intentions, before seeking any further order from the court, but must reserve the right to make application, without further notice, unless the earlier order has been complied with by 4pm on [*date*]. If it has not, then we are likely to ask the court to make an order that [the defence be struck out] [*details*].

If you face any particular difficulties, or otherwise have grounds for seeking relief from sanctions, please let us know no later than the deadline imposed in this letter so that we can consider whether any further time should be allowed for compliance.]

Yours faithfully

14.2   Letter to Client – Advising on Defendant's Failure to Comply with Court Order

The court made an order requiring [*name of opponent*] ('the Defendant') to [*details*], by 4 pm on [*date*]. The Defendant has not complied with these terms of the order.

Either

[This means the Defendant is now faced with the sanction of [*details*].

I should advise you, however, that the Defendant may apply to the court for relief from this sanction and, if it is fair to do so, the court will allow the Defendant additional time to deal with outstanding matters.

I have written to the Defendant making it clear that you will rely on the sanction that now applies and suggesting the longer the Defendant takes to rectify matters the more likely it is the court will consider it unfair to allow additional time.]

Or

[I have, accordingly, written to the Defendant's solicitors reminding them of the obligation to comply with the court order and warning that, unless this matter is now dealt with by [*date*], it will be necessary for you to seek a further order from the court enforcing the terms of the earlier order.

It may well be that, following this reminder, the Defendant will deal with this matter. I will let you know if the Defendant does comply but if not I will make an application to the court on your behalf seeking a further order either to ensure compliance or to make sure that the Defendant does not benefit from continued non-compliance.

I am sorry we have encountered this problem in dealing with the directions given by the court but I hope that, by following this up, we can ensure that the Defendant does now comply with the court order or, if not, will face appropriate sanctions.]

Yours sincerely

14.3   Letter to Opponent – Extending Time for Compliance with Court Order

Either

[We thank you for your [letter]/[telephone call] of [*date*].

We are, in all the circumstances, prepared to allow additional time[, but you will appreciate that we cannot put the overall court timetable at risk by deferring matters indefinitely].

Accordingly, you may have until 4 pm on [*date*] to deal with outstanding matters [failing which we shall have to proceed on the basis set out in earlier correspondence].

We consider that the correspondence we have exchanged amounts to an agreement varying the time for the purposes of CPR Part 2.11.]

Or

[We write to request that time for dealing with [*details*] be extended until 4 pm on [*date*] [because [*details*]].

If you are agreeable to extending time accordingly please confirm in writing for the purposes of CPR Part 2.11.

If a revised timescale cannot be agreed we must reserve the right to apply to the court for additional time but hope to avoid the costs of an application by reaching agreement with you.]

Yours faithfully

14.4   Letter to Client – Confirming Extension of Time for Compliance with Court Order

Either

[[*name of opponent*] ('the Defendant') has requested some additional time to deal with [*details*].

I consider, in all the circumstances, it is reasonable to agree the Defendant's request, though please let me know if you disagree.

This aspect of the case should now be dealt with by [*date*].]

Or

[It will take a little longer than originally planned to deal with [*details*].

Accordingly, I asked [*name of opponent*] ('the Defendant') to allow some additional time and am pleased to confirm that it has been agreed this stage should now be dealt with by [*date*].]

I hope this keeps you up to date.

Yours sincerely

ISSUE AND SERVICE OF APPLICATION NOTICE

14.5   Letter to Court – Issue of Application Notice

We enclose, on behalf of the Claimant, the following:

(1)   application notice [containing [evidence in support] [and] [draft of the order sought]];

[(2)   draft of the order sought;]

[(3)   evidence in support comprising the statement of [*name*];]

(4)   cheque for the court fee of £[*figure*];

[(5)   copies for return to us, for service and for our file;]

[(6)   statement of costs associated with the application.]

Either

[We have requested that the application be dealt with without a hearing under CPR Part 24.8.]

Or

[We have requested that the application be dealt with by telephone hearing. If this request is granted, we will, of course, make the appropriate arrangements.]

Or

[We have requested that the application be dealt with at a hearing as we do not consider it is suitable for the telephone.]

We look forward to hearing from you.

Yours faithfully

14.6   Letter to Client – Advising of Application (and Sending Supporting Statement)

Either

[When court proceedings were commenced, I wrote to you detailing the various stages of the case and mentioning that it might be necessary to ensure [*name of opponent*] ('the Defendant') complied with any timetable set by the court and, more generally, dealt properly with each stage of the case.

The Defendant has failed to [*details*].

The court expects each party to comply with the stages of the case by the date set in the timetable. If this does not occur sanctions will apply to the party in default.

Sometimes it is appropriate to rely on these sanctions and sometimes it is necessary to seek a further order from the court, in particular where inaction on the part of the Defendant might mean that you do not receive information to which you are entitled.

I consider that a further court order is required as, otherwise, information which may assist in dealing with the case may not become available.

I have, therefore, prepared an application asking the court to make an appropriate order.

[I am asking your insurers for their consent to this application being made.]

[I have asked the court, in the first instance, to consider making an order just on the basis of the paperwork in order to save time. The court may be prepared to make an order on this basis or may decide that a hearing should be arranged when the Defendant will have the opportunity of responding to the application. I will set out the procedure that will apply in the event that a hearing is necessary, although it is possible the court will make an order without the need for any such hearing.]

It may be, of course, that the Defendant deals with outstanding matters before any order is made. However, I think it right to proceed with an application in case this does not happen.]

Or

[[*name*] ('the Defendant') has made an application to the court seeking an order that [*details*].]

I do not need you to attend any hearing of the application [although of course you may attend if you wish] [which, in any event, I expect will be dealt with by telephone].

When any hearing of the application takes place the judge will be concerned only with matters relating directly to the application and will not make any final ruling on the issues in the case.

[It would be helpful, so that the court is aware of the background to the application, to have a statement from you outlining relevant matters.

Accordingly, I have prepared a statement dealing with these matters, a copy of which I enclose for your approval.

Please read the statement and check carefully that all the facts are correct. The final paragraph is your confirmation that the facts are true and, as you know, if you were to make a statement without an honest belief in the facts stated this could have serious consequences, as the court might treat it as a contempt of court.

If any amendments are required to the statement, please let [me]/[name] know as soon as possible and I will arrange for those amendments to be made.

If the statement is approved, I shall be grateful if you would sign it in the space provided at the end and then return it to me as soon as possible. I enclose a pre-paid envelope for your use.]

I will report to you as soon as I can on the outcome of the application or if there are developments meanwhile.

Whilst costs will usually be dealt with at the end of the case you need to be aware that, rather than leaving all costs to be dealt with at that stage, the court may order one party to pay to the other the costs associated with any specific application made meanwhile and for payment of those costs to be made within 14 days of the hearing. [However, the insurance cover you have should protect you against any such adverse costs order.] I consider it is, nevertheless, appropriate to [proceed with] [defend] the application.

Yours sincerely

14.7   Letter to Opponent – Serving Application Notice

We enclose, by way of service, notice of hearing, for [*date*] at [*time*], together with application notice [and draft order].

[Written evidence in support of the application [is set out on the notice itself] [is the statement of [*name*] which we also enclose] [will follow].

Kindly acknowledge safe receipt and let us know your intentions, concerning all aspects of the application, as soon as possible.

You will note the time estimate we have given to the court. Please let us know if you have any significant disagreement with that estimate.

Please let us have any details of any written evidence on which your client intends to rely at the hearing at the hearing of the application.

[We consider that it would be appropriate to invite the court to deal with the hearing on [*date*] by way of telephone hearing. If you are agreeable, perhaps you could write to confirm so that we can make the appropriate request to the court and, if this is granted, organise arrangements accordingly. We look forward to hearing from you.]

[We requested, when filing the application, that this be dealt with by way of telephone hearing. The court has agreed to that request. We are, therefore, making the appropriate arrangements for the hearing to be dealt with by telephone and it would be helpful if you could confirm the name, and telephone number, of the person who will be dealing with the hearing on behalf of your client.]

Yours faithfully

14.8   Letter to Opponent – Acknowledging Application Notice

Either

[We thank you for your letter of [*date*] and acknowledge safe receipt of the notice confirming the Defendant's application is to be heard on [*date*] at [*time*] [together with the application notice] [and supporting documentation].

Or

[We confirm we have received from the court notice that the Defendant's application is to be heard on [*date*] at [*time*] [together with the application notice] [and supporting documentation].

[We note that the time estimate you have given to the court but consider that a time estimate of [*details*] would be more realistic. Please let us know if the time estimate can be revised accordingly so that we may establish whether the court will have time to deal with the application at the present appointment or if the application will need to be re-listed when sufficient time is available.]

[We confirm that we are agreeable to [, and note the court has already provided for,] a telephone hearing.

We trust you will make the necessary arrangements for the hearing to be dealt with by telephone and shall be grateful if you would please confirm this has been done or if you wish us to make any such arrangements.

You may wish to know that the person who will be dealing with the hearing is [*details*] whose contact telephone number is [*number*].]

[We consider it would be appropriate to invite the court to deal with the hearing on [*date*] by way of telephone hearing.

If you are agreeable perhaps you could write to confirm so that we can make the appropriate request to the court and, if this is granted, organise arrangements accordingly.

We look forward to hearing from you.]

Yours faithfully

TELEPHONE HEARINGS

14.9   Letter to Opponent – Inviting Agreement/Agreeing to Telephone Hearing

Either

[Thank you for suggesting that the hearing on [*date*] be conducted by way of telephone hearing.

We confirm that we are content for the hearing on [*date of hearing*] to be dealt with in this way.

We assume, in the circumstances, you will invite the court to approve a telephone hearing but if you do wish us to deal with that request please advise as soon as possible.

Please confirm once you have heard from the court whether the request has been granted.]

Or

[We consider that it would be appropriate to invite the court to deal with the hearing on [*date*] by way of telephone hearing.

If you are agreeable, perhaps you could write to confirm so that we can make the appropriate request to the court and, if this is granted, organise arrangements accordingly.

We look forward to hearing from you.]

Yours faithfully

14.10   Letter to Court – Requesting Telephone Hearing

We write to request that the above hearing be dealt with by telephone.

We enclose a copy of a letter we have received from the Defendant's solicitors confirming agreement.

If the court considers it is appropriate to deal with the hearing by telephone we shall be grateful if you would confirm so that we can make the necessary arrangements.

Yours faithfully

14.11   Letter to Opponent – Confirming Telephone Hearing of Application

Either

[We are pleased to confirm the court has agreed to the hearing on [*date*] being dealt with by telephone.

We are, therefore, making the appropriate arrangements for the hearing to be dealt with by telephone and it would be helpful if you could confirm the name, and telephone number, of the person who will be dealing with the hearing on behalf of your client.]

Or

[Thank you for confirming that the hearing on [*date*] is to be dealt with by way of telephone hearing.

We trust you will make the necessary arrangements for the hearing to be dealt with by telephone and shall be grateful if you would please confirm this has been done or if you wish us to make any such arrangements.

You may wish to know that the person who will be dealing with the hearing is [*details*] whose contact telephone number is [*number*].]

Yours faithfully

HEARING OF APPLICATION NOTICE

14.12   Letter to Court – Dealing with Hearing by Consent

The parties are agreed on the terms of an order the court is invited to make [for case management directions]/[at the application listed for hearing on [*date*]].

[It may be useful if we explain the circumstances in which the parties are agreed on the terms of an order. These are [*reasons*].]

[We enclose a letter confirming agreement from the solicitors acting for the other party.]

[We enclose a draft order, duly endorsed with consent on behalf of the defendant.]

In the circumstances, the parties ask the court to make an order in the agreed terms [and, in order to save costs, vacate the hearing].

[The parties recognise that their agreement, of itself, does not mean that the hearing will be vacated. However, it is hoped that, in the circumstances, the court will be prepared to review the draft order prior to the hearing. If the order is approved, and the hearing vacated, we shall be grateful if you could let us know as soon as possible and we, in turn, will be happy to relay this information to the Defendant's solicitors.]

[As no application has been made for an order in these terms we enclose our cheque for the court fee of £[*figure*]]

We look forward to hearing from you.

Yours faithfully

14.13   Letter to Client – Confirming Successful Outcome of Application

I write to report on the outcome of the application made to the court [against]/[by] [*name of opponent*] ('the Defendant').

I am pleased to report that an order in your favour was made.

The court ordered [*details*].

Either

[Furthermore, the court ordered the Defendant to pay the costs of the application, whatever the final outcome of the case may be.]

Or

[Furthermore, the court ordered the Defendant to pay the costs of the application provided the claim is ultimately successful.]

I am pleased to be able to report in these terms.

Yours sincerely

14.14   Letter to Client – Confirming Unsuccessful Outcome of Application

I write to report on the outcome of the application to court [against]/[by] [*name of opponent*] ('the Defendant').

The court ordered that [*details*].

Because the Defendant was successful the court has ordered that the Defendant's costs, associated with the application, must be paid whatever the final outcome of the case.

[The court assessed the Defendant's costs at £[*figure*].]

[Those costs are payable now.]

[Those costs will not, however, be payable until the case is concluded.]

[I will make payment of those costs out of the monies kindly provided on account of costs.]

[I shall be grateful if you could arrange to let me have this sum so that these costs can be paid.]

[Those costs will be met by the insurance policy you have to guard against such outlays.]

I am sorry to have to write in these terms but I do consider that the prospects of [succeeding in] [resisting] the application outweighed the risk on costs.

Yours sincerely

14.15   Letter to Opponent – Sending Costs Statement for Hearing of Application

We enclose, by way of service, our statement of costs in readiness for the hearing on [*date*].

Yours faithfully

14.16   Letter to Court – Filing Costs Statement for Hearing of Application

We enclose, in readiness for the above hearing, the Claimant's statement of costs and confirm that a copy has been served upon the Defendant's solicitors.

Yours faithfully

SECTION 15

INTERIM PAYMENTS

CONTENTS

15.1   Letter to Client – Advising on Offer of Interim Payment

I have asked the insurers of [*name of opponent*] ('the Defendant') to put forward some proposals for [an]/[a further] interim payment, given that it is not yet possible to conclude an outright settlement of the claim.

I am pleased to report that the Defendant has accepted that there should be [an]/[a further] interim payment at this stage.

Either

[The Defendant has suggested that there be an interim payment of £[*figure*]. I think that this is a reasonable proposal and, as the level of interim payment has no bearing on any final award, am happy to recommend that this be agreed.]

Or

[The Defendant has suggested that there be an interim payment of £[*figure*]. I think that this is less than you might expect the court to award and, accordingly, would suggest that the offer be responded to by proposing a figure of £[*figure*] with a view to obtaining [such] an offer [of at least £[*figure*]].]

Or

[The Defendant has not suggested a figure for an interim payment at this stage but does invite proposals. In all the circumstances, I would suggest putting forward a figure of £[*figure*] with a view to obtaining [such] an offer [of at least £[*figure*]].]

[Under the terms of the conditional fee agreement you have entered with my firm, you have not been asked for outlays incurred to progress the claim, as arrangements have been made for these to be financed, but the agreement does provide for interim provision, in the first instance, to be used in clearing the outlays incurred to date. I have, therefore, tried to allow for this in the figures. Those outlays presently total £[*figure*] and so I should like to clear those, leaving a balance of £[*figure*] payable to you once the interim payment has been received. I would like to stress that, as outlays should be paid by the Defendant at the end of the case, you will then receive credit for this sum.]

If this letter enables you to reach a decision, would you please sign the enclosed confirmation, in the space provided. This can be completed either to confirm that you accept the advice given in this letter or to let me have any other specific instructions. I also enclose a pre-paid envelope for your use in returning this authority.

If you would prefer not to accept the advice given and are unable to give any specific instructions, or would like to discuss the matter with me before deciding how to proceed, please telephone [me]/[*name*].

I look forward to hearing from you.

Yours sincerely

15.2   Letter to Opponent – Making (Counter) Offer for Interim Payment

Our client [considers your proposal for an interim payment is on the low side but] is willing to accept an interim payment, at this stage, of £[*figure*].

This is on the strict understanding that our client may rely on losses and expenses incurred to date in support of any further applications that may be made for interim payments.

If terms for an interim payment cannot now be agreed our client must reserve the right to apply to the Court. If an application is necessary our client will need to seek the costs of that application.

We look forward to hearing from you.

Yours faithfully

15.3   Letter to Opponent – Confirming Agreement to Interim Payment

We confirm that our client is agreeable to accepting an interim payment of £[*figure*] at this stage on the strict understanding that losses and expenses incurred to date may be relied on in support of any further applications that may be made for interim payments.

[We enclose, accordingly, a draft order for you to endorse with consent and return to us for lodging at court so that an appropriate order may be made.]

Yours faithfully

15.4　Letter to Client – Following Order/Agreement for Interim Payment

Either

[I write to report on the outcome of the application made to the court on your behalf against [*name of opponent*] ('the Defendant') for an interim payment and am pleased to confirm that an Order in your favour has now been obtained.]

Or

[I am pleased to report that [*name of opponent*] ('the Defendant') has agreed to there being an interim payment.]

On account of the compensation you are likely to receive in due course the Defendant is to make you an interim payment of £[*figure*]. This is to be paid within [*number*] days by the Defendant, although I should warn you that it may sometimes take rather longer for the monies to become available. I will monitor the situation and chase the matter up if necessary.

I will, of course, let you have the interim payment once the monies have been received and explain, in more detail, the implications.

[The court ordered the Defendant to pay the costs of the application, [whatever the final outcome of the case may be] [provided the claim is ultimately successful].]

[Under the terms of the conditional fee agreement you have entered with my firm, you have not been asked for outlays incurred to progress the claim, as arrangements have been made for these to be financed, but the agreement does provide for interim provision, in the first instance, to be used in clearing the outlays incurred to date. I have, therefore, tried to allow for this in the figures. Those outlays presently total £[*figure*] and so I should like to clear those leaving a balance of £[*figure*] payable to you once the interim payment has been received. I would like to stress that, as outlays should be paid by the Defendant at the end of the case, you will then receive credit for this sum.]

I will report further once the interim payment has been made.

Yours sincerely

15.5 Letter to Client – Making Interim Payment

I am pleased to report that I have now received, from [*name of opponent*] ('the Defendant'), the interim payment which [was recently agreed] [the court recently ordered].

Accordingly, I am pleased to enclose a cheque for £[*figure*] as this [further] interim payment.

This is a [further] payment on account of the compensation it is anticipated will ultimately be received. When a final award of compensation has been agreed, or made by the court, the amount of this interim payment [together with all previous interim provision] will be deducted from that total when the sum due is paid over.

The very fact there has been an interim payment means that it is likely there will be, when the amount of compensation is finally assessed or agreed, a total which exceeds the amount already provided for by interim payment. However, until a final award has been made there can be no absolute certainties and, if no award were ultimately to be made or that award was less than the amount of interim payments, any overpayment would have to be refunded to the Defendant. This is most unlikely, but it is a possibility I should draw to your attention.

For the purposes of calculating, if necessary at a later stage, whether you have beaten an offer of settlement made by the Defendant the court will regard the sum which has to be beaten as the total offer including all interim payments.

[The enclosed cheque is less than the total interim payment of £[*figure*] as my firm has incurred outlays totalling £[*figure*] to progress the claim and, under the terms of the conditional fee agreement, these payments were met on the basis that the cost would be reimbursed as and when any interim payment was made. I confirm that it is my intention to try and recover these outlays as part of the costs of the claim from the Defendant, but I can only do that when the claim is concluded.]

If these points are not clear, or you require advice on any particular aspect, please let me know.

Yours sincerely

SECTION 16

REVIEW OF QUANTUM

CONTENTS

16.1   Letter to Client – Sending Up-to-date/Final Schedule of Expenses and Losses

I have now been able to prepare an up-to-date calculation of the expenses and losses claimed from [*name of opponent*] ('the Defendant'). I enclose a copy of that calculation.

May I ask you to bear in mind that the calculation of expenses and losses I have prepared puts forward the case on the most reasonably optimistic basis possible at this stage. Whilst it is still right to put the case at its best to the Defendant, it is likely that the Defendant will maintain that lower figures are appropriate on certain aspects of the claim. Accordingly, you do still need to keep an open mind on the level at which a settlement might be achieved, should reasonable proposals be put forward by the Defendant.

[My view is that, allowing for arguments the Defendant is likely to maintain, it is likely that the court would not award more than £[*figure*] for expenses and damages, and so you need to read the calculation with this in mind.]

Either

[This calculation of expenses and losses may still need to be updated. I will, of course, let you have a copy of any future calculation, but hope it is useful for you to have sight of this calculation meanwhile.]

Or

[This calculation brings the earlier calculation up to date taking account of all the information now available and is, I hope, now finalised.]

Once approved I will send the schedule to the Defendant with a request that matters of agreement and disagreement with each aspect of the claim be identified. I will let you know once I have the Defendant's response.

I would remind you that, in addition to the claim for expenses and losses, the court will also make an award of general damages [which I would expect to be in the region of £[*figure*]].

These calculations are all made on the basis of the Defendant being fully liable.

[The Defendant has, of course, admitted liability.]

[Liability has, of course, already been dealt with on the basis that the Defendant will pay [*figure*]% of any compensation ultimately agreed or awarded by the court.]

[The Defendant has suggested there should be an apportionment of liability and, although this remains subject to further negotiation, this is, therefore, something that you should bear in mind.]

[Liability is presently denied, although it may be that the Defendant's stance will change and some negotiations will be possible. Accordingly, despite the denial of liability, I think it right to let you have my views on the potential value of the claim.]

May I remind you that the advice given so far in this letter takes no account of the State benefits received as a result of the injuries. You will recall that, if corresponding benefits have been received, the Defendant can deduct those benefits from relevant parts of the claim. [In round terms, it may be necessary to give an allowance of £[*approximate figure of corresponding benefits*] against the claim for losses and expenses which would bring the appropriate figure for settlement of the case down to approximately £[*figure*].]/[However, the information received to date from the Compensation Recovery Unit indicates that no recoverable benefits have been paid as a result of the injuries, and so, if that remains the position, the rules relating to recoupment of benefits will not have any impact on the value of the claim.]

I hope it is useful for you to have this up-to-date information on the potential value of the claim.

I shall be grateful if you could check the calculation, and in particular let me know if there have been any further items of expenditure or losses incurred but not yet included.

Should the calculation be approved, as presently drafted, please would you sign the statement, to this effect, in the space provided between the marked crosses and then return the calculation to me.

The calculation, like other documents which are sent to the court on your behalf, is required to contain a statement of truth. Your signature amounts to confirmation that the facts in the calculation are true and I must remind you that if the court took the view any facts were stated without an honest belief in them proceedings for contempt of court could be taken against you.

I enclose a pre-paid envelope for you to return the calculation, either signed and approved or with details of amendments, and look forward to hearing from you accordingly.

Yours sincerely

16.2   Letter to Opponent – Serving Up-to-date/Final Schedule of Expenses and Losses

We enclose, by way of service, an up-to-date schedule of expenses and losses.

Either

[We look forward to receiving the counter-schedule, in accordance with case management directions, by [*date*].]

Or

[Now you have up-to-date details of the Claimant's claim for expenses and losses, we ask you to identify, precisely, points of agreement and disagreement with each item of claim and to identify, insofar as any item is not agreed, the reasons for this and the Defendant's calculation by counter-schedule.]

Meanwhile, kindly acknowledge safe receipt of the enclosed schedule.

Yours faithfully

16.3   Letter to Court – Filing Up-to-date/Final Schedule of Expenses and Losses

We enclose, for filing, the Claimant's up-to-date schedule of expenses and losses. A copy has been served upon the Defendant's solicitors.

Yours faithfully

16.4   Letter to Client – Advising on Defendant's Counter-schedule

I prepared an up-to-date calculation of financial expenses and losses suffered as a result of the injuries which I sent you, for approval, and to [*name of opponent*] ('the Defendant') as confirmation of the sums claimed.

The Defendant has responded to that calculation by sending a counter-schedule, a copy of which I enclose.

The Defendant's counter-schedule sets out the Defendant's case on the claim for expenses and losses which helps to identify, and to an extent narrow, the extent to which the sums claimed are disputed.

[It may be useful if I summarise, and where appropriate comment on, the respective positions of the parties on the various items of expenses and losses claimed.

Item	Sum claimed	Defendant's figure	Comment
1.			
2.			
3.			

Accordingly, in comparison with the calculation I prepared for you totalling £[*total from Claimant's schedule*], the Defendant suggests that the losses and expenses should be limited to £[*total from Defendant's schedule*].]

I would always expect the Defendant's calculation to suggest lower figures than those given in the schedule I have prepared for you. I consider, as I indicated when sending you the calculation, that it may be appropriate to accept, certainly for the purpose of any negotiations, some of the points taken by the Defendant, although not necessarily to the extent the Defendant suggests.

I hope it is useful for you to have, at this stage, an idea of the issues relating to the claim for expenses and losses.

Yours sincerely

16.5 Letter to Client – Reviewing/Updating Advice on Quantum

At an earlier stage, on the basis of the evidence then available, I advised on what I considered to be the appropriate level of compensation to be claimed from [*name of opponent*] ('the Defendant').

Further information has since become available and I think it is now appropriate to offer you my current advice on what I consider to be the value of the claim.

[I have, at this stage, prepared an up-to-date calculation of the financial losses and expenses resulting from the injuries.]

[There have been some negotiations towards settlement which makes it all the more important that the valuation of the claim is reviewed to see if further progress towards final settlement can be made.]

Compensation is, as you know, assessed by the Court under two main heads.

1.   General damages

Given all the evidence now available, I consider that the appropriate level of general damages is in the region of £[*figure*] to reflect pain, suffering and loss of amenity [and the disadvantage that might be faced on the labour market as a result of those injuries] [together with an award to reflect the loss of a job you enjoyed].

[This is lower than the earlier assessment but, given the up-to-date medical evidence, it seems that some of the problems anticipated have, fortunately, not occurred.]

[This is higher than the earlier assessment but, given the current evidence, it seems that the injuries have had a more significant effect than at first envisaged.]

This figure, again, is just for your information. [However, I would propose to base further negotiations towards settlement around this figure.]

2.   Expenses and losses

You are, in addition to general damages, entitled to seek financial losses and expenses resulting from the injuries.

Accordingly, these must be added to the figure already given to form a view on the total value of the claim.

Either

[When appropriate information became available, I made a detailed calculation of losses and expenses which I sent to you. Please can you telephone [me]/[*name*] to advise if you have incurred any further losses or expenses since that calculation was prepared.]

Or

[The losses and expenses detailed in your statement amount, in round terms, to £[*figure*]. Please can you telephone [me]/[*name*] to advise if you have incurred any further losses or expenses since that calculation was prepared.]

Or

[I made a calculation of expenses and losses at an earlier stage and mentioned that I might need to prepare an up-to-date calculation at a later stage.

On the basis of the information which is now available, I have been able to make a further calculation of the financial losses and expenses resulting from the injuries and enclose a copy of that.

May I ask you to bear in mind that the calculation of expenses and losses I have prepared puts forward your case on the most reasonably optimistic basis possible. Whilst it is right to put the case at its best to the Defendant, it is likely that the Defendant will argue that lower figures are appropriate on certain aspects of the claim. Accordingly, you do need to keep an open mind on the level at which a settlement might be achieved, should reasonable proposals be put forward by the Defendant.

I shall be grateful if you could check the calculation, and in particular let me know if there have been any further items of expenditure or losses incurred but not yet included in that calculation.

Should the calculation be approved, as presently drafted, please would you sign the statement, to this effect, in the space provided between the marked crosses and then return the calculation to me.

The calculation, like other documents which are sent to the court on your behalf, is required to contain a statement of truth. Your signature amounts to confirmation that the facts in the calculation are true and I must remind you that if the court took the view any facts were stated without an honest belief in them proceedings for contempt of court could be taken against you.

I enclose a pre-paid envelope for you to return the calculation, either signed and approved or with details of amendments, and look forward to hearing from you accordingly.

Or

[I appreciate that we have still only been able to form a broad view of those expenses to date and I will, of course, try to provide a detailed calculation once outstanding enquiries are complete.]

[Allowing for matters on which the Defendant may be able to persuade the court to award lesser expenses and losses than have been claimed, it seems reasonable to look for a figure of about £[*figure*] for expenses and losses.]

These figures are all given on the basis of the Defendant being fully liable for the injuries. An apportionment of liability, for any reason, means a reduction of the compensation by an equivalent percentage.

Either

[However, the Defendant has, of course, admitted liability.]

Or

[Liability has, of course, already been dealt with on the basis that the Defendant will pay [*figure*]% of any compensation ultimately agreed or awarded by the court.]

Or

[The Defendant has suggested there should be an apportionment of liability and, although this remains subject to further negotiation, this is something that you should bear in mind.]

Or

[Liability is presently denied, although it may be that the Defendant's stance will change and some negotiations will be possible. Accordingly, despite the denial of liability, I think it right to let you have my views on the potential value of the claim.]

May I remind you that the advice given so far in this letter takes no account of State benefits received as a result of the injuries. You will recall that, if corresponding benefits have been received, the Defendant can deduct those benefits from relevant parts of the claim.

Either

[In round terms, it may be necessary to give an allowance of £[*approximate figure of corresponding benefit*] against the claim for losses and expenses which would bring the appropriate figure for settlement of the case down to approximately £[*figure*].]

Or

[However, the information received to date from the Compensation Recovery Unit indicates that no recoverable benefits have been paid as a result of the injuries, and so, if that remains the position, a recoupment of benefits will not have any impact on the value of the claim.]

I hope it is useful to have this up-to-date view on the potential value of the claim.

Yours sincerely

SECTION 17

LISTING AND FURTHER CASE MANAGEMENT

CONTENTS

17.1   Letter to Client – Explaining the Pre-trial Checklist (and Checking Availability)

Following exchange of evidence with [*name of opponent*] ('the Defendant'), the court now expects further reports on the case from both me and the Defendant's Solicitors.

The court will, when reviewing the reports at this stage, check that all earlier directions have been dealt with and that the case is now ready for hearing so that a date can be fixed.

So that I can ensure that any hearing date is convenient I shall be grateful for confirmation of your availability between [*date*] and [*date*].

I enclose an acknowledgment and shall be grateful if you would kindly complete and return this, in the pre-paid envelope provided, to confirm either that you are available for all dates or to identify any dates you [and your [*details eg husband, wife or partner*]] will be unavailable with brief reasons.

It would be helpful if you could return the acknowledgment even if you are available on all dates as, once arranged, the court would be very reluctant to change a hearing date.

I will let you know once I hear from the Court.

Yours sincerely

17.2   Letter to Witness – Checking Availability

You kindly provided a statement concerning my client's claim which has been disclosed so that your evidence can be relied on.

It has not been possible to agree terms of settlement so arrangements are now being made for a final court hearing.

At this stage, although I hope it may not prove necessary, I must ask you to be available to attend that final hearing. Your written statement will be provided to the court but you will need to be present in case any questions have to be put on the content of the statement.

The court intends to arrange a hearing date between [*date*] and [*date*].

I enclose an acknowledgment and shall be grateful if you would kindly complete and return this, in the pre-paid envelope provided, to confirm either that you are available for all dates or to identify any dates you will be unavailable with brief reasons.

It would be helpful if you could return the acknowledgment even if you are available on all dates as, once arranged, the court would be very reluctant to change a hearing date.

I will, of course, let you know as soon as a firm hearing date has been arranged.

[Once a date has been arranged, to safeguard all interests, I will obtain an order from the court confirming that your attendance is required and send a copy to you.]

Finally, for the moment, I confirm that, if you do need to attend court, your expenses will be reimbursed.

Yours sincerely

17.3   Letter to Expert – Checking Availability

You kindly prepared a report dealing with our client's claim a copy of which has been disclosed so that your evidence can be relied on.

The court is now making arrangements to list the case and hopes to fix the hearing on a date between [*date*] and [*date*].

It may be necessary for you to attend court at the hearing to give oral evidence. Accordingly, we shall be grateful if you can let us know if any of the proposed dates present a difficulty for you in attending court. We enclose an acknowledgment which, if you wish, you can complete with details of unavailability, and brief reasons, though we are happy to let us have this information in any format you wish.

The court will need to be notified of any inconvenient dates by [*date*], after which the court is likely to list the case on the basis that any of the dates given are convenient for the parties and their witnesses.

We will advise further as and when a hearing date has been fixed.

Yours faithfully

17.4   Acknowledgment

[address]

I acknowledge receipt of your letter dated *[date]* requesting details of availability to attend court between *[date]* and *[date]*.

Please tick the appropriate box.

☐	Available throughout.
☐	Not available on these dates for the reasons given:
Date(s)	*Brief Reasons for Unavailability*

Dated:

17.5   Letter to Counsel's Clerk – Checking Availability

The court is now arranging a date for the trial of our client's claim. We propose to brief *[name of Counsel]* for that trial.

It is proposed that the hearing be arranged between *[date]* and *[date]* with a time estimate of *[time estimate]*.

If any of these dates present difficulties for Counsel we shall be grateful if you could let us know as soon as possible and, in any event, by *[date]*.

Yours faithfully

17.6   Letter to Court – Filing Pre-Trial Checklist

We enclose, for filing, the following:

(1) Pre-trial Checklist, duly completed;

(2)   estimate of costs;

[(3)   proposed timetable for trial;]

[(4)   the documents we were directed to file with the Checklist comprising:
 (i)   the statement of [*name*];
 (ii)   the report of [*name*];]

[(5)   case summary;]

[(6)   Application Notice;]

[(7)   draft directions;]

(8)   cheque for the court fee of £[*figure*] [comprising the listing fee of £[*figure*] and the hearing fee of £[*figure*]].

[We shall be grateful if you could send us copies of the Defendant's checklist together with any accompanying information or documentation.]

We look forward to hearing from you in due course.

Yours faithfully

17.7   Letter to Opponent – Enclosing Pre-Trial Checklist

We enclose the Claimant's Pre-trial Checklist, as filed at court, for your information.

[We also enclose documentation filed at court along with the checklist.]

[We shall be grateful if you could let us have a copy of the Defendant's checklist, and any accompanying documentation or letters you ask the court to consider at this stage.]

Yours faithfully

17.8 Letter to Client – Enclosing Completed Pre-trial Checklist

I have now made a further report to the court on progress by completing and returning a checklist.

I enclose a copy of checklist for your information.

The checklist has to be accompanied by a costs estimate and so it is right to let you have a copy of this as well.

May I remind you that the main purpose of this estimate is, again, to appraise [*name of opponent*] of the costs that are likely to be claimed following a settlement or successful conclusion of the case and this does not affect in any way the funding arrangements already made to pursue the claim.

Yours sincerely

17.9 Letter to Opponent – Acknowledging Defendant's Pre-trial Checklist

We thank you for your letter of [*date*].

Thank you for the Defendant's Pre-trial Checklist [and accompanying documentation].

[The Defendant does not appear to have given a costs estimate. Section 6 of the Practice Direction About Costs requires a costs estimate at this stage and we shall be grateful, therefore, if you would provide such an estimate failing which we reserve the right to seek an appropriate order from the court.]

Yours faithfully

SECTION 18

TRIAL

CONTENTS

REVIEW AND ADVICE ON EVIDENCE

18.1 Letter to Client – Ahead of Review of Evidence

We have now dealt with most of the stages in the court proceedings against [*name of opponent*] ('the Defendant'). These stages are intended to ensure that the case of each party is disclosed as this is the best way of allowing a settlement to be achieved or, if that is not possible, of ensuring that the issues to be resolved at any hearing have been narrowed.

Whilst any negotiations can continue the case has reached the stage at which, if agreement cannot now be achieved, a hearing can take place.

It is, of course, important that all the information now available is carefully assessed so that the case can be reviewed and if there are any further matters to be dealt with ahead of the hearing these can be followed up as soon as possible.

[I will arrange for you to be represented by Counsel, your barrister, at the hearing and, accordingly, I think it is appropriate for Counsel to look at all the information now available and to advise, following this review.]

I will let you know once this review has been carried out and advise on any matters arising.

Yours sincerely

18.2 Letter to Client – On Review of Evidence/Receipt of Counsel's Advice on Evidence

Following exchange of evidence with [*name of opponent*] ('the Defendant') I arranged to review all the information now available.

[As you will be represented by Counsel (your barrister) at any hearing, I asked Counsel to carry out this review. Counsel has now had the opportunity of reviewing and advising on the case.]

Accordingly, I now write to deal with the matters arising from this review which I will look at in turn.

1. *Statements of case*

Either

[I consider these still, in the light of all the evidence now available, provide appropriate detail of each party's case.]

Or

[On the basis of all the evidence now available an amended statement of your case has been prepared so that the Defendant cannot be said to have been taken by surprise on any point at a final hearing.

I enclose the amended document for you to check. If this is correct, as presently drafted, please sign the statement to this effect. If any corrections are required please could you let [me]/[*name*] know. Please return the document to me, as signed and approved or with any corrections, by the pre-paid envelope also enclosed.

I must remind you that if the court took the view facts were stated without an honest belief in the truth of those matters there would be a risk of proceedings for contempt of court.]

2.   Documents

Either

[Disclosure of relevant documentation appears to be complete.]

Or

[The Defendant has not dealt fully with outstanding requests for disclosure of all documentation and it seems appropriate, at this stage, to press the Defendant for disclosure of any further documentation there may be relating to the issues in the case.]

May I remind you that if any further documentation relating to the issues in the case has become available you should let me have this so that I can disclose it to the Defendant.

3.   Factual evidence

The factual evidence has been reviewed to ensure that the statements relied on cover all relevant matters which will have to be decided by the court.

Either

[All available and appropriate evidence does appear to have already been obtained and disclosed.]

Or

[It would be helpful to have your further instructions, at this stage, on [*details*].]

And/Or

[It would be helpful, at this stage, to know whether [*name*] would be able to give evidence that might help to ensure that the court has all available factual evidence to assist it in deciding the matters in dispute.]

4. Expert evidence

The expert evidence has also been reviewed to ensure that this deals with matters to be decided by the court which are likely to be determined by expert opinion.

Either

[All available and appropriate expert evidence does appear to have been obtained and disclosed.]

Or

[It would be helpful, at this stage, to obtain further expert opinion relating to [*details*].]

Permission to rely on all necessary expert evidence has [not yet] been given by the court [and so that permission will now be sought].

5. Value

This has also been a useful opportunity to review the appropriate level of compensation.

Compensation is, as you know, assessed under two main heads.

(1) *General damages*
     Given all the evidence now available, I consider that the appropriate level of general damages is in the region of £[*figure*] to reflect pain, suffering and loss of amenity [and the disadvantage that might be faced on the labour market as a result of those injuries] [together with an award to reflect the loss of a job you enjoyed].
     [This is lower than the earlier assessment but, given the up-to-date medical evidence, it seems to me that the recovery has been quite good and some of the problems anticipated have, fortunately, not occurred.]
     [This is higher than the earlier assessment but, given the up-to-date evidence, it seems to me that the injuries have had a more significant effect than at first envisaged.]

This figure is still just for your information and for any offers of settlement to be properly assessed. [However, I would propose to base any further negotiations towards settlement on this figure.]

(2)   *Expenses and losses*

In addition to general damages, you are, of course, entitled to seek financial losses and expenses resulting from the injuries. Accordingly, these must be added to the estimate just given to form an overall view of the potential value of the claim.

Either

[When appropriate information became available, I made a detailed calculation of losses and expenses which I sent to you. Please can you write or telephone [me]/[*name*], to advise if you have incurred any further losses or expenses since that calculation was prepared.]

Or

[The losses and expenses detailed in your statement amount, in round terms, to £[*figure*]. Please can you write or telephone [me]/[*name*], to advise if you have incurred any further losses or expenses since that calculation was prepared.]

Or

[I made a calculation of expenses and losses at an earlier stage and mentioned that I might need to prepare an up-to-date calculation at a later stage.

On the basis of the information which is now available, I have been able to make a further calculation of the financial losses and expenses resulting from the injuries and enclose a copy of that.

May I ask you to bear in mind that the calculation of expenses and losses I have prepared puts forward your case on the most reasonably optimistic basis possible. Whilst it is right to put the case at its best to the Defendant, it is likely that the Defendant will argue that lower figures are appropriate on certain aspects of the claim. Accordingly, you do need to keep an open mind on the level at which a settlement might be achieved, should reasonable proposals be put forward by the Defendant.

I shall be grateful if you could check the calculation, and in particular let me know if there have been any further items of expenditure or losses incurred but not yet included in that calculation.

Should the calculation be approved, as presently drafted, please would you sign the statement, to this effect, in the space provided between the marked crosses and then return the calculation to me.

The calculation, like other documents which are sent to the court on your behalf, is required to contain a statement of truth. Your signature amounts to confirmation that the facts in the calculation are true and I must remind you that if the court took the view that any facts were stated without an honest belief in them proceedings for contempt of court could be taken against you.

I enclose a pre-paid envelope for you to return the calculation, either signed and approved or with details of amendments, and look forward to hearing from you accordingly.]
Or
[I appreciate that we have still only been able to form a broad view of those expenses to date and I will, of course, try to provide a detailed calculation once outstanding enquiries are complete.]

[Allowing for matters on which the Defendant may be able to persuade the court to award less than the sums claimed, it seems reasonable to look for a figure of about £[*figure*] for expenses and losses.]

This assessment is made on the basis of the Defendant being fully liable for the injuries. An apportionment of liability, for any reason, means a reduction of the compensation by an equivalent percentage.

May I remind you that the advice given so far in this letter takes no account of state benefits received as a result of the injuries. You will recall that, if corresponding benefits have been received, the Defendant can offset those benefits against relevant parts of the claim.

Either

[In round terms, it may be necessary to give an allowance of £[*approximate figure of corresponding benefit*] against the claim for losses and expenses which would bring the appropriate figure for settlement of the case down to approximately £[*figure*].]

Or

[However, the information received to date from the Compensation Recovery Unit indicates that no recoverable benefits have been paid as a result of the injuries and so, if that remains the position, recoupment of benefits will not have any impact on the value of the claim.]

[May I also remind you that you have received interim provision of £[*figure*] which I have included in the calculations already set out but for which, of course, allowance will have to be made for the purposes of any settlement.]

6.   *The merits*

This is a good opportunity, on the basis of all the information now available, to assess the overall merits of pursuing the claim further.

Either

[Liability has, of course, been admitted in full.]

Or

[Liability has, of course, already been dealt with on the basis that the Defendant will pay [*figure*]% of any compensation ultimately agreed or awarded by the court.]

Or

[The Defendant has suggested that there should be an apportionment of liability and, although this remains subject to further negotiation, this is something that you should bear in mind.]

Or

[Liability is denied by the Defendant.]

[Although liability is disputed, there are good prospects of the claim succeeding given the evidence available to support it.

[Unfortunately, I must conclude that, on the evidence available, the claim is more likely to fail than succeed if it had to be decided by a court.]]

[Terms proposed by the Defendant for settlement do not adequately reflect the likely outcome and the prospects of doing better seem likely to outweigh the risks of doing worse.]

[Proposals made by the Defendant do appear to reasonably reflect the likely outcome and, accordingly, the prospects of doing better are outweighed by the risks of doing worse.]

7. *Summary*

Either

[Accordingly, I have now been able to make a detailed review of the information that has become available through the stages of the court case now completed. As you can see, this helps to identify the main issues and hence the likely outcome. All of this will assist in any negotiations and, of course, means that we are now well prepared for any hearing should it not be possible to negotiate a settlement. None of this prevents negotiations taking place, but I think the best way of forcing the Defendant into entering sensible negotiations is to deal with all outstanding matters and ensure we press on with the case towards a hearing. I recommend that we proceed on that basis.]

Or

[Accordingly, I think we must now look at settlement in the terms proposed by the Defendant unless any further effort at negotiation results in improved settlement terms.]

Or

[Accordingly, I consider that the claim cannot be pursued in accordance with the conditional fee agreement. You may, of course, give instructions to proceed on a private basis if you wish, although I would be reluctant to recommend that you incur the costs of this, given the assessment of the case already set out in this letter. However, if you do wish to have an estimate of the costs that would be incurred on a private basis, please let me know. By dropping the claim at this stage you do not incur any responsibility for costs as my firm will not be paid for the work undertaken, as we agreed at the outset by entering the conditional fee agreement, and any other outlays will be met by the insurance policy you took out.]

Or

[Accordingly, I do not think it is appropriate to recommend that any further costs be incurred, although this does, of course, mean that costs, in accordance with earlier estimates, have been incurred. [This is unless a final effort at negotiation results in settlement.]]

Or

[Accordingly, I consider the claim cannot be pursued in accordance with the legal expenses insurance as that cover depends upon the claim still being assessed as likely to succeed.

You may, of course, give instructions to proceed on a private basis if you wish, although I would be reluctant to recommend that you incur the costs of this, given the assessment of the case already set out in this letter. However, if you do wish to have an estimate of the costs that would be incurred on a private basis, please let me know.

By dropping the claim at this stage you do not incur any responsibility for costs as my firm will be paid for the work undertaken by the cover you have for legal expenses. [This is unless a final effort at negotiation results in settlement.]]

And/Or

[I consider that negotiations to see if a settlement can be achieved should be pursued, and I will write further, concerning this, as soon as I can.]

If you are prepared to accept the advice in this letter, I shall be grateful if you would kindly sign and return the enclosed acknowledgment to confirm as much. If, before reaching your decision, you would like to review matters, please telephone [me]/[*name*].

I hope this letter brings you fully up to date.

Yours sincerely

TRIAL DATE

18.3 Letter to Client – Confirming Date of Trial

I write to confirm that the court has now fixed a hearing date for your case against [*name of opponent*] ('the Defendant') and also to provide information about the arrangements for that hearing.

The hearing will take place on [day(s) and date(s) for trial] at [*name and address of court*].

I enclose, for your information, a map confirming the location of the court.

The case is due to commence at [*time*] on [*first date of hearing*] although, in practice, it may be necessary for the hearing to begin later in the day, depending upon other work the court has to deal with on that occasion.

Please would you be at court for, say, [*time*] that morning to allow sufficient time for a full review of the case before the hearing begins.

[I have arranged for you to be represented by a barrister ('Counsel') at the hearing. My role has been to fully investigate and prepare your case for the final hearing whilst Counsel's role is to present the case at court.

Either

[By briefing Counsel to appear at court on your behalf, my firm will become committed to paying Counsel's fee and you are responsible, ultimately, for this cost. I estimate that Counsel's fee will be in the region of £[*figure*]. Please let me know, as soon as possible, if you do not wish to be committed to this fee. If your claim is successful I will try to recover Counsel's fee as part of the costs of the claim from the Defendant.]

Or

[Counsel can, as my firm has done, enter a conditional fee agreement with you so that Counsel is also acting on a 'no win – no fee' basis. Counsel has, of course, already made a conditional fee agreement concerning the claim.]

Or

[Counsel can, as my firm has done, enter a conditional fee agreement with you so that Counsel is also acting on a 'no win – no fee' basis. Very often, when we have entered such an agreement, Counsel will agree to enter an agreement with you in the same terms. However, as that will involve Counsel running the risk of being unpaid in the absence of a success under the terms of the agreement, it is right to let Counsel look at the papers (on the basis there will be no charge for doing just this) to decide whether Counsel is prepared to enter a conditional fee agreement. I should know Counsel's views on this in the near future and will report further once I hear.]

Either

[I will, by the time of the hearing, have completed my work on the case [although myself or one of my colleagues will be at court just in case any further matters do arise at that stage]/[and so I shall leave Counsel to deal with that hearing].]

Or

[At the hearing [I] [my colleague [*name*]] will be representing you.]

You are, of course, aware of the issues that have emerged as the case has gone through all the preparatory stages. The purpose of this hearing is for the judge, after reading each party's case, considering the documents and hearing the evidence, to reach a decision on the matters in dispute [concerning liability].

It may be helpful if I summarise the procedure the court hearing will follow.

(1)   The judge will be told about the general background to the case. The judge will probably be familiar with the matter from a reading of the papers relating to the case filed at court.

(2)   You, followed by any witnesses you rely on, will give evidence. The judge may read your written statement or may ask you to give evidence confirming that statement. The Defendant's representative will then have the opportunity of putting any questions.

(3)   The Defendant, and any witnesses relied on by the Defendant, will, similarly, give evidence and your representative will put any questions.

(4)   Each party's representative will address the judge, stressing the main points each party relies on and dealing with any points of law.

(5)   The judge will decide the case, giving reasons for the decision.

It is, of course, still possible for the parties to negotiate a settlement, even on the day of the hearing, so I still do not rule out that possibility.

Either

[A complete bundle of documents relating to the case has now been prepared and filed at court, and I enclose a bundle for your information. Please bring the bundle of documents to court with you so that you have it to refer to when necessary.]

Or

[A complete bundle of documents relating to the case will be prepared prior to the hearing. I will send you that bundle as soon as I can and shall be grateful if you would bring it with you to court so that you could have it to refer to when necessary.]

Finally, for the moment, I shall be grateful if you could return the enclosed acknowledgment to confirm that you [and your [*details, e g husband, wife or partner*]] will attend the hearing.

I enclose a pre-paid envelope for your use in returning the acknowledgment.

Yours sincerely

18.4   Letter to Witness – Confirming Date of Trial

I write to confirm that the court has now arranged for the final hearing of [*name of client*]'s case which is to take place on [*day(s) and date(s) for trial*] at [*name and address of court*].

I enclose, for your information, a map confirming the location of the court.

The case is due to commence at [*time*] on [*first date of hearing*] and I shall be grateful if you could be at court for, say, [*time*].

[I confirm that, as it is important to ensure the availability of all important witnesses, the court will be issuing a witness order which you should receive in the near future. You will receive, with the order, a payment to cover your expenses in attending court. If this is not sufficient to cover all your expenses, for example lost earnings, please let me have a full breakdown of expenses after the hearing.]

Finally, for the moment, I shall be grateful if you could return the enclosed acknowledgment to confirm that you will attend the hearing. I enclose a pre-paid envelope for your use in returning the acknowledgment.

Yours sincerely

18.5   Letter to Expert – Confirming Date of Trial

We write to confirm that the court has now arranged for the final hearing of [*name of client*]'s case which is to take place on [*day(s) and date(s) for trial*] at [*name and address of court*].

The case is due to commence at [*time*] on [*first date of hearing*] and we shall be grateful if you could be at court for, say, [*time*].

Either

[A complete bundle of documents relating to the case has now been prepared and filed at court. We enclose a bundle for your information. Please bring the bundle of documents to court with you so that you have it to refer to when necessary.]

Or

[A complete bundle of documents relating to the case will be prepared prior to the hearing. We will send you that bundle as soon as we can and shall be grateful if you would bring it with you to court so that you have it to refer to when necessary.]

Either

[Unless you would prefer us to do so we do not propose to serve you, as an expert witness, with a witness order. However, if you would prefer us to obtain a witness order, please let us know and we shall be happy to make the appropriate arrangements.]

Or

[We recognise that you may receive requests to attend other court hearings and, whilst reluctant to serve witness orders on expert witnesses, think it may be prudent to take the precaution of obtaining a witness order. If you have any objection please let us know, otherwise we will make the necessary arrangements.]

We confirm that we shall, of course, be responsible for your reasonable fee in attending court.

It would be helpful if you could confirm your current terms for attending court, including details of any cancellation charges. We will then arrange to forward these details to the Defendant's solicitors so that they are aware of those terms.

Finally, for the moment, we shall be grateful if you could return the enclosed acknowledgment to confirm that you will attend the hearing.

Yours faithfully

18.6   Acknowledgment of Hearing Date

[address]

I acknowledge receipt of your letter dated *[date of letter]* and confirm that I am aware of the hearing at *[name of court]* on *[date]*, which I will attend.

[title, initials and surname]

Dated:

18.7   Letter to Counsel's Clerk – Confirming Date of Trial

The trial of the [issue of liability in the] above action, in which we propose to brief *[Counsel's name]*, has now been fixed for *[date(s)]* at *[name and address of* court].

The brief will follow but, meanwhile, we shall be grateful if you would make a note of the hearing in your diary.

Our client is the Claimant and [is legally aided]/[we [and counsel] are acting under a conditional fee agreement] [is privately funded [with the support of legal expenses insurance]].

Yours faithfully

WITNESS ORDERS

18.8 Letter to Court – Requesting Issue of Witness Summons

We enclose, for your kind attention, the following:

(1) witness summons, for service upon [*name of witness*], for issue;

(2) cheque for the court fee of £[*figure*].

We shall be grateful if the summons may be served on the witness by post, at the address shown in the summons, and, accordingly, enclose a cheque in the sum of £[*figure*] to be tendered to the witness with the summons.

We shall be grateful if you can let us have a copy of the summons with confirmation of service in due course.

We look forward to hearing from you.

Yours faithfully

18.9 Letter to Witness – Advising about Impending Service of a Witness Summons

The court has now issued a witness summons for your attendance at the hearing on [*date(s)*].

You should receive from the court, in the next few days, a copy of the witness summons together with some explanatory information.

Please make contact if you need any further information.

Yours [sincerely]/[faithfully]

BUNDLES OF DOCUMENTS

18.10 Letter to Opponent – Enclosing Index to Trial Bundle

We have reviewed this matter in readiness for the trial.

We have prepared a bundle of documents and enclose a copy of the draft index for your information. Please confirm that the bundle is agreed or let us know if there are any further documents you wish to be included, identifying any such documents. We should like to be ready to file the bundle by [*date which is 7 days ahead of the trial date*] and so look forward to hearing from you prior to then.

Please note that if a settlement has not been achieved by 4 pm on [*date*] we reserve the right to deliver a brief without further notice. This will, obviously, increase the costs.

[We enclose details of the terms for [*name of expert(s)*] for attending court and shall be grateful if you would note these, in particular cancellation fees.]

[We are also mindful of the time limits that apply for a refund of the hearing fee in the event of settlement.]

We look forward to hearing from you.

Yours faithfully

18.11 Letter to Client/Witness/Counsel – Sending Bundle of Documents

Preparation of an indexed and paginated bundle of documents, in readiness for the final hearing, has now been completed.

Accordingly, a copy of the bundle is enclosed.

[The bundle includes a case summary.]

[A [folder of photographs] [and a] [sketch plan], to accompany the bundle, is also enclosed.]

Yours [sincerely]/[faithfully]

18.12   Letter to Court – Filing Bundles of Documents Prior to Trial

In readiness for the trial of the above action, we now enclose, duly indexed and paginated, the bundle of documents in duplicate. One bundle is for use of the judge and the other for use by witnesses.

[The bundle includes a case summary.]

[We also enclose a [folder of photographs] [and a] [sketch plan], to accompany the bundle of documents, again in duplicate.]

Yours faithfully

18.13   Letter to Opponent – Sending Bundle of Documents

[Thank you for confirming that the draft index to the trial bundle is agreed.]

[We confirm that we are agreeable to amending the trial bundle as proposed.]

[We note your comments on the draft index but consider that the present format of the bundle is appropriate.]

[We do not appear to have heard from you in response to the draft index to the trial bundle and we assume, therefore, that there is no objection to the proposed format.]

Accordingly, we enclose, duly indexed and paginated, a bundle of documents for your use and confirm that two bundles have been filed at court, one for use by the judge and one for use by witnesses.

[The bundle includes a case summary.]

[We also enclose a [folder of photographs] [and a] [sketch plan], to accompany the bundle of documents, again in duplicate.]

Yours faithfully

FINAL CHECKS

18.14   Letter to Client – Final Reminder of Date of Trial

I write just to remind you that the hearing date of your case against [*name of opponent*] ('the Defendant') is now approaching.

As you know, the hearing will take place on [*date(s)*] at [*name and address of court*].

May I remind you that it will be helpful if you can be at court for [*time*] on [*date*] to allow sufficient time for a full review of the case [with your barrister, [*name of Counsel*],] before the hearing begins.

When you arrive at court it would be helpful if you could give your name to the court usher and ask for [me]/[*name of person attending Counsel or name of Counsel if no one is attending*].

I will, of course, let you know if there are any late developments.

Finally, for the moment, I shall be grateful if you would write or telephone [me]/[*name*] to confirm that you have received this letter and will be able to keep to these arrangements.

Yours sincerely

18.15   Letter to Witness/Expert – Final Reminder of Date of Trial

This letter is just a reminder that the hearing of [*name of client*]'s case is to take place on [*date(s)*] at [*name and address of court*].

It will be helpful if you could be at court for [*time*] on [*date*] to allow time for review of any final matters before the hearing begins.

When you arrive at court it would be helpful if you could give your name to the court usher and ask for [me]/[*name of person attending Counsel or name of Counsel if no one is attending*].

Yours [sincerely]/[faithfully]

18.16   Letter to Court – Enclosing Costs Statement for Trial

We enclose, in readiness for the hearing on [*date*], the Claimant's costs statement.

[The statement may include matters the trial judge will not wish to be made aware of until the conclusion of the hearing. Accordingly, we have placed the statement in an envelope and think it is a matter for the court whether the envelope is opened or the statement left within the envelope for opening once all matters arising at the hearing, save for costs, have been dealt with.]

Yours faithfully

18.17   Letter to Opponent – Enclosing Costs Statement for Trial

We enclose, in readiness for the hearing on [*date*], the Claimant's costs statement.

Yours faithfully

18.18   Letter to Counsel's Clerk – Enclosing Costs Statement for Trial

We enclose, in readiness for the hearing on [*date*], the Claimant's costs statement. We confirm this has been filed and served.

[We also enclose the Defendant's costs statement served on us.]

We shall be grateful if this information can be placed with the papers already before Counsel.

Yours faithfully

FOLLOWING TRIAL

18.19   Letter to Non-expert Witness – Following Trial

Thank you for attending court on our client's behalf.

[We are pleased to confirm that an order was made in our client's favour.]/[Unfortunately the court did not make an order in our client's favour.]

Either

We trust the payment you received with the witness order covered your expenses in attending court.

Or

[We confirm that you are entitled to be reimbursed for:

(1)   travel expenses to and from court; and

(2)   any loss of earnings.

It will be helpful to have details of mileage, if you travelled by private transport, or tickets, if you went by public transport, together with a letter from work confirming any lost earnings. We will then try to reimburse you as soon as possible.]

May we take this opportunity to thank you for your assistance.

Yours faithfully

18.20   Letter to Expert Witness – Following Trial

Thank you for attending court on our client's behalf.

[We are pleased to confirm that an order was made in our client's favour.]/[Unfortunately the court did not make an order in our client's favour.]

[Thank you for details of your fee for attending court. Payment will follow under separate cover.]/[We look forward to receiving details of your fee for attending court.]

Many thanks for your assistance throughout the case.

Yours faithfully

18.21   Letter to Client – Following Trial (Successful Outcome)

Thank you for attending court when your case against [*name of opponent*] ('the Defendant') was heard.

I am pleased to confirm that a final court order has been made in your favour.

The terms are that the Defendant will pay compensation totaling £[*figure*] [as a lump sum with periodical payments of [*details*]] [and] [with [no] provisional damages [if [*details*]]].

[May I remind you that out of the total of £[*figure*], you have already received interim payments of £[*figure*]. Accordingly, that leaves £[*figure*].]

[The Defendant is entitled, under the scheme for recoupment of State benefits, to deduct corresponding benefits from relevant heads of the claim. The Defendant has been allowed to make a deduction of £[*figure*] from the claim accordingly.]

[Please bear in mind that, out of the compensation, there will need to be refunded to [*employer*] [£[*figure*] being] monies paid during the absence from work] [and] [to [*insurer*] [£[*figure*] as] outlays incurred for treatment].]

The compensation should be available for me to make a payment of £[*figure*] in, I hope, the next [*number*] months.

In addition to the compensation, the Defendant is also to pay the costs of pursuing the claim. Those costs are calculated, as you know, on the basis of the time it has been necessary to spend on bringing the matter to a conclusion, together with court fees and the cost of payments made to other people involved in the case on your behalf. I will try, now, to agree the costs payable by the Defendant, with a view to recovering as much of those costs as I can. If agreement cannot be reached, costs will have to be assessed by the court.

[Finally, for the moment, I should mention that the Defendant might appeal the order. An appeal is not possible on any factual matter decided by the judge, but only on the grounds the judge made a mistake on the law. It is unusual for there to be any such point of law and I would not expect there to be an appeal, although it is right just to mention the possibility.]

I am pleased to be able to report to you in these terms at this stage.

Yours sincerely

18.22   Letter to Client – Following Trial (Unsuccessful Outcome)

Thank you for attending court when your case against [*name of opponent*] ('the Defendant') was heard.

Unfortunately, after hearing the evidence, the judge concluded that the Defendant was not legally liable for the injuries suffered. Accordingly, a final court order was made dismissing the claim.

[The court also allowed the Defendant the costs of defending the claim [though these should be dealt with by the insurers providing cover for the risk of such costs].]

I am sorry that this has been the outcome but, as you know, a careful decision was made to pursue the matter to a final hearing, mindful of the risk that the claim could fail.

Either

[Whilst, in certain circumstances, the decision of the judge could be appealed, I must tell you that an appeal is not possible against any factual matter decided by the judge, but only on the grounds that the judge made a mistake of law. In the circumstances, I do not think there are any grounds to appeal the decision.]

Or

[The decision of the judge can be appealed, but only in limited circumstances. An appeal is not possible against any factual matter decided by the judge, but only on the grounds that the judge made a mistake of law. I am presently considering whether we have sufficient grounds to argue that there has been a mistake of law. As only 4 weeks are allowed for an appeal, I will advise further as soon as I can on whether I think there are good grounds to appeal.]

I shall write to let you have a final report [, or to confirm if an appeal can be pursued,] as soon as I can.

Yours sincerely

SECTION 19

SETTLEMENT AND FINAL REPORTS

CONTENTS

ACCEPTANCE OF OFFERS

19.1   Letter to Opponent – on Acceptance of Offer on an Issue

Either

[Our client hereby accepts your client's [Part 36] offer made on [*date*] on the issue of [liability that there be an apportionment on the basis our client will receive [*figure*]% of the damages and interest that would be awarded on full liability]/[*details of issue*].

Or

[We thank you for your letter of [*date*].

We are pleased to note your client accepts our client's [Part 36] offer made on [*date*] on the issue of [liability that there be an apportionment on the basis our client will receive [*figure*]% of the damages and interest that would be awarded on full liability]/[*details of issue*].

[We think it would be sensible to record the agreement reached in a consent order. Accordingly, we enclose a draft order which we invite you to approve and then return to us, endorsed with consent, for filing at court so that we can obtain an order confirming the terms agreed.]

[This is, of course, subject to the court's approval of a settlement on these terms and we are, therefore, now [taking steps to make the appropriate application and will advise further as soon as we can] [asking the court to deal with approval at the hearing already arranged for [*date*] which, we consider, will allow the time estimate to be amended to [*details*]].

[Finally, and given the agreement that has now been reached, we consider that it is appropriate for our client to receive an interim payment. Please let us have your proposals, failing which we must reserve the right to make application to the court and if that should be necessary we would, of course, have to seek the costs of such application.]

Yours faithfully

19.2   Letter to Opponent – on Acceptance of Offer in Settlement

Either

[Our client hereby accepts your client's [Part 36] offer made on [*date*] of £[*figure*] damages in settlement of the whole claim [inclusive of deductible benefits of £[*figure*] [and] [interim provision already made of £[*figure*]] [net of any recoverable benefits].

Or

[We thank you for your letter of [*date*] and are pleased to note your client accepts our client's [Part 36] offer made on [*date*] of £[*figure*] damages in settlement of the whole claim [inclusive of deductible benefits of £[*figure*] [and] [interim provision already made of £[*figure*]] [net of any recoverable benefits].]

Either

[This is on the basis that our client's costs [in accordance with Part 36.10] will be paid by your client, to be the subject of a detailed assessment by the court if not agreed.]

Or

[This is on the basis that the damages are part of an entire agreement under which costs calculated on the predictable basis provided for in Part 45, as calculated at the time of the offer, are paid with the damages so that sum payable is £ [*figure*].]

We calculate that in accordance with [Part 36]/[the terms of the offer] the monies due to our client should be paid by [*date*] and look forward to hearing from you accordingly.

[We think it would be sensible to record the agreement reached in a consent order. Accordingly, we enclose a draft order which we invite you to approve and then return to us, endorsed with consent, for filing at court so that we can obtain an order confirming the terms agreed.] [Pending detailed assessment we would expect there to be a payment on account of costs and [invite your proposals] [and are pleased to note the sum of £[*figure*] has been agreed].]

[This is, of course, subject to the court's approval of a settlement on these terms and we are, therefore, now [taking steps to make the appropriate application and will advise further as soon as we can] [asking the court to deal with approval at the hearing already arranged for [*date*] which, we consider, will allow the time estimate to be amended to [*details*]].

Yours faithfully

19.3   Letter to Court – Filing Acceptance of Part 36 Offer

We enclose for filing, in accordance with the Practice Direction to Part 36, a copy of a letter dated [*date*] sent [to]/[from] the Defendant's Solicitors accepting a Part 36 offer.

[In the circumstances we would ask that the hearing arranged for [*date*] be [vacated] [used just for the purposes of the court considering whether to approve the settlement which would allow the time estimate to be reduced to [*time estimate*].]

We have paid the hearing fee of £[*figure*] and as this letter gives notice the case has settled more than [28 days before the hearing we request 100% of that fee be refunded]/[14 days before the hearing we request 75% of that fee be refunded]/[7 days before the hearing we request 50% of that fee be refunded].

Yours faithfully

JUDGMENT AFTER ACCEPTANCE OF PART 36 OFFER

19.4 Letter to Court – Requesting Judgment on Defendant's Failure to Pay Damages After Acceptance of Part 36 Offer

On [*date*] a Part 36 offer was accepted, and we filed a copy of the acceptance, under which the Defendant was to pay the Claimant damages of £[*figure*].

In accordance with CPR Part 36.11(6) that sum became payable within 14 days of [*date*].

Payment has not been made by the Defendant and, accordingly, the Claimant seeks judgment for the unpaid sum in accordance with Part 36.11(7).

On acceptance of the offer the Claimant also became entitled to costs in accordance with Part 36.10.

Accordingly, we respectfully invite the court to enter judgment, in accordance with Part 36.11.

We do not think, under the terms of Part 36, this request requires an application notice nor do we consider any fee is payable.

We shall be grateful, given that our client is otherwise prejudiced in losing interest on the agreed sum, if judgment may be entered at the earliest opportunity.

We look forward to hearing from you.

Yours faithfully

19.5 Letter to Opponent – on Failure to Pay Damages After Acceptance of Part 36 Offer

A Part 36 offer was accepted on [*date*] for payment of £[*figure*] to our client.

In accordance with Part 36.11(6) that sum became payable by [*date 14 days after above date*].

Payment does not appear to have been made and, accordingly, our client is now applying for judgment in accordance with Part 36.11(7).

Please would you make payment as soon as possible. As and when judgment is entered we reserve the right to seek interest, at the judgment debt rate, on the unpaid sum and to enforce the judgment should it remain unpaid.

Yours faithfully

IMPLEMENTING SETTLEMENT

19.6   Letter to Court – Confirming Settlement Ahead of Filing Consent Order

We write to give you immediate notice that terms of settlement have been reached between the parties.

A consent order is being prepared and will be filed as soon as possible.

[We are concerned to let you know of this development without delay, given the hearing fixed for [*date of hearing*].]

[We have paid the hearing fee of £[*figure*] and as this letter gives notice that the case has settled more than [28 days before the hearing we request 100% of that fee be refunded]/[14 days before the hearing we request 75% of that fee be refunded]/[7 days before the hearing we request 50% of that fee be refunded].]

Yours faithfully

19.7   Letter to Court – Enclosing Draft Order on Settlement

We confirm that the parties are agreed on terms of settlement in the above action.

Those terms are reflected in a draft order which we enclose herewith for the court's approval.

Either

[In the circumstances, we would ask that the hearing arranged for [*date of hearing/appointment and time*] be vacated.]

Or

[In the circumstances, we would ask that the hearing arranged for [*date of hearing/appointment and time*] be used just for the purposes of seeking approval of the settlement which would allow the time estimate to be reduced to [*time estimate*].]

[We enclose our cheque for the court fee of £[*figure*] for considering the draft order.]

Yours faithfully

19.8   Letter to Counsel's Clerk – Confirming Settlement

We are pleased to report that terms of settlement have now been agreed in the above matter.

Our client is to receive damages of £[*figure*], together with payment of costs.

Either

[Accordingly, the hearing on [*first date of hearing*] (and any subsequent days) has been cancelled and we shall be grateful if you could please note that Counsel will not, therefore, need to attend that hearing.]

Or

[It is now proposed to deal with the hearing on [*date*] for the purposes of approval only with a revised time estimate of [*details*].]

Please let us have a complete and up-to-date fee note [following the approval hearing] so that we can try to agree costs.

Yours faithfully

19.9   Letter to Witness – Confirming Settlement

I am pleased to confirm that a settlement has been reached in [*client's name*]'s case.

[Accordingly, the hearing on [*date*] (and any subsequent days) has been cancelled.]

I do not, therefore, need you to attend any court hearing and should not need to trouble you further.

May I take this opportunity of thanking you for your assistance with this matter.

Yours sincerely

19.10   Letter to Expert – Confirming Settlement

We are pleased to confirm that a settlement has been reached in [*client's name*]'s case.

Our client is to receive damages of £[*figure*] together with payment of costs.

[Accordingly, the hearing on [*date*] (and any subsequent days) has been cancelled and we will not, now, need you to attend any court hearing.]

[If you have incurred any further fees, we shall be grateful if you could let us have details as soon as possible as we shall now try to agree costs with the other side.]

May we take this opportunity of thanking you for your valuable assistance in bringing this matter to a satisfactory conclusion.

Yours faithfully

19.11   Letter to Client – Confirming Settlement

Either

[I write to confirm your instructions that you are prepared to accept the offer made by [*name of opponent*] ('the Defendant').]

Or

[I am pleased to confirm that [*name of opponent*] ('the Defendant') has accepted your offer.]

Settlement of the whole claim has, therefore, been reached and I should like to confirm the terms.

The terms are that the Defendant will pay compensation totalling £[*figure*] [as a lump sum with periodical payments of [*details*]] [and] [with [no] provisional damages [if [*details*]]].

[May I remind you that out of the total of £[*figure*], you have already received interim payments of £[*figure*]. Accordingly, that leaves £[*figure*].]

[The Defendant is entitled, under the scheme for recoupment of State benefits, to deduct corresponding benefits from relevant heads of the claim. The Defendant has made a deduction of £[*figure*] from the claim accordingly.]

[Please bear in mind that, out of the compensation, there will need to be refunded to [*employer*] [£[*figure*] being] monies paid during the absence from work] [and] [to [*insurer*] [£[*figure*] as] outlays incurred for treatment].]

The compensation should be available for me to make a payment of £[*figure*] in, I hope, the next [*number*] months.

The Defendant is also, in addition to the compensation, to pay the costs of pursuing the claim.

Either

[Those costs, in a case of this kind, are calculated on a straightforward, predictable, basis which I have been able to deal with as part of the settlement negotiations.]

Or

[Those costs are calculated on the basis of the time it has been necessary to spend on bringing the matter to a conclusion, together with court fees and the cost of payments made to other people involved in the case on your behalf. I will try, now, to agree the costs payable by the Defendant but if necessary those costs will be assessed by the court.]

Either

[In the circumstances, the hearing date on [*date*] (and any subsequent days) will be cancelled and you will not need to attend court.]

Or

[The settlement will need to be approved by the court [and I will let you know when a hearing has been fixed]/[and the hearing scheduled for [*date*] can now be used just for that purpose].]

I am pleased to be able to report to you in these terms at this stage.

Yours sincerely

19.12   Letter to Client – Advising on Will/Trust

The claim against [*name of opponent*] ('the Defendant') has now been finalised and you will soon be receiving the compensation due.

If you already have a will, I think you should, at this stage, be reviewing its terms and ensuring that these are up to date. If you do not yet have a will, I think this is the time to consider making one. The procedure, either to make or to update a will, is straightforward and, if you would like me to arrange this, I will be happy to do so.

[It is important, at this stage, to mention the possible effect, of the compensation if you are, or become entitled to, any means-tested State benefits.

In assessing entitlement to such benefits, the Government:

(1)   will not take into account any capital below £[*figure*];

(2)   will, if your capital is between £[*figure*] and £[*figure*] once you have received the compensation, treat every £[*figure*] of capital over £[*figure*], as producing £[*figure*] per week in income, and reduce payment of benefits accordingly;

(3)   will not pay means-tested benefits at all, if your capital exceeds £[*figure*] once you have received the compensation (although there is some discretion in the event of elderly or severely disabled people).

If you think receipt of the compensation may now, or in the future, affect entitlement to benefits you may wish to consider putting the damages in a trust. Such a trust will still allow you ready access to the funds but will mean that these are not treated as part of your capital for the purpose of assessing means-tested benefits and will allow you to remain entitled to those benefits so far as your financial circumstances are concerned.

I will be happy to advise you further if you would like advice on this aspect of the matter.]

It would be helpful if you could confirm your wishes by completing and returning the enclosed authority accordingly.

I enclose a pre-paid envelope for your use.

Yours sincerely

19.13   Authority Confirming Instructions on Will/Trust

[client's address]

I acknowledge receipt of your letter dated *[date of letter]*.

Please tick the appropriate box.

☐   I would like further information about making or updating a Will.

☐   I do not need information about making or updating a Will.

[☐   I should like information about a Trust.]

[☐   I do not need information about a Trust.]

[client's title, initials and surname]

Dated:

FINAL REPORTS

19.14   Letter to Client – Final Report (Monies Due)

I am pleased to advise that I am now able to let you have a final report on the claim against [*name of opponent*] ('the Defendant').

The compensation has been paid by the Defendant and arrangements have now been made to recover the costs of the claim from the Defendant in addition to the compensation payable.

Accordingly, I am pleased to enclose a cheque for the [balance of the] sum due of £[*figure*].

[I should also like to confirm how this sum has been calculated.

(1)   The total compensation payable by the Defendant is £[*figure*].

[(2)   Out of that total, the Defendant has deducted benefits of £[*figure*].]

[(3)   I have, of course, already released the sum of £[*figure*].]

[(4)   I have made a refund to [[*employer*] of £[*figure*] for wages paid during the absence from work] [and a refund to] [*insurer*] of £[*figure*] for outlays incurred in respect of treatment].]

(5)   Accordingly, that leaves due the sum of £[*figure*].]

I am pleased to let you have this final report on what I believe to be a satisfactory resolution of the case. May I take this opportunity of thanking you for your instructions.

As your case is now concluded, the file of papers will be placed in storage and kept for at least 6 years. After 6 years, unless there is some reason to retain them, the papers may be destroyed. As a general rule, you are entitled to have the papers now or in the future should you so require. If you do require the papers, or wish to consult them, it would be helpful to have advance notice so that they can be retrieved from storage. You are welcome to arrange for anyone else to collect the papers, although, in this event, your signed authority for release of the papers to that person and proof of identity of the person making the collection will be necessary.

[I have extracted from the papers the original documents you kindly provided during the case and these are returned with this letter.]

[May I remind you that, under the terms on which this matter has been concluded, the settlement can be reviewed if [*details*].]

Of course, if you should need advice on any legal matter in the future, please do not hesitate to contact me.

[Finally, as part of the firm's commitment to improving the quality of service, I enclose a feedback questionnaire. I would be grateful if you could help us monitor our service by completing the questionnaire and returning it in the pre-paid envelope also enclosed.]

Thank you, once again, for your valued instructions.

Yours sincerely

19.15 Letter to Client – Final Report (No Monies Due)

Either

[I write to confirm your instructions that, given the information now available, you have accepted that I should not proceed with the claim. I am sorry that it has not been possible to pursue the claim further, but I do think it was quite proper that the matter should have been fully investigated in order to make a considered decision as to whether the claim ought to have been taken to a conclusion. I hope, at least, that you feel you have been able to make a considered decision and that we have fully explored all the ways in which the claim might have been pursued.]

Or

[I write to confirm that, having carefully considered the prospects of an appeal against the judgment entered against you, I must advise that any appeal would not have sufficient prospects of success to justify the risks of further costs in pursuing any appeal. Accordingly, I think we must accept the judgment. If, however, there are any aspects of the matter that you would like to review with me before I close my file, I shall be happy to see you again. If I do not hear from you I shall assume that I may now close my file.]

Either

[Accordingly, this seems an appropriate point to submit my firm's final account, which I therefore enclose herewith.]

Or

[You entered a conditional fee agreement with my firm and, as the outcome of the case has not been a 'success', under the terms of that agreement, I confirm that no costs are payable by you. Any outlays and costs of the Defendant for which you would otherwise be liable will be met under the insurance policy taken out on your behalf.]

Or

[The costs of dealing with the claim will be met under the policy covering legal expenses and, accordingly, no further costs are payable by you.]

As your case is now concluded, the file of papers will be placed in storage and kept for at least 6 years. After 6 years, unless there is some reason to retain them, the papers may be destroyed. As a general rule, you are entitled to have the papers now or in the future should you so require. If you do require the papers, or wish to consult them, it would be helpful to have advance notice so that they can be retrieved from storage. You are welcome to arrange for anyone else to collect the papers, although, in this event, your signed authority for release of the papers to that person and proof of identity of the person making the collection will be necessary.

[I have extracted from the papers the original documents you kindly provided during the case and these are returned with this letter.]

Of course, if you should need advice on any legal matter in the future, please do not hesitate to contact me.

[Finally, as part of the firm's commitment to improving the quality of service, I enclose a feedback questionnaire. I would be grateful if you could help us monitor our service by completing the questionnaire and returning it in the pre-paid envelope also enclosed.]

Thank you, once again, for your valued instructions.

Yours sincerely

SECTION 20

COSTS

CONTENTS

20.1   Letter to Opponent – Sending Details of Costs (and Notice of Commencement)

We are now able to provide details of costs.

Accordingly, we enclose details of those costs [in the format of a bill of costs] [and Notice of Funding, statement of reasons for the percentage increase and copy insurance details] [together with notice of commencement of detailed assessment proceedings].

Either

[If you consider proposals for settlement can be made which may avoid the need for assessment by the court, please let us have these within the next 21 days. If we consider the proposals are such that we may be able to reach agreement, we would then be content to consider extending time for you to serve points of dispute and, consequently, the date by which we would ask for issue of any default costs certificate.

If, having reviewed the bill, you consider that it is likely that the matter will have to proceed to an assessment by the court, we trust you will send points of dispute by the date given in the notice.

Unless we receive points of dispute or reach agreement for an extension of time on the basis that negotiations can proceed, in either event within the relevant timescale, we reserve the right to apply for a default costs certificate without further notice.]

Or

[If you consider proposals for settlement can be made which may avoid the need for assessment by the court, please let us have these within the next 21 days.

If we do not hear from you, or do not hear with proposals which suggest that agreement on costs is likely, we reserve the right to [issue Part 8 (costs only)] [commence detailed assessment] proceedings without further notice.]

Yours faithfully

20.2   Letter to Court – Issue of Costs Only Proceedings

We are instructed by [*client*].

We enclose, for your kind attention, the following:

(1)   Part 8 claim form (costs only proceedings) for filing together with two copies for sealing and return (one for service and one for our file) to which we have attached a bill of costs and documentation confirming the agreement referred to;

[(2)   copy legal aid certificate [and amendments];

(3)   notice of issue for filing together with copy for service;]

[(4)   notice of funding;]

(5)   draft order;

(6)   cheque for the court fee of £[*figure*].

The purpose of the claim is to allow for the detailed assessment of the costs which, as part of a pre-action settlement, it was agreed that the Defendant would pay but which have not yet been agreed. In the circumstances, we consider that these costs only proceedings, in accordance with section 17 of the Practice Direction About Costs, can be commenced by claim form under Part 8 CPR.

Either

[We should like to arrange for service of the claim form upon the Defendant ourselves and, accordingly, shall be grateful if you would return to us, after issue, the claim form, duly sealed, together with a response pack and, if a date for hearing has been fixed, notice of the hearing.]

Or

[We shall be grateful if you would serve the claim form upon the Defendant and let us have confirmation in due course with, if a date for hearing has been fixed, notice of the hearing.]

We look forward to receiving the sealed copy claim form for our file.

We anticipate that directions will be required from the court as and when the Defendant has either acknowledged service or the time for doing so has elapsed.

Yours faithfully

20.3   Letter to Opponent – Serving Part 8 Claim Form (Costs Only Proceedings)

We enclose, by way of service, the following documents:

(1)   Part 8 claim form;

(2)   bill of costs;

(3)   documentation confirming the agreement;

[(4)   notice of issue;]

[(5)   notice of funding;]

(6)   draft order;

(7)   form for acknowledging service.

Either

[We have been in correspondence with the relevant insurers [*name of insurance company*] of [*address of insurance company*] (under reference [*reference number of insurance company*]) to whom you may care to refer these papers.]

Or

[We shall be grateful if you would kindly acknowledge safe receipt and confirm that service is accepted on behalf of the Defendant.]

Yours faithfully

20.4   Letter to Court – Requesting Detailed Assessment Hearing

We write to request a detailed assessment hearing [and an interim costs certificate].

Accordingly, we enclose:

(1)   request for a detailed assessment hearing (giving appropriate details of the receiving party, the paying party and time estimate);

(2)   copy of the notice of commencement of detailed assessment proceedings;

(3)   copy of the bill of costs;

(4)   copy of the document giving the right to detailed assessment, namely [*details*];

(5)   copy of the points of dispute;

[(6)   copy of the replies to the points of dispute;]

(7)   copies of fee notes and other vouchers for disbursements;

[(8)   copies of further orders relating to the costs which are to be assessed;]

[(9)   legal aid documentation;]

(10)   cheque for the court fee of £[*figure*].

[We also ask that the court issues an interim costs certificate, for such sum as the court considers appropriate, now this request for a detailed assessment hearing has been filed.]

We look forward to hearing from you in due course.

Yours faithfully

20.5   Letter to Opponent – Confirming Detailed Assessment Hearing Requested

We write to confirm that we have now requested a detailed assessment hearing.

Yours faithfully

20.6   Letter to Opponent – Acknowledging Points of Dispute

We thank you for your letter of [*date*] and acknowledge safe receipt of the Defendant's points of dispute.

Either

[We will serve replies to the points of dispute in due course].

Or

[On the basis that the Claimant's case is effectively set out in the bill of costs, we do not propose to re-state this by replies to the points of dispute.

We would suggest a time estimate of [*details*] for a detailed assessment hearing, but please let us know if you disagree.]

Yours faithfully

20.7   Letter to Opponent – Serving Replies to Points of Dispute

We now enclose, by way of service, replies to the points of dispute. Kindly acknowledge safe receipt.

We would suggest a time estimate of [*details*] for a detailed assessment hearing, but please let us know if you disagree.

Yours faithfully

20.8   Letter to Court – Requesting Default Costs Certificate

We enclose, for your kind attention, the following:

(1)   request for a Default Costs Certificate;

(2)   copy Notice of Commencement;

(3) copy of the document giving the right to detailed assessment;

(4) cheque for the court fee of £[*figure*].

Yours faithfully

20.9 Letter to Opponent – Responding to Offer on Costs

We thank you for your letter of [*date*].

We are grateful for your observations on the Claimant's costs and for your [further] proposals.

[Thank you also for the enclosed cheque in the sum of £[*figure*], which we confirm is being presented for payment on the strict understanding that it represents a payment on account of costs, so as to mitigate interest, and does not amount to an agreement on costs.]

[We shall be grateful, so that we can properly assess and respond to the offer, if you would clarify that offer by confirming how this breaks down between base profit costs; the success fee element of the additional liability; disbursements (and insofar as any are not agreed indicating what figure is proposed and the reasons for this); and the insurance premium element of the additional liability.]

We consider the costs claimed are reasonable but to take account of the inevitable risks of proceeding to detailed assessment we are prepared to enter [further] negotiations on costs. Accordingly [, and doing the best we can pending clarification of the offer,] we are prepared, if it will allow us to agree costs, to accept an offer of £[*total in respect of profit costs, VAT, disbursements and interest*].

[We hope it will assist, in considering the matter further, to have a breakdown of the figure. We have, at this stage, approached the figures as follows:

(1) base profit costs of £[*figure*];

(2) VAT thereon of £[*figure*];

(3) disbursements of £[*figure*];

(4) VAT thereon of £[*figure*];

(5)   success fee (at [*figure*]%) of £[*figure*];

(6)   VAT thereon of £[*figure*];

(7)   insurance premium of £[*figure*].]

This offer is open to acceptance for 21 days from the day you receive this letter on the basis that, if agreed, payment will be made within 28 days.

This is an offer under Part 47.19 CPR and so will be referred to, should this be necessary, in connection with the costs of any detailed assessment.

[We invite you to try and agree with us base costs or the level of success fee independently of each other. Please let us know whether or not your instructions allow you to try to reach agreement on either of these issues, leaving the other to be resolved by the court if terms cannot subsequently be agreed.]

[Whilst we note the information sought we have signed the appropriate certificate on the bill, confirming that the indemnity principle has not been breached, and do not consider you have raised any genuine issue which would justify going behind that certificate.]

We look forward to hearing from you.

Yours faithfully

20.10   Letter to Opponent – Confirming Agreement of Costs

We are pleased to confirm that [base] costs have been agreed at a total of £[*figure*] (inclusive of disbursements, [the additional liability,] VAT and any interest) [on the basis those costs will be paid by [*date*]].

[We have advised the court of the agreement reached and asked that the hearing fixed for the detailed assessment be vacated.]

We expect the costs to be paid by [*date*] [and if not calculate interest will accrue at £[*figure*] per day up to the date of payment].

Yours faithfully

20.11   Letter to Court – Requesting Detailed Assessment Hearing be Vacated

We are pleased to report that the parties have been able to reach agreement on costs.

We shall, in the circumstances, be grateful if the detailed assessment, scheduled for [*date and time of detailed assessment hearing*] can be vacated.

Yours faithfully

20.12   Letter to Opponent – Enclosing Final/Default Costs Certificate

We now enclose, by way of service, [final]/[default] costs certificate.

You will note that, under the certificate, the sum of £[*figure*] is due by [*date*].

Please note that further interest is now payable accruing at £[*figure*] per day up to and including the date of payment. To date, therefore, that brings the total payable to £[*figure*].

We look forward to hearing from you accordingly and must, of course, reserve the right to take steps to recover costs without further notice, unless payment in full has been received by the due date.

Yours faithfully